Austria 1945–95

Austria 1945–95

Fifty Years of the Second Republic

Edited by
KURT RICHARD LUTHER
Keele University

and

PETER PULZER
All Souls College, Oxford

Routledge
Taylor & Francis Group
LONDON AND NEW YORK

First published 1998 by Ashgate Publishing

Reissued 2018 by Routledge
2 Park Square, Milton Park, Abingdon, Oxon, OX14 4RN
711 Third Avenue, New York, NY 10017, USA

Routledge is an imprint of the Taylor & Francis Group, an informa business

A Library of Congress record exists under LC control number: 97039130

Typeset by Manton Typesetters, 5-7 Eastfield Road, Louth, Lincolnshire, UK.

ISBN 13: 978-1-138-61062-0 (hbk)
ISBN 13: 978-1-138-61065-1 (pbk)
ISBN 13: 978-0-429-46329-7 (ebk)

Contents

Part III External Relations

Part IV Whither Austria?

List of Figures

List of Tables

Notes on Contributors

Ernst Bruckmüller is Professor of Economic and Social History at the Institute of Economic and Social History of the University of Vienna. His research interests embrace Austrian social, agrarian and middle-class history, as well as the development of Austrian national identity. His publications include *Landwirtschaftliche Organisationen und gesellschaftliche Modernisierung. Vereine, Genossenschaften und politische Mobilisierung der Landwirtschaft Österreichs vom Vormärz bis 1914* (Salzburg: Neugebauer, 1977); *Nation Österreich. Sozialhistorische Aspekte ihrer Entwicklung* (Vienna: Böhlau, 1984); *Sozialgeschichte Österreichs* (Vienna: Herold, 1985); *Österreichbewußtsein im Wandel. Idenitität und Selbstverständnis in den 90er Jahren* (Vienna: Signum, 1994); and *Nation Österreich. Kulturelles Bewußtsein und gesellschaftlich-politische Prozesse* (Vienna-Cologne-Graz: Böhlau, 1996), which is a second edition of his 1984 volume.

Lázló J. Kiss is a Professor at the Hungarian Institute for International Affairs, Budapest and the Budapest University of Economic Science.

Robert Knight is a Lecturer in European Studies at the University of Loughborough. He has published numerous articles and essays on Austrian politics and recent history, as well as *'Ich bin dafür, die Sache in die Länge zu ziehen', Wortprotokolle der österreichischen Bundesregierung von 1945–52 über die Entschädigung der Juden* (Frankfurt am-Main: Athenäum Verlag, 1988).

Helmut Kramer studied at the University of Vienna and the Institute of Advanced Studies, Vienna. He held posts at Stanford University, the Institute of Advanced Studies, Vienna and the Austrian Institute of International Politics, Laxenburg, before becoming Professor of Political Science at the Institute of Political Science of the University of Vienna. His teaching and research interests are in the field of international politics, foreign policy and political theory. His recent publications include *Politische Indeengeschichte* *im Gespräch* (Vienna: WUV-Universitätsverlag, 1995) (editor) and *Handbuch des politischen Systems Österreichs. Die Zweite Republik* (Vienna: Manz 1997) (co-editor).

Walter Lukan taught at a primary school in the bilingual area of Carinthia before studing history and German language and literature at the University of Vienna. In 1971 he joined the Austrian Institute of East and South-East European Studies as head of its library and documentation centre and, since 1980, has edited the interdisciplinary periodical *Österreichische Osthefte.* He wrote his PhD on the Slovenian social reformer Janez Ev. Krek and has produced numerous publications on the history of the South-Slavs, especially Slovenia, on national stereotypes and on the First World War. Since 1990 he has lectured on recent history at the University of Vienna and, in 1997, the University of Ljubljana awarded him a *venia legendi* for recent Slovenian history.

Kurt Richard Luther lectures in Politics at Keele University. His publications include *Politics in Austria. Still a Case of Consociationalism*? (London: Frank Cass, 1992) (co-editor), as well as numerous essays and journal articles on his research interests, which include the Austrian party system, the *Freiheitliche Partei Österreichs*, federalism and consociationalism. He was recently awarded a Leverhulme Fellowship for research into the FPÖ and is currently working on a book-length manuscript on the party.

Hanspeter Neuhold is Professor of International Relations at the University of Vienna and was until 1996 Director of the Austrian Institute for International Affairs, Laxenburg. His publications include *Neutrality and Non-Alignment in Europe* (Laxenburg, 1982) (co-editor); *CSCE: N+N Perspectives. The Process of the Conference on Security and Cooperation in Europe from the Viewpoint of the Neutral and Non-Aligned Participating States* (Vienna 1987) (editor); *The Pentagonal/Hexagonal Experiment: New Forms of Cooperation in a Changing Europe* (Vienna: Braumüller, 1991) (editor); *Das außenpolitische Bewußtsein der Österreicher* (Vienna, 1992) (co-editor); *Internationaler Strukturwandel und staatliche Außenpolitik. Das österreichische Außenministerium vor neuen Herausforderungen* (Vienna: Braumüller, 1993); *Austria on the Threshold of the Twenty-first Century: Another Change of International Status?* (Oslo: Europa-progranimet, 1996); and *Österreichisches Handbuch des Völkerrechts* (Vienna: Manz, 1996) (co-editor).

Oliver Rathkolb is Co-Director in the Ludwig Boltzman Institute for History and Science at the Institute of Contemporary History of the University of Vienna. He is also the Academic Director of the Bruno Kreisky Archives in Vienna. His research specialities include Austrian post-war diplomatic and security history.

Anton Pelinka is Professor of Political Science at the University of Innsbruck and Director of the Institute of Conflict Research in Vienna. His extensive list of publications on Austrian politics include *Demokratie und Verfassung in Österreich* (Vienna-Frankfurt-Zürich: Europa Verlag, 1971) (co-edited with Manfred Welan); *Sozialdemokratie in Europa. Macht ohne Grundsätze, oder Grundsätze ohne Macht?* (Vienna-Munich: Herold, 1980); *Modellfall Österreich? Möglichkeiten und Grenzen der Sozialpartnerschaft* (Vienna: Braumüller, 1981); *Windstille, Klagen über Österreich* (Vienna-Munich, 1985); *The Austrian Party System* (Boulder, Col.: Westview Press, 1989) (co-editor); *Die Kleine Koalition: SPÖ–FPÖ; 1983–1986* (Vienna: Böhlau 1993); *EU-Referendum. Zur Praxis direkter Demokratie in Österreich* (Vienna: Signum, 1994) (editor). Since 1993 he has co-edited *Contemporary Austrian Studies* (New Brunswick and London: Transaction Publishers).

Peter Pulzer was, until 1996, Gladstone Professor of Government and Public Administration and Fellow of All Souls College, Oxford. He has held various visiting professorships in the USA and continental Europe, most recently in Dresden, and published widely on Austrian and German history and politics. His books include *The Rise of Political Anti-Semitism in Germany and Austria* (New York: 1964, London: Peter Halban and Cambridge MA: Harvard University Press, 1988), *German Politics 1945–1995* (Oxford: Oxford University Press, 1995) and *Germany 1870–1945: Politics, State-Building and War* (Oxford: Oxford University Press, 1997).

Edward Timms is Professor of German at the University of Sussex and Director of the Centre for German–Jewish Studies. Since 1990 he has been co-editor of the Austrian Studies series. His study of Karl Kraus, *Karl Kraus – Apocalyptic Satirist* (New Haven: Yale University Press 1986), appeared in German translation in 1995 (Böhlau Verlag) and has also been translated into a number of other languages.

Erika Weinzierl is Emeritus Professor of History, University of Vienna. She has published very widely on the history of the Austrian First and Second Republics. Examples include *Die österreichischen Konkordate* (Vienna, 1960); *Österreich 1918–1938*, 2 vols (Vienna, 1983) (co-editor); *Österreich, Zeitgeschichte in Bildern* (Vienna, 1975); *Emanzipation? Österreichische Frauen im 20. Jahrhundert* (Vienna, 1975); *Vertreibung und*

Neubeginn. Israelische Bürger österreichischer Herkunft (Vienna-Cologne-Weimar, 1992) (co-editor); *Zu wenig Geschichte. Österreicher und Judenverfolgung 1938–1945* (4th edn, Vienna, 1997). Since, 1973, she has been Editor of the journal *Zeitgeschichte.*

Series Foreword

The Association for the Study of German Politics (ASGP) was established to encourage teaching and research in the politics and society of the German-speaking countries. Since its formation in 1974, the ASGP has brought together academics from a variety of disciplines – politics, languages, history, economics and other social sciences – who, along with others with practical and personal interests, are concerned with contemporary developments in these countries. Through its conferences, research seminars, and its journal *German Politics*, the ASGP has proved itself to be an invaluable forum for discussion and research. This series represents a significant extension of ASGP activities. The Association believes that its wide range of expertise will ensure that the series will be of value to teachers, students, and those involved in policy and research, providing them with readily accessible material on current issues.

Preface

In June 1995 we organized a highly successful conference on the Second Austrian Republic which was, that year, celebrating its fiftieth anniversary. The conference was designed to look back at the evolution of Austrian politics from occupation to independence; to evaluate the development of Austria's national identity and political institutions; and to look forward to the impact on Austria of the end of the Cold War, European Union membership and the secularization of the political culture. We were fortunate in being able to recruit some of the most distinguished specialists in Austrian affairs. They were drawn from a wide range of disciplines and included historians, political scientists, economists, international relations specialists and literary historians.

This volume brings together, under one cover, 12 of the 13 papers delivered at the conference. The first four essays offer a reassessment of 'The Origins of the Second Republic' and include: Erika Weinzierl's detailed retrospective on the genesis of the Second Republic; Robert Knight's consideration of the first post-war coalition government headed by Dr Karl Renner; Edward Timms' illustration of how Austrian literature sought to overcome the divided 'schizophrenic spiritual condition' it faced after the traumas of the National Socialist period; and Oliver Rathkolb's analysis of superpower assessments of the geopolitical and economic context of Austrian neutrality during the first two post-war decades. Part II on 'Society and Politics' contains contributions from Ernst Bruckmüller, who documents the bases and gradual development of a sense of an Austrian national identity; from Anton Pelinka, whose essay considers whether the orientation of Austria's political culture has become less subject and more participant; and from Kurt Richard Luther, whose chapter provides a detailed analysis of the extent to which the Second Republic's party system has moved from accommodation towards competition. In the first of the four chapters in Part III, 'External Relations', Helmut Kramer charts the development of Austrian foreign policy from the 1955 State Treaty to European Union membership in 1995. There are then two contributions on Austria's relationship with her Eastern and Southern neighbours: Lázló Kiss reflects on the evolution of

Austro-Hungarian relations during and since the Cold War, whilst Walter Lukan outlines the development of Austria's relations with the territory that now constitutes Slovenia. Hanspeter Neuhold then considers whether Austria ever really was 'between the blocs' and how, in light of the recent profound changes to the international system, Austria appears to have embarked on the road to full Western integration. He concludes with a consideration of the challenges which Austria now faces as a result of the (non-) decisions of the European Union's Amsterdam summit, on the one hand, and, on the other hand, its unresolved future relationship to NATO. The final Part is entitled 'Whither Austria?' and contains just one essay, namely, that by Peter Pulzer, which offers a summing up, and puts the post-war Austrian experience into its developmental perspective.

We owe a great debt of gratitude to the Austrian Ambassador, His Excellency, Dr Georg Hennig and to the then Director of the Austrian Institute, Dr Peter Marginter, both for their enthusiastic responses to our initial proposals for the conference upon which this volume is based, and for their generous financial support. The organizational assistance of Dr Marginter's successor, Magister Ulla Krauß-Nußbaumer and of the other staff at the Austrian Institute and the Austrian Embassy was essential in ensuring the success of the conference. We are also indebted to Howard Machin, Director of the European Institute of the London School of Economics, who enabled us to stage the conference at the LSE, and to the Association for the Study of German Politics (ASGP) for supporting the venture.

The process of converting the original conference papers into the finalized manuscripts of this volume was somewhat lengthier than we had anticipated. We should like to express our appreciation to all our contributors for the work they undertook on their chapters, as well as to the editors of the ASGP series for their patience. We hope that this volume, which examines the post-war Austrian experience from a multidisciplinary perspective that embraces the latest research, will be of interest not only to specialists in Austrian affairs but also to students and scholars concerned with the evolution of small democracies, their place in an integrated continent and the shape of post-communist Central Europe.

Kurt Richard Luther

Peter Pulzer

List of Abbreviations

APEC	Asian-Pacific Economic Cooperation
BBC	British Broadcasting Corporation
CFSP	Common Foreign and Security Policy
CIA	Central Intelligence Agency
CIS	Confederation of Independent States
COCOM	Coordinating Committee
COMECON	Council for Mutual Economic Assistance
CSCE	Conference on Security and Cooperation in Europe
EAC	European Advisory Commission
ECSE	European Coal and Steel Community
EEC	European Economic Community
EFTA	European Free Trade Association
EU	European Union
FPÖ	*Freiheitliche Partei Österreichs* Austrian Freedom Party
GDP	gross domestic product
IAEA	International Atomic Energy Agency
IGC	Intergovernmental Conference
KPÖ	*Kommunistische Partei Österreichs* Communist Party of Austria
LiF	Liberales Forum Liberal Forum
MBFR	Mutual and Balanced Force Reduction
MI6	Military Intelligence 6
NAFTA	North American Free Trade Association
NATO	North Atlantic Treaty Organization
NS	National Socialist
NSDAP	*Nationalsozialistische Deutsche Arbeiterpartei* National Socialist German Workers Party
ÖAAB	*Österreichischer Arbeiter- und Angestelltenbund* Austrian League of Workers and Employees

ÖGB	*Österreichischer Gewerkschaftsbund* Austrian Trade Union Federation
OECD	Organization for Economic Cooperation and Development
OSCE	Organization for Security and Cooperation in Europe
ÖVP	*Österreichische Volkspartei* Austrian People's Party
POEN	*Provisorisches Österreichisches National Kommitee* Provisional Austrian National Committee
SPÖ	*Sozialistische* (since 1991 *Sozialdemokratische*) *Partei Österreichs* Socialist (since 1991 Social Democratic) Party of Austria
SWS	*Sozialwissenschaftliche Studiengesellschaft*
UN	United Nations
USA	United States of America
USSR	Union of Soviet Socialist Republics
VdU	*Verband der Unabhängigen* League of Independents
VÖI	*Vereinigung Österreichischer Industrieller* Union of Austrian Industrialists
WEU	Western European Union
WTO	Warsaw Treaty Organization

PART I
THE GENESIS OF THE SECOND REPUBLIC

1 The Origins of the Second Republic: A Retrospective View

Erika Weinzierl

Adolf Schärf and Lois Weinberger, prominent and influential representatives of the two parties to the 1945–66 Grand Coalition, affirmed the independence of the new Austria long before the Allies' Moscow Declaration of November 1943. Agreements to work together after the war were made from 1943 onwards, particularly in the talks conducted by Dr Felix Hurdes and Lois Weinberger with Dr Adolf Schärf and Dr Alfred Migsch. All four had been prisoners during the Nazi regime. Migsch had founded his own resistance group (*Wahrheit*) and had good connections with the communists and Catholic circles (Stadler, 1982, p.174). Hurdes, formerly in the youth league of the *Vaterländische Front* (Reichhold, 1984, p.366) and a member of the Carinthian provincial government from 1936 to 1938, was imprisoned longest and under the direst conditions. Plans for post-war Austria were also being made prior to the Moscow Declaration by Austrian exile groups. In Paris and then in London, Moscow and New York, they had not just been concerned to help fellow refugees, but had also disseminated anti-Nazi propaganda, directed at Austria through journals and radio, and had debated plans for the period 'afterwards'. Helene Maimann is right in stating that the Austrian emigrant movement 'can certainly be placed alongside the domestic struggle for liberation', as she is in concluding that, given the animosity between socialists and communists, the émigré community in Great Britain did not achieve the 'political impact' it could have attained (Maimann, 1975 p.236). Unfortunately, this also holds true for the other exile nations.

At the risk of oversimplification, the politically active exile groups can be characterized along geographical lines as follows. In London the strongest organizations were the 'Free Austrian Movement', which included both socialists and bourgeois-conservative activists, but was clearly dominated by communists and the socialist 'London Office'. Until at least 1943, both were unable to attain any real official backing from the British. That Moscow was the centre of communist exile needs no further elaboration. In Sweden Bruno Kreisky headed a very active socialist emigrants' group which would have also been willing to collaborate with the communists. After the Moscow Declaration, it developed very concrete concepts for rebuilding post-war Austria. In the USA, especially in New York, all groups were, of course, represented. There, the monarchist movement under Otto Habsburg – or 'Otto of Austria' as he later called himself – made itself particularly noticeable with its hopes for restoring at least a Danubian confederation. Yet the only tangible result of their efforts was rather inconsequential. In the autumn of 1942, President Roosevelt let Otto persuade him to establish in the US army a separate Austrian unit, the so-called Autonomous Infantry Battalion No. 101. However, on 3 May 1943 the battalion – which on 2 April had consisted of only 193 men, many of whom were not Austrians – was disbanded. This was largely a result of resistance to the battalion from American government circles, from representatives of the former successor states and, in particular, from within the Austrian exile groups, which did not cooperate with each other. The symbolic impact which the initiators had intended the battalion to have on the restoration of an independent Austria was not achieved. On the contrary, it had made all the more apparent the division among Austrian exiles, who had been unable to generate an exile government recognized by all groups. Be that as it may, one cannot deny that allowing this battalion to be created marked the 'only requisite attempt of a political emigration group from Austria to effect, in some kind of way, the recognition of Austria's independence' (Goldner, 1977, p.236).

Even more decisive in bringing about a change of mood within the Austrian resistance and among Austrian exiles was, however, the 'Moscow Declaration'. It dates back to a memorandum on 'The Future of Austria', written in the spring of 1943 by the British Foreign Office diplomat Geoffrey W. Harrison. In it, he explored four possible 'solutions' to the Austrian issue:

1. Linking Austria with Germany, either via full integration, or on the basis of a federation;
2. Austria's inclusion in a Southern German confederation;
3. the restoration of Austria as a free and autonomous state;
4. Austria's inclusion in a Central or Eastern European confederation.

Harrison weighed up the advantages and disadvantages of the various solutions and finally opted for the restoration of Austrian state autonomy as a first, necessary step, ultimately to be followed by an association with a Central, or Southern European confederation. On 16 June 1943 Winston Churchill's War Cabinet decided, on the basis of Harrison's memorandum, to prioritize preparations for the fourth solution and Foreign Minister Eden was put in charge. Acting on this decision, Harrison a few days later drew up the first draft for a declaration on Austria, to be published after consultations with the USA and USSR. Because it was intended to strengthen Austrian resistance, it referred to the inescapable responsibility of the Austrians and specified that their war-time position would be taken into account (Stourzh, 1988, pp.1–3). After the British–American agreement at the Moscow Conference at the end of October 1943, this point became more crucial since, in compliance with Soviet wishes, the text now spoke of Austria's responsibility, which meant a possibility of 'moving the issue of Austrian responsibility from the moral level … to the legal level of international law' (Stourzh, 1988, p.3). Moreover, responsibility was defined in more precise terms: participation in the war on the German side. Even though the British and the Americans were not very satisfied with these modifications, they agreed to them. The conference of foreign ministers deleted a reference to the spirit of the 'Atlantic Charter', replaced 'union' with Germany with 'annexation' and referred specifically to the war as that of 'Hitler Germany'. The reference to Austria's association with its successor states had been deleted long before that.

The final formulation of the 'Moscow Declaration', signed and published on 1 November 1943 as Appendix 6 of the protocol of the Moscow Conference had thus been decided upon and was later to be integrated *ad verbatim* into the Declaration of Independence of 27 April 1945 by the responsible Austrian politicians 'of the first hour'. On 16 November 1945 the French Committee for National Liberation under Charles de Gaulle had also accepted this declaration. Indeed as early as December 1941, in an exchange of ideas at a conference in Moscow on the post-war order of Europe, Anthony Eden had reported on the British considerations regarding a division of Germany, stating that the British government in any case favoured a separation of Austria from Germany. At the same time he conceded that he had no concrete ideas on how this was to take place. Stalin answered in writing, suggesting that Austria be restored as an autonomous state within its pre-war boundaries (Aichinger, 1977, pp.22ff). It is worth stressing that this document, so crucial for the establishment of the Second Republic, was dealt with belatedly and marginally in Moscow in 1943.[1] This shows both the limited significance which the Austrian issue had for the Allies at the time (Fellner, 1972) and the extent to which the Austrians' use of the Moscow Declaration in 1945 was tactically shrewd.

Another resolution of the Moscow Conference in 1943 extended far beyond Austria – the appointment of a committee of diplomats to discuss measures to be taken after victory over Germany, the European Advisory Commission (EAC), based in London. It began its work at the beginning of 1944 and finished in July 1945. The main issue was the delineation of the occupation zones, with regard to which the Western Allies showed only little interest as far as Austria was concerned. It was the USSR which finally suggested a division of zones at the end of 1944; this provided for 'a strong participation of the Americans', amounting essentially to the occupation as carried out in the summer of 1945 – with the exception of the French zone. The head of the Soviet commission for issues related to a ceasefire had on 25 May 1944 sent to Foreign Minister Molotov a statement of the commission pointing out that:

> ... the Soviet zone is connected, through train lines, to the north with Czechoslovakia, to the south with Yugoslavia, and to the east with Hungary. The commission does not consider it appropriate to mark the borders between the British and the American occupation zones. Since, in their first memorandum, the British had suggested handing over their territory in Austria to the Americans, while they (the British) in principle accepted our suggestion to have Austria occupied by troops of all three powers, it seems expedient to let the British and the Americans decide themselves who will occupy what part.
>
> We have suggested that the City of Vienna be occupied by troops of all three powers, with the Eastern part of the city being occupied as far as the Danube Canal by troops of the Soviet Union and the rest of the city creating the Anglo-American zone. The commission did not suggest any lines of demarcation between the British and the American zone in the Vienna region, assuming that the British and Americans would settle this themselves.
>
> The demarcation line which marks the Soviet zone on Austrian territory was drawn so that the Anglo-American zone in Austria bordered directly onto the area of Vienna that was to be occupied by British and American troops.[2]

President Roosevelt, who in September 1943 was still sure that Austria would become a Soviet protectorate like Hungary and Croatia, did not agree to the creation of an American occupation zone in Austria, bordering on Bavaria, until 9 December 1944 (Stourzh, 1988, pp.6ff). On 23 January 1943 the Deputy People's Commissar A. Lozovsky outlined the plans then existing for a post-war order in Austria, in which the intervention of the Vatican is mentioned, and summed up the possibilities of Soviet decisions in five points:

> 1. We basically declare ourselves in favour of changing the borders at the expense of German Territory. 2. We can also endorse the annexation to Austria of Tyrolean areas in which German is spoken. 3. We must resolutely oppose the slightest attempt to create a Danubian confederation, a Danubian state, an

> economic bloc, etc. since the Catholic Danubian bloc would be an instrument of anti-Soviet policy. 4. The administration of Austria should be modelled after Romania and Hungary. Only when British and American troops advance into German and Austrian territory can the necessary changes be effected in the administrative system. 5. We must categorically oppose the re-establishment of the Habsburg Monarchy. The issues regarding a domestic order of Austria must be solved by the Austrians themselves under the supervision of the Allied (Soviet) command. [3]

At the beginning of 1945 the situation was that Austria was to become a sovereign nation again and to be denazified and democratized under the protectorate of the occupation forces. The Austrian exile organizations had also agreed to regaining sovereignty (Molden, 1970, pp.205–10; Luza, 1984 pp.227ff). Since early 1944 the resistance group 05 (code name for Austria), founded by Hans Becker, had been seeking to create an all-Austrian resistance organization. An initiative by Fritz Molden in Vienna brought this about on 18 December 1944 when the Provisorisches Österreichisches Nationalkommitee (POEN – Provisional Austrian National Committee) was created (Molden, 1976, p.299). It initially consisted of Catholic conservatives, but had, from the outset, maintained contacts with the socialists, primarily with Dr Adolf Schärf, and with the communists. It was also able to form links with the military and political leaders of the Allies. Fritz Molden was charged with these tasks (Thalberg, 1984, pp.136ff). The illegal *Arbeiter-Zeitung*, printed in Zürich, made an appeal in its first 1945 issue for support for 05 as a supraparty Austrian resistance movement. As early as November 1944, the so-called *Siebenerausschuß* (Committee of Seven) comprising representatives of all political movements within the 05 was set up. It was at first directed by Becker. After he was arrested in March 1945, Raoul Bumballa headed the committee, which during the struggle for Vienna in April 1945 assumed the political leadership of the resistance (Rathkolb, 1985, pp.295ff).

The course of military operations in Austria can only be alluded to here, even though it was of great significance for the early history of the Second Republic (Rauchensteiner, 1970; Jedlicka, 1972, pp.129–45). After the fall of Budapest in February 1945, it was clear that the next goal of the Russian troops would be to occupy Vienna. Even though SS divisions tried to stop the Russian troops from advancing on Lake Balaton, the Soviet troops were able to cross the former Austro-Hungarian border at Güns on 28 March. On 5 April *Reichsstatthalter* Baldur von Schirach left the city of Vienna, which had been declared a 'defended area'. The following day the first Russian troops reached Vienna from the south. The commander of the 3rd Ukrainian Front, Marshal Tolbukhin, had already followed Moscow's order in letting leaflets be distributed over Vienna in which he assured the citizens of the city that the Red Army was not marching into Austrian territory as conquerors, and that its goal was only to crush the German fascist troops and to liberate Austria from dependence on Germany.

> The Red Army stands on the ground of the Moscow Declaration of the Allied forces on the independence of Austria. It will help in restoring the conditions which existed in the country until 1938, i.e., before the Germans invaded Austria. The Red Army fights against the German occupiers but not against the Austrian population.

The rumour spread by the Nazis that the Red Army liquidating all members of the NSDAP was a lie. The party was to be dissolved, and the ordinary members, provided they acted loyally, were to be left alone. In order 'To preserve the Austrian capital, its historic monuments of art and culture', the Viennese were not to leave the city; to prevent the Germans from trying to defend themselves; to organize the battle against the Germans themselves; and to try to stop the Germans from removing production goods and foodstuffs (Weinzierl and Hofrichter, 1975, p.332). The Russian troops were initially welcomed with genuine joy as liberators, especially in working-class districts, where at times the German soldiers came under greater fire from the Viennese than from the Russians (Käs, 1965, p.19).

On the day the Red Army crossed the Austrian border, 29 March, Smirnov, Novikov, Roshchin and S. Bazarov presented to Deputy Foreign Minister Vyshinsky their ideas of how the occupation zones in Austria were to be divided. The USSR was to accept the British suggestion 'regarding the division of Austria into four zones on condition that the Soviet Union was not to receive the northern part including Upper Austria, but the southern part with all of Styria and Carinthia'. According to this scheme the USSR and not Britain was to share borders with Yugoslavia and Italy. This way, not only could the British influence on Yugoslavian affairs be limited, but Yugoslavia would also gain a real opportunity to acquire a small area of southern Austria. Furthermore, the stationing of Soviet troops in the Austrian region bordering on Yugoslavia and Italy would reinforce Soviet influence on the Balkan peninsula, 'as a result of which the issues related to Yugoslav border claims on Austria, now a matter of concern for Britain, would no longer figure'. With regard to the duration of the stationing of Soviet troops in Romania, that was to be 'significantly shorter than the period during which Austria was occupied as part of Germany'. A map of Austria drawn up by the Red Army reconnaissance service shows that the economically most prosperous zone included Carinthia and Styria, assigned to the British according to the British plan. For all these political and economic considerations 'the British plan of zonal division was to be accepted on condition that the Soviet Union receive the southern zone, including Styria and Carinthia', which, as is known, is not what happened.[4]

The initially friendly manner in which the Russian troops were received and supported by the Austrian population was expressly and positively noted by the Soviet Union in its appeal to the Austrians published on 9 April 1945 in *Pravda.* Hitler, on the other hand, telephoned from Berlin with an instruction 'to proceed against the insurgents in Vienna with the most brutal measures' (Molden, 1970, p.247). By 8 April the Russians, advancing from the West, had already occupied the outer western districts of the city. In attacking Vienna from the south-west, they were following a resistance movement suggestion which had been conveyed to them in their headquarters at Hochwolkersdorf by acting Sergeant-Major Käs. However, at the last minute, treason prevented the Austrians from making the contribution they had announced – that is, the uprising of the replacement army in Vienna (Käs, 1965, pp.14ff; Vogel, 1977, pp.60ff).

After occupying Vienna, the Russians advanced further to the west and the north. By the end of April, Burgenland, Lower Austria and a significant part of Styria was under their control. At the same time, French troops advanced in Vorarlberg and American troops in Tyrol, Salzburg and Upper Austria. A few days later, British troops moved into Carinthia from the south. However, the Yugoslav partisans had already marched in and occupied Carinthia in order to reverse the result of the referendum of 1920. Only under Russian pressure did Yugoslavia turn over southern Carinthia to British occupation. Fighting stopped throughout Austria on 7 May, one day before the ceasefire was enforced. At this time, Austrian interests were already being represented by a provisional national government established in Vienna by Chancellor Karl Renner before the end of April 1945. The prerequisite for creating this government was the cooperation of the Russians with Karl Renner and the founding of Austrian political parties.

The Russians' 'discovery' of the 75-year-old Renner was not, it should be noted, as coincidental as was assumed up to the 1970s. The first Chancellor of the First Republic had retreated to Gloggnitz in Lower Austria after the *Anschluß*, where he dedicated himself for the most part to personal affairs. At the end of March 1945 when the National Socialists had already left Gloggnitz, Renner immediately appeared in public and encouraged the people of Gloggnitz not to flee from Russian troops. On 1 April 1945 these troops marched into Gloggnitz. The very next day, Renner asked two former socialist functionaries to create a democratic municipal government. On 3 April he made representations to the local Soviet commandant in Gloggnitz in connection with offences by Russian soldiers against the population 'and offered in very concrete terms his services to re-establish the Republic of Austria' (Nasko, 1982, pp.31ff; Rauscher, 1995, pp.308ff). He was also recognized by an officer of the 103rd Guards Division. Renner was thus immediately led on foot to the command post in Köttlach, from where he was driven by car to the main headquarters of the 9th Guards Division in Hochwolkersdorf. There he was received on 5 April by Colonel-General Alexei Zeltov who, following Stalin's orders of 4 April, expressed to him the Soviets' trust and the willingness of the Russians to support him in rebuilding democratic order in Austria.[5] Renner immediately declared himself willing, drawing on his experiences as Chancellor in 1918–20 and as the last President of the Austrian parliament. Renner himself later declared that, in Hochwolkersdorf, he committed himself only to summoning the old parliament 'so that it could appoint a provisional government and immediately call for a referendum on the autonomy and independence of Austria'. He was then brought back to Gloggnitz where he wrote a total of eight appeals and acted as a 'fully competent Chancellor' (Nasko, 1982, p.32). On 9 April, the Russians brought Renner and his family to Eichbüchl castle near Wiener Neustadt, which had been furnished specially for him. There he drafted his first proclamations and wrote his first long letter to Stalin on 15 April. In this letter, he first emphasized his personal contacts with Lenin, Trotsky (!) and other Russian 'pioneer fighters', expressing his gratitude for the welcoming treatment he had received from the Red Army and declaring himself, given his personal history and the existing situation, called on 'to speak for the Austrian people' and capable 'of assuming the task of rebuilding a resurrected Austria'. Here he already spoke explicitly of the Second Republic. Two passages in this almost effusive letter, however, were more than problematic, even given that they could be seen as reflecting Renner's special tactical abilities. The first is Renner's request that Stalin take Austria under his protection in the Council of Great Powers; the second is in the concluding sentences:

> The special trust of the Austrian working class in the Soviet Republic has become boundless. The Austrian Social Democrats will debate fraternally with the K.P. [Communist Party] and work together on equal footing in rebuilding the Republic. That the future of the country belongs to socialism is beyond dispute and does not need to be stressed. (Nasko, 1982, pp.14ff)

By this time, Marshal Tolbukhin had issued an order from Vienna that Renner be located. The then lieutenant-colonel of the 4th Viennese Guards Division, Yakov Starchevsky, finally met Renner on 19 April in Gloggnitz, to which he had returned for this purpose. Starchevsky was accompanied by Leo Hölzl, the lieutenant of former Communist Party leader, Franz Honner. That same day, Renner was brought to Vienna to Tolbukhin and was given a villa in Vienna-Hietzing, Wenzgasse 2 as a residence.

What motivated the Russians to carry out a veritable search for Renner? According to the memoirs of the Soviet army general, S.M. Chernenkov, Stalin himself had, at the beginning of April 1945, asked for Karl Renner, a student of Karl Kautsky, at a discussion of the situation at the headquarters only to find that no one knew what had become of him. Stalin commented that one should not 'disregard the influential forces taking an anti-fascist position. Hitler's dictatorship had certainly also taught the Social Democrats something' and the 3rd Ukrainian Front thus received a telephone order to look for Renner. As early as the evening of 4 April, a report regarding a meeting and conversation with Renner was sent from the Front. In response Stalin dictated a telegram to the War Council of the 3rd Ukrainian Front, stating the following: first, Renner was to be given expressions of confidence; second, he was to be informed that the Supreme Command of the Soviet troops would support him in restoring democratic order; third, it was to be explained to him that the Russian troops would not annex Austria, but only drive off the fascist occupiers. The telegram was signed by Stalin and A.J. Antonov.[6] What Stalin expected from Renner might become clear when the relevant Soviet files become accessible but, until then, the room for interpretation is fairly wide. Even if the opinion expressed by a British journalist and published many years later in the *Observer* were to turn out to be correct, namely that Renner seemed to be the man the Russians needed: 'old, very old, very popular, long out of contact with practical politics, a link with the past, a respectable facade for a popular front government, which could be quickly conquered by a young Communist ...' (Jochum, 1982, pp.5ff), the Russians' presumed objectives were not achieved.

Renner had penned another important letter while still in Eichbüchl. On 17 April 1945 he informed the former Christian-Social minister of finance and mayor of Baden, Josef Kollmann, that he, together with the Red Army commander's headquarters and through them with Moscow, was now ready to organize the 'Second Republic of Austria', as he had organized the First in 1918. He assumed that, in so doing, the Social Democratic as well as Communist workers would follow him and would be willing to collaborate primarily with the farmers, as well as with the sincere Christian-Social workers and middle-class citizens, so that all political debates were deferred to the general elections to be expected at a later date. However, he conceded that one could not expect the Social Democratic workers to forget 'that Fascism, in Austria, was a "Dollfuß growth" imposed on the country by Mussolini', that Dollfuß had robbed the workers of their autonomous institutions and that he had incarcerated all leading Social Democrats, of whom a not inconsiderable number had been executed. He, Renner, had always assumed that a discernable, albeit not very large majority of Christian-Social MPs 'had not approved of this policy of Dollfuß, but had merely proved too weak to resist it'. He thus asked Kollmann to contact Kunschak, Buchinger and other Christian-Socials who had remained democratic, give them a copy of his letter and bring them to him as soon as he got to Vienna. 'Those, however, who were active as Fascists in a provocative manner, that is, the inner Dollfuß clique as well as committed Heimwehr leaders, I ask to let sink into oblivion.' He himself resolutely adhered to the Constitution of 1920 and contested both the legality and rationale of all amendments. In this context, it is noticeable how similar Renner's ideas were to those of the London Social Democratic emigrants who endorsed the re-establishment of the Republic of Austria on the basis of the constitution of 1920, but with the amendment of 1929 (Maimann, 1975, p.218).

In conceiving this letter, however, Renner did not know that the political parties had already been formed in the few days since the defeat of Vienna. Adolf Schärf, who had spent the last phase of the war at the general hospital, conducted the first political discussions as early as 12 April. On this day, former Social Democratic district councillor, Anton Weber, invited him to the Palais Auersperg, which was, as already mentioned, the headquarters of 05, and on 13 April to the City Hall. Other leading Social Democrats, including Oskar Helmer and Paul Speiser, were informed and met at the City Hall, where the Viennese mayor was to be appointed. Weber had been selected for this post by 05, whilst the Russians and Communists had chosen Rudolf Prikyl for the post of deputy mayor. However, from the outset, both were willing to withdraw in favour of a more suitable candidate. After intensive negotiations, this candidate was found in the person of Theodor Körner who was appointed on 14 April and was also recognized by the Russian city commandant. The official refounding of the Socialist Party took place on the same day, when the Revolutionary Socialists (among them the later Mayor Felix Slavik), reunited with Social Democrats such as Josef Afritsch. The name 'Socialist Party of Austria (Social Democrats and Revolutionary Socialists)' was chosen. Both groups were represented in the provisional party committee. The chairman was to be Karl Seitz, but since he was not yet in Vienna, Schärf was appointed provisional party chairman. (Helmer, 1957, pp.211ff). He was immediately asked by Renner to begin making arrangements for a new provisional government.

Felix Hurdes, Leopold Figl, Lois Weinberger and Hans Perntner were released from the Vienna *Landesgericht* (provincial court) on 5 and 6 April. Before then, Figl and other friends had been summoned to Marshal Tolbukhin and asked to collaborate in rebuilding Austria. The first centre for the people who were later to become the founding members of the new bourgeois party was the Palais Auersperg (Reichhold, 1975, pp.72ff), where Lois Weinberger, who had in the meantime become chair of the *Arbeiter- und Angestelltenbund* (Workers' and Employees' League), was the first to name the new party the

Österreichische Volkspartei (Austrian People's Party, ÖVP) (Weinberger, 1948, p.245). Preparatory talks for its foundation had been conducted on 15 April, when work was begun at the Vienna Schottenstift. The actual inaugural meeting took place on 17 April and was attended by some 20 people. Leopold Kunschak took the chair and Hans Perntner acted as executive chairman. The meeting essentially consisted of reports by Weinberger and Hurdes on the preceding years and on the resolutions that originated during that period. There was complete unanimity on these – the collaboration with all democratic forces for a new Austria – and on the name of the party which, in contrast with the inter-war period, was no longer to be the secular arm of the Church. Kunschak became chairman, Perntner executive chairman, Bumballa the representative of the Liberals and the deputy chairman of the resistance movement and Hurdes became general secretary. In addition, two more representatives of the Farmers', Employees' and Business Leagues, among them Figl, Weinberger and Raab, were elected to the executive. The organizational department was taken over by Johannes Eidlitz, and Herbert Braunsteiner became secretary of the general secretary (Reichhold, 1975, pp.72ff). Retrospectively, Hurdes declared in 1956 that the ÖVP emerged 'from a belief in Austria and in its right' (Jochum, 1982, p.15).

Even though the Communist Party did not see itself prompted to change its name or its programme, there was still no central party leadership in Austria in April 1945. On 13 April Johann Koplenig and Ernst Fischer arrived in Vienna from Moscow; on 21 April, Franz Honner and Friedl Fürnberg arrived from Yugoslavia. They all had serious misgivings about the preparations already made to create a government under Renner, but finally expressed their willingness to cooperate actively as representatives of the *Kommunistische Partei Österreichs* (Austrian Communist Party – KPÖ) (Autorenkollektiv, 1977, pp.239ff).[7]

In the meantime, Renner was already planning the formation of a government which, in the interests of maintaining constant liaison, was to include a representative from each party, as well as a member of the *Antifaschistischer Landbund* (Anti-fascist Farmers League), which soon became affiliated to the ÖVP. Moreover, he planned to create four political and five economic departments, each of which would include a state secretary, an under-secretary and an expert head of office. He allocated the Communists one contact person and a state secretary, believing that he had thereby 'done enough in this direction'. However, on the very day he arrived in Vienna (19 April) Renner had had a long conversation with Marshal Tolbukhin, Colonel General Sheltov, General Major Blagodatov (commander of the City of Vienna), Colonel Piterski and the reporter, chargé d'affaires and political consultant of the commandant of the 3rd Ukrainian Front, Koptelev. A record of this conversation was passed on to Dekanosov, the representative deputy of the People's Commissariat for External Affairs of the USSR under the heading, 'On the Issue of the Creation of a Provisional Government in Austria'. Prior to this, Tolbukhin had a short conversation with the secretary of the Central Committee of the Austrian Communist Party, Koplenig, on the latter's opinion regarding the creation of a future Austrian government. Koplenig agreed to Renner becoming the head of the government. The cabinet was to consist of 15 persons, including Chancellor Renner, a deputy chancellor who was to be a representative of the Christian-Social Party, and a second deputy chancellor, who was to be a representative of the Communist Party. Koplenig also considered it to be:

> … necessary to reserve the posts of Minister of Interior Affairs and Minister of External Affairs for the Communists. According to what he says, Renner is perfectly willing to reach an agreement with the Communists, but he is very reluctant to accept Catholics in the government, notwithstanding the fact that the Catholics behave considerably better than the Social Democrats.

Afterwards, the Soviet group under Tolbukhin gave a reception for Renner. Renner first thanked the marshal for liberating Austria 'whereby the country had become independent and free' and then explained his programme. He suggested creating an executive committee in which all democratic parties were to be represented. The task of this committee was to be to re-create all government institutions which had been dissolved as a result of the flight of the Nazis. In addition, he suggested directing several appeals to the Austrian population and to various groups of the population on his behalf and to establish 'some model districts so as to organize the joint work of the local authorities with the Red Army'. Renner believed that 'the military command should give the necessary instructions via the commandant, instructions which would then be followed by the local authorities'. He then described the catastrophic situation in Austria – no food supplies, no other supplies, no means of transportation, no doctors, the danger of epidemics, no seeds and no livestock. He pointed out that starting up industrial production required permission, instructions from the Red Army and extensive executive powers.

Tolbukhin then explained to Renner that the difficulties in that situation mainly resulted from the overhasty installation of a provisional government consisting of representatives of all democratic parties! 'As former head of the Austrian government, we will entrust you with the task of forming a provisional government.' The appeal would have to be made to the population on behalf of the government. The Red Army would provide all conceivable assistance for all democratic efforts. Moreover, the provisional government would have to prepare National Assembly elections on a democratic basis and to ensure that they were carried out, and to then create a constitutional government. After listening to Tolbukhin's suggestions, Renner reflected on this and then asked whether it would be possible to issue a decree through the Red Army, by virtue of which he, Renner, would be asked to create the provisional Austrian government. The answer he received was that the Red Army would not appoint the government by order as this was the task of the Austrians, above all of the leading representatives of the democratic parties. Renner agreed to this and asked to be given five days for all the necessary negotiations. He promised to 'present a list of the future composition of the Austrian government on 23 April'. He then asked for a security force to be supplied by all parties, but learned, in a further conversation, that this would prove to be too complicated, given the interests of Marshal Tito. He then asked for all Austrian railway workers to be released from wartime captivity and for the rail system to start up again as soon as possible. 'In the course of the talk, Renner underlined that he now has to save Austria for the second time' (Stadler, 1982, p.196).

This conversation was followed by a lunch attended also by Koplenig (secretary of the Central Committee of the KPÖ), Kunschak (leader of the ÖVP), and Körner (the Social Democratic former general of the Austrian Army), who had 'provisionally' been appointed Mayor of Vienna. During this lunch, the Austrians stressed that it was necessary to create a really democratic government and to forget the 'squabbles between the parties'. Renner suggested that three government seats should be allocated to the Social Democrats, two to the Communist Party who were the junior party, one each to the Landbund and the Revolutionary Socialists, plus two seats to those with no party membership. The Soviets responded that these issues had to be settled with the leaders of the democratic parties. Renner appeared optimistic and very satisfied, particularly with becoming chancellor again. It is not entirely clear what was meant by Koptelev's cryptic statement to the effect that Renner 'has still not understood the meaning of our suggestions and drawn the necessary conclusions'. After lunch, Kunschak, the leader of the 'Social Democratic [*sic*] Party' declared 'that Renner was to a large degree responsible for Austria's *Anschluß* to Germany and that he had welcomed it. Renner then answered that he would now like to come to terms with this error.' Prior to this, Kunschak had committed himself to restoring the unity of the Austrian people.[8]

On 21 and 22 April, Renner negotiated with Schärf, the former parliamentary secretary of the Social Democratic group 'whom Renner had appointed Minister of the Interior', and with other earlier Social Democratic parliamentary representatives such as Schneidmadl, Helmer, and Böhm. He then negotiated with the Christian-Social Kunschak and Kollmann and other prominent politicians. He did not conduct any concrete dialogues with the Communists until 23 April.

> Renner wishes to do without Deputy Chancellors and does not wish to be subject to any control through them. With the Communists there were many differences with regard to the Ministry of the Interior. Renner, however, agreed to let this office be occupied by the Communist Party. In the suggested declaration, Renner followed a certain line for creating the 'Second Republic' and restoring the pre-1938 state in Austria.[9]

On 23 April a cabinet list was prepared at a meeting of the democratic parties under Renner's leadership; the list differed from the first version only with regard to some names, none of them central. Honner had already been intended as an under-secretary of state. The second list was presented to Tolbukhin and Sheltov and conveyed to Stalin at 1.30 pm on 24 April.[10] When Renner presented his proposal, which widely corresponded with the Russian wishes, to the party representatives Körner and Mentasti (SPÖ), Kunschak and Kollmann (ÖVP), Kopelnig and Fischer (KPÖ) at the Wenzgasse on the afternoon of 22 April, he encountered energetic resistance from the Communists who demanded a deputy headship of the government, as well as the Departments of the Interior, Education and *Volksaufklärung* ('popular enlightenment'). The Russians, who had already been informed beforehand, fully backed these demands. Renner then thought of a considerably more complicated solution in terms of checks and balances: the chancellor was to be joined by four state secretaries without portfolio who were to act as his deputies. Together with him they created the so-called 'political cabinet', while the other state secretaries were heads of secretariats. In each state office, those parties whose representatives were not entrusted with the leadership were to be represented by state under-secretaries. Finance and Justice were to be headed by non-party persons, and the Communists were to take over the Interior and Education. This construction was largely implemented. The political Cabinet Council (*Kabinettsrat*) comprised Schärf (SPÖ), Figl (ÖVP) and Koplenig (KPÖ). Its decisions had to be taken unanimously. Even though the government consisted of ten Socialists, nine members of the ÖVP, seven Communists and three non-party persons or experts, Russian pressure ensured that, in terms of power, the KPÖ came off best (Stadler, 1982, p.197).

These are the circumstances under which a provisional government was finally created. Of its 33 members, 13 had been persecuted during the Nazi period (Enderle-Burcel, 1995). It is incidentally of interest to note Renner's authoritarian style of directing negotiations in all 16 sessions of the Cabinet Council prior to 9 July. The provisional government officially presented itself to Marshal Tolbukhin on 27 April 1945 and submitted the Declaration of Independence, consisting of five articles, written by Karl Renner which became the founding charter of the Second Republic. In compliance with Ernst Fischer's demand, the full text of the Moscow Declaration, with the postscript on Austria's responsibility for its participation in Hitler's wars, was included in this document. For Austria's resurrection, however, only the first two succinct articles are significant in that they differed decisively from the those of the proclamation of the First Republic on 12 November 1918:

> Article I: The democratic republic of Austria is restored and established in the spirit of the constitution of 1920.
> Article II: The *Anschluß* forced onto the people of Austria in the year 1938 is null and void. (*Neues Österreich*, 28 April 1945, p.1)

On 28 April the Viennese were able to read the declaration signed by Renner, Schärf, Kunschak and Koplenig in *Neues Österreich*, the 'Organ of Democratic Unification'. On the very same day, Chancellor Renner informed Molotov and the USA that a provisional government had been created and that it had begun its activities that day. He also requested that the restored statehood, about which the USSR had already informed the USA and Great Britain on 24 April 1945, be recognized.[11] Austria had re-emerged with the decisive help of the USSR. Although the first step to founding a state had been taken, the path to full freedom and sovereignty, however, was still long and arduous. Most arduous were no doubt the months following 27 April 1945, which can only be described here in very general terms.

There were primarily three seemingly insoluble problems for the Viennese in an Austria occupied by the Russians. One was the recognition of the provisional government as a government of all of Austria within and outside of Austria, for which a connection with all other Austrian zones was a prerequisite. These were zones in which there was still fighting at the time that independence was proclaimed. Further problems were the resolution of the constitutional issue, the holding of democratic elections and ensuring that all Austrians were provided with minimum foodstuffs. The Russians helped in the summer of 1945 with supplies of, among other things, peas, for which Renner offered emotional thanks (Nasko, 1982, pp.151ff). That this assistance was not a gift, but rather functioned as 'pea debts' in the negotiations leading up to the 1955 State Treaty – debts which Austria sought to eliminate in these negotiations (Stourzh, 1988, pp.71ff) – was something Renner could not have known at the time.

The constitutional issue was settled the most quickly. The provisional government spared itself a struggle for the constitution by accepting the

Verfassungsüberleitungsgesetz (constitutional transition law) and the so-called 'Provisional Constitution' of Austria on 13 May (Rauchensteiner, 1979, pp.112ff). The Federal Constitution Law in its 1929 version and all other constitutional laws as they had existed prior to 5 March 1933 – the day after the suspension of parliament – came back into force. All laws passed after this date were repealed. The 'Provisional Constitution' was the basis of the government's powers for the period prior to the establishment of representative parliamentary bodies. On 19 December 1945, the day the new national parliament convened, it ceased to be effective.

A second issue concerned matters related to the installation of the occupying forces (Rauchsteiner, 1979, pp.30ff; Jedlicka, 1972, pp.112ff). The greater part of Lower Austria, as well as Vienna, had been conquered by Russian troops by 8 May; the remainder of the country was not occupied until after 8 May, which, at Tolbukhins request, Koptelev reported to Renner on 9 May, also informing him that the territory between the line of Enns, Bruck-Graz and Leibnitz on the one hand and Vienna on the other was to be handed over to the administration of the provisional government.[12] As in Vienna, mayors were immediately appointed. In the Wiener–Neustadt area, parish priests were even granted the right to nominate candidates. A Lower Austrian provisional government comprising Leopold Figl (ÖVP), Oskar Helmer (SPÖ) and Otto Mödlagl (KPÖ) was appointed as early as 18 April and, on 11 May, Lower Austria was handed over to Austrian civil administration. In Burgenland, the former *Landesrat* (provisional minister) and *Landesstatthalter* (governor) Lorenz Karall had already met with politicians from the pre-war period in Mattersburg during the battle for Vienna to discuss the re-establishment of Burgenland which had been split up between the Gaue Niederdonau and Styria during the Nazi period. In Vienna and Lower Austria there was an unwillingness, for tactical reasons, to dwell on this at that time, due to concern about the revival of the idea of a Slavic corridor between Hungary and Austria. Nevertheless, the Russians had definitely planned to re-establish Burgenland, although the people of Burgenland were as ill-informed of this as of the fact that their fate had often been discussed by the European Advisory Commission in London. In Styria, part of which had been occupied by the Russians and part of which had been conquered or occupied by Bulgarian units of the Red Army, Yugoslav partisan units and American troops, there was a real 'transfer of administration from National Socialist functionaries to Austrian representatives' (Rauchensteiner, 1979, p.84). The *Gauleiter* and *Reichsstatthalter* (Reich Governor) of Styria, Siegfried Uiberreither, had fled from the Russians on 8 May, whereupon the *Gauhauptmann*, Armin Dadieu, took over affairs. However, since news of the creation of a national provisional government had already arrived in Styria, above all via the BBC, Styrian Social Democrats and Christian-Socials had already decided to cooperate prior to that date. Nine of them, led by Reinhard Machold, demanded that the mayor of Graz and Dadieu hand over competencies to them. They created the Styrian provincial Executive (*Landesausschuß*) which comprised five SPÖ, two ÖVP, two KPÖ members and established a provisional division of duties and ensured that Graz was handed over to the Russians without a struggle. However, the Russians initially dissolved the executive, before eventually recognizing it on 15 May after protracted negotiations with Machold. The provisional *Land* government was now made up of three representatives from each of the parties (SPÖ, ÖVP and KPÖ). Four days later, Karl Renner came to Graz, where he gave Machold the authority to issue the necessary decrees on all provincial matters 'on behalf of the national government' (Rauchensteiner, 1979, p.85). The Vienna–Graz connection functioned well until July. Once the whole of Styria had been occupied by British troops, however, these troops sealed off the zonal borders.

All of the Allies' plans envisaged Carinthia being occupied by the British, yet from January 1945 Tito, too, made claims on Southern Carinthia. In Carinthia, politicians from the pre-1938 period had also created a provisional provincial government (two Socialists, two former Christian-Socials and one non-party) before 8 May. Nevertheless, despite the mediation of *Gauhauptmann* Meinrad Natmeßnig, *Gauleiter* Friedrich Rainer was not prepared to resign and stipulated that no Communist was to become a member of what was now the Carinthian Executive Committee.

After the Executive Committee had effected an intervention by telegram on the part of the British military government for Austria in Rome and by the former Austrian ambassador in London, Sir George Franckenstein, Rainer finally resigned and asked Natmeßnig to carry on with affairs, which he, in turn, immediately transferred to the Executive Committee. We cannot go into greater detail here on the conflicts between the British or Western Allies and Tito. The Western Allies finally turned to Stalin who, as mentioned above, intervened successfully. On 16 May the units of the 3rd Yugoslavian People's Liberation Army were put under the military command of the 3rd Ukrainian Front and between 19 and 23 May, Marshal Tolbukhin withdrew these troops from Carinthia. Since, in agreement with the Americans, the British wanted to build up the Austrian administration from below, they dissolved the provisional provincial government on 4 June and, with two exceptions, nominated its members to form an 'advisory provincial committee'. The appointment of the mayor and the district *Hauptleute* was based on complicated guidelines and was not finished until the end of January 1946.

Tyrol was destined to become part of the American zone, yet from February 1945 on, there were also debates about a possible French occupation.

However, the region had numerous resistance groups, the leadership of which Dr Karl Gruber had taken over in mid-March. He also organized a military group which systematically appropriated all German military offices and the NS administration. When, on the evening of 3 May, American troops marched into Innsbruck, they arrived in a city which had already been liberated from the Nazi regime and was festively adorned with red, white and red flags. At the *Landhaus*, the traditional seat of the provincial government, the executive committee of the Tyrolean resistance movement presented itself as a sort of Tyrolean provincial government (Gruber, Hans Gamper and Eduard Reut-Nicolussi). This, of course, also led to conflicts of authority which were not settled by the Allied military government under Lieutenant-Colonel Watts until the end of May. The Tyrolean politicians knew almost nothing about events in Vienna. Dr Karl Gruber thus acted on his own initiative when he appealed – in vain – to the State Department in Washington that Tyrol be left in the American zone (Rauchensteiner, 1979, p.84).[13]

On 30 April French troops marched into Vorarlberg. They had not been properly prepared for their task and were asked by the Americans and British to comply with their guidelines, which stipulated a ban on fraternization and rebuilding the administration from the bottom up. The commanding general of the French 1st Corps, however, had a sign erected at the border of Vorarlberg which said that Austria, 'a friendly country', begins here (Rauchensteiner, 1979, pp.94ff). When the French began to appoint their mayors, numerous Vorarlberg mayors asked for a provincial executive to be appointed. This took place on 24 May, and one of its first resolutions was to reclaim the autonomy of their province – that is, to separate it from Tyrol.

The city of Salzburg was handed over to the Americans on 4 May without a struggle, although this had been preceded by critical conflicts between German military officials and Salzburg politicians (Lackerbauer, 1977), of whom *Gauleiter* Scheel proved to be reasonable. Since the preliminary talks held in Salzburg among former Austrian politicians on the way the future was to be shaped did not take proceed smoothly and the American military government lacked a constructive outlook, a provisional provincial government was not appointed until 23 May. The Americans constantly interfered in the agenda of this government, even on the issue of denazification. Austrian political parties were permitted again on 1 June. At the end of June, the military government had also been consolidated.

As a result of the efforts of the Nazi Mayor Franz Langoth and contrary to the will of Gustav Eigruber, *Gauleiter* of Oberdonau (Upper Danube), the city of Linz had not been defended. Langroth was thus replaced by Ernst Koref (SPÖ) on 7 May; Koref had been unanimously suggested by the representatives of the Austrian parties for the position of mayor, and his appointment was recognized by the US commander for Upper Austria, Colonel Snooke, the very next day. The consolidation of the US occupation authorities took place very quickly, especially since they were prepared for an active role in Austria. The provincial government, made up of representatives from the three parties under the leadership of the socialist Alois Oberhummer, was not accepted by the Americans, who also banned political parties on 14 May. They asked an official of the Nazi period, *Regierungsdirektor* Adolf Eigl, to create a government of civil servants, which he headed until he was arrested in August 1945.

Even though the European Advisory Committee had, to all intents and purposes, already accepted the British zone plan for Austria in December 1944, there were complicated negotiations from January to June 1945 (Fellner, 1972, pp.81, 86ff). These negotiations resulted in the Russians being given all of Burgenland and the Mühlviertel region of Upper Austria. The main item of contention, however, was Vienna. Otto Habsburg had emphatically warned President Truman[14] against the Renner government in a letter, but this sentiment could also be traced back to Russian knowledge of a British memorandum dated December 1944 that took the same line. For the Western Allies this was a reason to be distrustful, as was the Russian condition that they dispense with sending American and British representatives to Vienna. The Russians had already informed the Americans about Renner's appointment on 24 April, and Chancellor Renner had officially notified the governments of the USSR and the USA of the creation of the provisional government on 28 April (Schilcher, 1980, p.1).

Marshal Tolbukhin had expressed '*de facto* recognition' of the provisional government through the Red Army on behalf of the Red Army (Schärf, 1948, p.101) whereas the Americans wanted to wait for the time being. This was undoubtedly the first sign of the Cold War which was initially more strongly evident among the British than among the Americans (Fellner, 1972, p.89). Thus it was not until the beginning of June 1945 that the first commission of the Western Allies came to Vienna via Judenburg to check the situation. The commission's findings enabled the Western Allies to reach agreement by 19 June, and the EAC was therefore able to resume its consultations on 22 June. The Russians, too, finally agreed to the last suggestion for the four-zone division of Vienna that came from the French and to joint control of Vienna's First District (the 'four men in a jeep'). Thus the First Control Agreement was signed on 4 July and the agreement on zones on 9 July 1945.

With that, Allied rule via the Allied Council, in which resolutions had to be passed unanimously, was settled and free access by the Western Allies to Vienna ensured. The four-power occupation of Vienna came into effect on 1 September 1945 and remained unchanged (as did joint control of the inner city of Vienna) until 1955, surviving even the height of the Cold War. The first meeting of the Allied Council took place in Vienna on 11 September and a further 200 meetings followed.

With regard to the occupation forces, the first phase of Austrian post-war history was completed in the summer and early autumn of 1945. The question of the recognition of the Renner government and the question of elections had yet to be settled. Regarding the former, the final protocol of the Potsdam Conference stated:

> The conference has examined a suggestion of the Soviet Government as to the expansion of the Austrian provisional government to all of Austria. The three governments agreed that they would examine this issue after British and American troops had pulled into Vienna. It was agreed on that no reparation demands were to be made on Austria. (Fellner, 1972, p.89)

In the first session of the Allied Council on 11 September, the prime issue was the Austrian rejection of a bilateral Soviet–Austrian petroleum company (Schärf, 1955, pp.68ff) – a rejection which was massively backed by the Western Allies. Nonetheless, the acceptance of political parties was decided pending approval of the Allied Council. Marshal Koniev asked that the power of the Renner government be extended to all of Austria, but this was rejected on account of the vehement British objection. The Americans and the French sought a compromise, which was undoubtedly the result of a conversation Renner had immediately before the session with General Clark regarding his further plans. As had been the case after the First World War, these included the appointment of provincial conferences for negotiations with the provinces, then the broadening of the government to lessen the influence of the Communists, and the holding of elections by the end of November at the latest, since they would then not be possible before March for weather reasons. This conversation won Clark over to Renner and his policy (Rauchensteiner, 1979, pp.118ff). This was more difficult with the British, as Renner's correspondence in October 1945 with his London delegate, Walter Wodak, shows (Wodak, 1976, pp.147ff).[15] Renner's conversations with the military and political representatives had resulted only in the acceptance of a reorganization of government, for which the British, however, made maximum demands. There were also suspicions in Austria, especially in the 'golden West'. The most influential figure in this respect was the Tyrolean Governor Gruber, who had already met with Herbert Braunsteiner in May in Salzburg. He had swum across the river Enns as a 'messenger of the federal ÖVP' to inform Eastern Austria about the situation. After this, Gruber merged his *Demokratische Staatspartei* (Democratic State Party) and all other non-socialist resistance groups with the *Tirolische*

Volkspartei (Tyrolean People's Party) (Gruber, 1953, p.28). Renner came to the fore within Austria only through the *Länder* conferences in Vienna (Feichtenberger, 1965).

Preliminary conferences of the representatives of the western *Länder* had already taken place in Salzburg, where there was agreement on the demand that Gruber be appointed foreign minister in the Renner government. Even if the first *Länder* conference, which took place in Vienna from 24 to 26 September, did not reach complete consensus on all issues, it was possible to reach an agreement on all of the most important questions. The Renner government, recognized for all of Austria, was expanded by three under-secretaries, who all belonged to the ÖVP, among them Karl Gruber at the Foreign Ministry. The date for elections in all of Austria was set for 26 November 1945.

These results, and the intervention of Austrian emigrants such as Bruno Kreisky, the chairman of the Organization of Austrians in Sweden, who had on 22 May 1945 already asked the press attaché of the Soviet Mission in Stockholm to provide him with pro-Austrian material for circulation in the press of the Nordic countries,[16] prompted the Allied commander-in-chief to suggest that their governments recognize Renner's cabinet at their session on 1 October. This took place so quickly that Renner was invited to the session of the Council on 20 October and received formal acceptance of the extension of his government's competence to all of Austria – that is, the *de facto* recognition of the Western Allies. In addition, elections were to be held subject to the Control Law of the Allied Council.

At the second *Länder* Conference, which took place in Vienna from 9–11 October, the main issue was how the elections, in which the Nazis were not to be permitted to take part, were to be held. At the third Conference on 25 October, there was a change in the registration requirements. The law banning the NSDAP had already been passed by the provisional government on 8 May; the law on war criminals on 26 June 1945. Gruber's demand that there be a distinction between active Nazis and fellow travellers in every single case before the elections was not fully accepted, any more than the demand made by the Americans to exclude the leading men of the 'pre-Nazi Fascist Regime' and its paramilitary organizations from leading positions for a short time (Stiefel, 1981, p.31; Meissl *et al.*, 1985). On 22 September, Renner had already confidentially informed the British High Commissioner of the intention to create an SPÖ-ÖVP coalition government after the elections (Rauchensteiner, 1979, p.132).

The elections duly took place on 26 November. The results surprised the occupational forces, especially the Russians. Despite – or maybe because of – the massive support which the Russian troops in Austria and Vienna provided the KPÖ (the 'Russian party'), the Austrians who had been afflicted by suffering, hunger, cold and all sorts of deprivations made an impressive pledge to parliamentary democracy. Since the majority of prisoners of war had not yet returned home and the National Socialists could not vote, 64 per cent of the 3 449 605 eligible voters were women. The free and secret elections, which took place in all of Austria, resulted in the following distribution of seats: 85 for the ÖVP, 76 for the SPÖ and 4 for the KPÖ. As a consequence, in December, a Grand Coalition was created, consisting of the two major parties which 11 years earlier had fought each other in a civil war. A Communist minister (Altmann) was accepted into the first coalition government under Figl and Schärf. He retired from office in 1947, in protest against the currency reform. With the election of Renner as the first federal president by the National Assembly on 20 December 1945, the first reconstruction phase of the new Austria had been successfully completed. After his election, Renner thanked President of Parliament, Leopold Kunschak, and expressed his delight at the fact that, after the Republic's most difficult times, it was he and Kunschak who had been the first Austrians to meet each other in the Wenzgasse and come to an understanding:

> In this encounter of Socialists and Christian-Socials and in the understanding I saw a sign of things to come. I drew optimism from the fact that the co-operation of these two parties as well as all other democratic parties would lay the foundation of a new, happier Austria. (Fischer, 1970, p.402).

This marked the end of the first, decisive, phase in the history of the 'Second Republic', as Renner had apparently been first to call it.

On the basis of the minutes (published in three volumes) of the Cabinet Council of Karl Renner's provisional government of 1945, it would be possible to describe its arduous work in a difficult period in greater detail. Here I will only quote from the introduction to the first volume by Gertrude Enderle-Burcel (1995, pp.xff) on the relationship of Renner's provisional government with the Soviet occupying power – that is, the 3rd Ukrainian Front:

> The Cabinet Council minutes contain numerous examples of positive co-operation. There was constant help in questions regarding social administration and food. The Austrian government did not follow the Soviet order to not make too many laws, but rather to focus on important practical work. In addition to the necessary economic reconstruction measures, the whole administration was rebuilt as quickly as possible with the help of numerous laws. … Within the period of the present volume [April–July 1945] Renner's Provisional Government could at first only become effective within the 3rd Ukrainian Front and its impact was limited to Vienna, almost all of Lower Austria and the large part of Styria after the German capitulation. However, all legal measures were intended to be applied to the entire state.

Notes

1 *Postwar Foreign Policy Preparation 1939–1945*, Department of State publication 3580, Washington, 1948, p.198.
2 25 May 1944, Archive of the Russian Foreign Ministry, hereinafter RFM. Photocopies of originals in the Archive of the Bruno Kreisky Foundation, *Ländersammlung: Sowjetunion, Projekt: Russisch Akten 1945–1962*. The author would like to thank Dr Oliver Rathkolb for the copies of these documents.
3 A. Lozovsky, memorandum of 23 January 1945, ibid.
4 29 March 1945, Smirnov, Novikov, Roshchin, Barazov, to Vyshinsky, FM.
5 4 April 1945, Reports by Tolbukhin and Sheltov to Stalin and Stalin's directions to them, RFM.
6 This report by Shtemenko was published in *Neue Zeit*, 1972 (21), pp.18ff and Rauchenstein (1972; 1979) mentioned its contents. For a detailed account, see Shtemenko 1977 pp.325ff which quotes the *Neue Zeit* text published by Nasko (1982 pp.259ff). See also footnote 5.
7 Ernst Fischer (1969, p.470), claims that he had already arrived in Vienna on 10 April.
8 19 April 1945, Koptelev to Dekanazov, FM.
9 23 April 1945, accepted at 1.20 am.
10 Koptelev to Dekanazov. FM. 24 April 1945, Tolbukhin and Sheltov to Stalin, ibid.
11 28 April 1945, report by Renner to Molotov; 24 April 1945, Foreign Minister Vyshinsky to the American and British representatives, RFM. The significant aspect of Vyshinsky's communications is that all initiatives for forming the provisional government are attributed to Renner. The Soviet Union evidently did not wish to emphasize its own decisive role in Austria in 1945.
12 9 May 1945, M. Koptelev, summary of conversation with Chancellor Renner, RFM.
13 While Gruber reports in both his memoirs (1953 pp.21ff; 1976 pp.63ff) of good relations with the Americans, Rauchensteiner makes no mention of these representations.
14 'The Russians have unilaterally set up a regime in Vienna that is subject to Communist pressure. There were rumours that the Allies might under certain circumstances recognise this Communist regime, the so-called Provisional Government. I can assure you that the overwhelming majority of Austrians is opposed to such a government.' Text in Stadler (1982, p.208).
15 For Wodak's personality, see Wagnleitner (1980, pp.5ff).
16 25 May 1945, notes by the press attaché of the USSR in Sweden, F. Malgin, concerning his conversation with Bruno Kreisky, RFM.

Bibliography

Aichinger, W. (1977), *Sowjetische Österreichpolitik 1943–1945*, Vienna.

Enderle-Burcel, G. (1995), '"Einleitung", Österreichische Gesellschaft für historische Quellenstudie', (ed.), *Protokolle des Kabinettsrates der Provisorischen Regierung Karl Renner 1945*, vol. I, *'Im eigenen Haus Ordnung schaffen', Protokolle des Kabinettsrates, 29 April 1945 bis 10 Juli 1945*, Vienna: Horn.

Feichtenberger, F.J. (1965), *Die Länderkonferenzen 1945. Die Wiedererrichtung der Republik Österreich*, unpublished PhD thesis, Vienna.

Fellner, Fritz (1972), 'Die außenpolitische und völkerrechtliche Situation Österreichs 1938. Österreichs Wiederherstellung als Kriegsziel der Alliierten', Erika Weinzierl and Kurt Skalnik (eds), *Österreich. Die Zweite Republik*, vol. I, Graz/Vienna/Cologne.

Fischer, E. (1969), *Erinnerungen und Reflexionen*, Rheinbeck.

Fischer, H. (ed.) (1970), *Karl Renner. Porträt einer Evolution*, Vienna/Frankfurt/Zürich: Europa-Verlag.

Goldner, F. (1977), *Die österreichische Emigration 1938 bis 1945*, 2nd edn, Vienna/Munich.

Gruber, K. (1953), *Zwischen Befreiung und Freiheit. Der Sonderfall Österreich*, Vienna.

Gruber, K. (1976), *Ein politisches Leben. Österreichs Weg zwischen den Diktaturen*, Vienna/Munich/Zürich.

Helmer, O. (1957), *50 Jahre erlebte Geschichte*, Vienna.

Jedlicka, L. (1972), *Die letzte Kriegsphase*, Erika Weinzierl and Kurt Skalnik (eds), *Österreich. Die Zweite Republik*, Graz/Vienna/Cologne.

Jochum, M. (1982), *Die Zweite Republik in Dokumenten und Bildern*, Vienna.

Käs, F. (1965), *Wien im Schicksalsjahr*, Vienna.

Lackerbauer, I. (1977), *Das Kriegsende in der Stadt Salzburg im Mai 1945*, Militärische Schriftenreihe 35, Vienna.

Luza, R. (1984), *The Resistance in Austria 1938–1945*, Minneapolis.

Maimann, H. (1975), *Politik im Wartesaal. Österreichische Exilpolitik in Großbritannien 1938 bis 1945*, Vienna/Cologne/Graz.

Meissl, S. *et al.* (1985), *Verdrängte Schuld, verfehlte Sühne. Entnazifizierung in Österreich 1945–1955*, Vienna.

Molden, F. (1976), *Fepolinski und Waschlapski auf dem berstenden Stern. Bericht einer unruhigen Jugend*, 3rd edn, Vienna/Munich/Zürich.

Molden, Otto (1970), *Der Ruf*, 3rd edn, Vienna.

Nasko, S. (ed.) (1982), *Karl Renner in Dokumenten und Erinnerungen*, Vienna.

Rathkolb, Oliver (1985), 'Raoul Bumballa, ein politischer Nonkonformist 1945. Fallstudie zur Funktion der 0–5 im Widerstand und in der Parteienrestauration', Rudolf G. Ardelt *et al.* (eds), *Unterdrückung und Emanzipation. Festschrift für Erika Weinzierl*, Vienna/Salzburg.

Rauchensteiner, M. (1970), *Krieg in Österreich*, Vienna.

Rauchensteiner, M. (1972), 'Nachkriegsösterreich', *Österreichische Militärische Zeitschrift*, (6).

Rauchensteiner, M. (1979), *Der Sonderfall. Die Besatzungszeit in Österreich 1945 bis 1955*, Graz.

Rauscher, W. (1995), *Karl Renner. Ein österreichischer Mythos*, Vienna.

Reichhold, L. (1975), *Geschichte der ÖVP*, Graz/Vienna/Cologne.

Reichhold, L. (1984), *Kampf um Österreich. Die Vaterländische Front und ihr Widerstand gegen den Anschluß 1933–1938*, Vienna.

Schärf, A. (1948), *April 1945 in Wien*, Vienna.

Schärf, A. (1955), *Österreichs Erneuerung 1945–1955. Das erste Jahrzehnt der Zweiten Republik*, 7th edn, Vienna.

Schilcher, A. (1980), *Österreich und die Großmächte. Dokumente zur österreichischen Außenpolitik 1945–1955*, Vienna/Salzburg.

Shtemenko, S.M. (1977), *The Last Six Months. Russian Final Battles with Hitler's Armies in World War II*, transl. Guy Daniels, New York.

Stadler, K.R. (1982), *Adolf Schärf. Mensch–Politiker–Staatsmann*, Vienna/Munich/Zürich.

Stiefel, D. (1981), *Entnazifizierung in Österreich*, Vienna/Munich/Zürich.

Stourzh, G. (1988), *Geschichte des Staatsvertrages 1945–1955. Österreichs Weg zur Neutralität*, 2nd edn, Graz/Munich/Cologne.

Thalberg, H.J. (1984), *Von der Kunst, Österreicher zu sein. Erinnerungen und Tagebuchnotizen*, Vienna, Cologne, Graz.

Wagnleitner, R. (ed.) (1980), *Diplomatie zwischen Parteiproporz und Weltpolitik, Briefe, Dokumente und Memoranden aus dem Nachlaß Walter Wodaks*, Salzburg.

Weinberger, L. (1948), *Tatsachen, Begegnungen und Gespräche. Ein Buch um Österreich*, Vienna.

Weinzierl, E. and Hofrichter, P. (1975), *Österreich. Zeitgeschichte in Bildern*, 2nd edn, Innsbruck/Vienna/Munich.

Wodak, W. (1976), *Diplomatie zwischen Ostund West*, Graz/Vienna/Cologne.

2 The Renner State Government and Austrian Sovereignty

Robert Knight

Introduction

Austria's first post-war government, the provisional state government (*Staatsregierung*) was established under the chancellorship of Karl Renner on 27 April 1945 and functioned until the end of the year. Recent publications, from the popular to the scholarly, suggest that neither the government's actions nor its historical position are now a matter for much discussion, let alone controversy (Portisch, 1986; Ableitinger, 1992; Rauscher 1995). The chancellor himself, though he may still be attacked for his legendary 'adaptability' and, more specifically, for his public support of the *Anschluß* (Pelinka, 1989) is generally seen, even by his critics, as having played a vital and patriotic role in re-establishing the Austrian state in the ruins of the Third Reich. This lack of controversy, and what Anton Pelinka has described as Renner's 'beatification', (Pelinka, 1992, p.117) is surely in itself reason for a re-examination of the government's record. An additional one is provided by the new availability of an important primary source, the first volume of the cabinet minutes of the government (*Kabinettsrat*).[1] These, and the invaluable diary of Josef Schöner, who observed political affairs at the start of the Second Republic closely, albeit from a junior position, now make it possible to escape from the overreliance of most discussions on the account of the socialist leader Adolf Schärf, only partly offset by the counterversion offered by the communist leader Ernst Fischer. In the following discussion these published sources will be supplemented by my own research in the remaining, as yet unpublished, cabinet papers for the period July to December 1945.

For reasons of space, I concentrate here on the first of the three broad areas, within which most discussion of the Renner government has taken place – sovereignty, reconstruction, and continuity. Broadly speaking, sovereignty, its restoration and possible threats to it, have been discussed in three distinct perspectives; the first and most common one is that of a communist attempt – real or imagined – to 'sovietize' Austria; the second, which originated in the post-war communist party and has received a wider resonance since the 1960s, centres on Western policy towards Austria; the third one contrasts the Allied occupation as a whole with Austrian efforts to regain its sovereignty. After discussing these perspectives and some of their problems I will argue here for a more historical and 'relativist' understanding of the sovereignty issue, based on the ambiguity of Austria's intermediate position between defeat and liberation.

The Renner Government and the Soviet Authorities

During and after Austria's ten-year occupation, the Renner government was often seen as the 'one which got away', narrowly escaping the clutches of the Soviet Union and its Austrian communist fifth column. And although opinions may vary about the part played in this by resolution, toughness, luck or cunning, this sense of a narrow escape remains in much of the literature (for example, Brook-Shepherd, 1957; Bader, 1966; Kurth Cronin, 1986). Renner himself still tends to be seen, by friends and critics alike, as the 'old fox' who, unlike other Eastern European leaders, outwitted the Soviet authorities (Portisch, 1986, p.300; Rauscher, 1995, p.316).

Yet this interpretation is questionable on a number of grounds. First, it assumes a fixed Soviet master plan to expand wherever and whenever possible. While Stalin's foreign policy, despite some opening of Soviet archives, is still far from clear, this view should itself be seen as a product of the era of 'containment'. It is surely less plausible than the kind of interpretation recently advanced that, beyond a 'minimum core' of Poland and Rumania, Soviet policy before 1947 was marked as much by indecision or uncertainty as by a purposeful will to expand (Swain and Swain, 1993). In the case of Austria three particular hypotheses about Soviet goals can be advanced:

1 Strategically the Soviet Union favoured a re-established Austrian state in order to weaken Germany and prevent any Catholic and anti-communist federation in Central Europe, such as that often considered by Churchill (Aichinger, 1977).
2 Beyond the elimination of Nazi rule, the political composition of Austria was not a matter of major Soviet concern in 1945 but its working

assumption was that a four-power occupation and administration would continue for some time.

3 Whatever its ultimate political aims may have been the Soviet Union was determined to extract what it could economically from Austria, in the form of plant and raw materials.

Second, and more counterfactually, we do not know how Renner might have reacted if he had been subjected to a similar pressure as that exerted on Beneš or Mikolajzkyk (Fischer, 1973, pp.75–6). Can it be assumed that he would have put up stiffer resistance? The evidence of Renner's servile letter to Stalin in May 1945, not to mention his previous history of 'adaptability' or, as Gerald Stourzh more charitably puts it, his inability to stand aside (*abseits stehen*) (cited in Pelinka, 1989, p.70) hardly suggests so, although Renner's resistance to the Soviet interpretation of the Potsdam Agreement in September should not be ignored either (KR 29, 5 September).

Third, several particular aspects of the 'escape' can be questioned. The Soviet choice of Renner itself appears to have been essentially an act of administrative convenience which happened to coincide with Renner's own self-confident assertion of leadership (Rauscher, 1995, pp.307ff, Aichinger, 1977, pp.132–9; Rathkolb, 1985, pp.116–17). It certainly was not a sign of concern to advance the interests of the Austrian Communist Party. The comments of the Soviet General Scheltov to Austrian ministers some months later (albeit made in the context of the attempt to gain western recognition for the Renner government at the Potsdam Conference) reinforce this impression. According to Renner, Scheltov had told him:

> For the Red Army the most important thing had been not to leave the country without an administration ... all we want is an improvement of your situation. He refused to defend one party or another.[2]

Lack of personnel and limited use of Austrian communists meant that, throughout the life of the provisional government, the Soviet authorities were unable to interfere in any systematic way in the government's legislative activities. This does not mean, as has sometimes been argued (for example, Rauscher, 1995, pp.325, 339) that they were indifferent about everything which the government was doing, at least until the November elections produced a government unpalatable to them. For example, there were complaints about the slow progress in denazification; after three months the Red Army generals complained 'it was time to see some major heads roll' (*da müsse man endlich einige grosse Köpfe rollen sehen*) (KR 22, 31 July) and, in general, Scheltov complained 'Your laws may be good, but the practice leaves something to be desired ... between the government and the masses there is a blank sheet of paper' (*Ihre Gesetze mögen gut sein, aber die Praxis lasse zu wünschen übrig ... zwischen Regierung und den Massen ein leeres Blatt Papier stehe)* (KR 23, 7 August). Despite this criticism, there is little sign of the kind of concentrated application of pressure seen elsewhere, for example in East Berlin.

In addition, new evidence suggests that the role played by the communist ministers in the state government was more complex than the caricature of a Soviet Trojan horse suggests. Their acceptance of, and participation in, Stalinist repression should not, of course, be ignored. But neither should their nationalism – or patriotism – be dismissed as merely Machiavellian and instrumental. Rather, anti-fascist and anti-Nazi commitment were inextricably linked with Austrian emotion (and a large dose of anti-Prussian feeling) (Knight, 1994, pp.181–3). Scepticism about the 'escape thesis' is further supported by a re-examination of two issues, which, ever since Adolf Schärf, have been seen as crucial turning-points which led away from Austria's 'sovietization': the return to the 1929 Constitution and Soviet economic confiscations.

After the government's initial declaration of its intent to return to the 1920 Constitution, the decision was taken on 13 May to include in the transitional Constitution (*Verfassungsüberleitungsgesetz*) the amendments which had been made in 1929. Schärf claims not only that the decision was taken in the teeth of communist opposition, but that the result prevented Austria becoming a 'people's democracy' (Schärf, 1955, pp.56–7). The record of the cabinet meeting on 13 May, (Protokolle, p.66) certainly broadly confirms Schärf's account of a confrontation between Renner and the communist ministers. Instead of letting the principle of unanimity be used as a blocking veto against him, Renner effectively turned it on its head, confronting the communists with an ultimatum to either accept the draft law or resign. In getting his own way he showed not only his forceful personality but also his dexterity as a chairman, behind which lay a lifetime of political experience.

Seeing this confrontation as a crucial turning-point nevertheless blurs the point that it was not in fact a defeat of a communist initiative but rather a successful attempt by Renner (apparently under pressure from Schärf and the leading constitutional lawyer Ludwig Adamovich) to move from the original declaration of independence (27 April). Second, as the (non-party) justice minister, Josef Gerö, argued at the time, there were respectable constitutional objections to a non-elected provisional government taking the constitutional decision proposed by Renner. Third, the lack of Soviet coordination, or even interest, in the issue is clear. Their lack of concern had already been demonstrated by Marshal Tolbuchin's lapse, when he declared on the entry of the Red Army into Vienna that the Soviets intented to restore the conditions which had existed before 1938, for this ignored the undemocratic nature of the 1934–38 regime. It was further confirmed by the fact that two months elapsed after the confrontation of May before the Soviet political adviser Kissilev asked Renner 'why we had taken the constitution of 1929 and not that of 1920 as our starting point and whether attempts were being made in the cabinet to implement a constitutional reform' (*warum wir die Verfassung von Jahre 1929 und nicht 1920 zum Ausgangpunkt genommen haben und ob Bestrebungen nach einer Verfassungsreform im Kabinett bestünden*). In reply Renner – on his own account – simply said they were not (KR 23, 7 August) It was this lack of coordination between the Trojans and their horse which surely explains why the communists had been unable to call Renner's bluff at the May confrontation. Last but not least, the insignificance of the constitutional changes made in 1929 (Ucakar, 1987, pp.440–41) surely undermines the great interpretative weight put on the decision to keep them (and, in any case, the most significant change – direct presidential elections – was put in abeyance in December 1945). (It is striking that, while most accounts agree with Schärf that a communist threat was averted by the decision, they differ widely as to what its constitutional significance was.)[3]

If the controversy over the Constitution has been distorted, or at least overinterpreted, so has a second major issue – Soviet confiscations. As already suggested, the basic Soviet aim of extracting as many economic resources from Austria as possible is not in dispute (Aichinger, 1977, pp.52–3), neither is the extent of looting by Red Army soldiers and its effect on Soviet popularity among the Austrian population. However, the Cold War led to insufficient weight being given to the purely economic imperatives behind Soviet policy – that is, the goal of reconstructing the shattered Soviet economy (Herz, 1982, pp.183–4). This was expressed by Marshal Tolbuchin with clarity, not to say brutality, when he told Austrian ministers in May (according to the Austrian translation):

> The law of war is, who gains the booty also exploits it. ... You all know, gentlemen, that the Soviet Union has lost all its industry up to the Volga and in particular its heavy industry.[4]

The consequences of this stance plagued the provisional government from the outset, but its full implications only emerged after the Potsdam Conference when the decision was made to allocate German external assets located in East and West Austria (and Europe) to the respective occupation power. The decision apparently reinforced the Soviet Union's 'maximalist' interpretation of its rights. As the crisis deepened throughout August, the Renner government was faced by an almost impossible choice – whether to negotiate in order to make the best of a bad situation or to resist and risk a damaging conflict. The first line led to the start of negotiations on a Soviet-Austrian joint stock company (Sanaphta) to produce oil and on a bilateral trade agreement (Aichinger, 1977, pp.308 ff). The second produced a first attempt, at least on paper, to nationalize German property. A row between Renner and the Soviet political representative, Kissilev, followed (KR 29). Kissilev declared the Austrian move to be in violation of Potsdam, reprimanded the government for not consulting the Soviet Union and reaffirmed that:

> The Soviet Union had to insist on reparations for all the losses which she had suffered and he was convinced that all the reparations which might be offered could not re-place these losses.[5]

Renner responded that:

> Germany has seized much of our wealth, which is now German property, but because of the unusual position of our country we cannot live without it.[6]

He vowed to 'fight against' [*sic*] the Potsdam decision. Although he conceded that the Soviet Union had not so far taken everything which had a German title he added:

> It is not enough to possess what is demonstrably old-Austrian. We must possess a certain amount of industries to be able to live, for we have to export in order to live. We have to obtain a third of our food needs from abroad and can only buy it. For this reason we will decide in cabinet what we consider necessary for the existence of our country, even if this contradicts some interpretation or other of the Potsdam agreement.[7]

This conversation (as reported by Renner) certainly supports Kissilev's comment that 'we are both talking from different platforms, which makes it fruitless to carry on discussing' (*Wir sprechen beide von einer verschiedenen Plattform aus, es wird also unfruchtbar sein, weiter zu diskutieren*). The massive gap between the Soviet and Austrian priorities could not have been made clearer. Yet it is also worth noting that although the Soviet authorities gave the needs of the Austrian reconstruction a low priority they did not discount them altogether. Another important point, which has nearly always been glossed over, is that Renner's case was that Austria's future depended on being able to keep the investments made by the Germans after the *Anschluß* under relatively 'normal' conditions as well as those taken over by forcible methods. Most importantly here, whatever their actual and potential damage to Austrian economy, Soviet confiscations cannot be assumed to have been *intended* as an instrument to undermine Austria and pave the way to a communist takeover.

The Austrian government's discussions of Soviet claims shows a greater range of opinion than might be expected. Several ministers saw some advantage in concluding a bilateral trade agreement in a situation where economic exchange had almost ground to a halt. And Renner pointed out that the proposed oil deal had to be viewed against the possibilities that the Soviet authorities would simply take away all the petroleum resources anyway:

> If now Russia instead offers a treaty, which will allow us to participate in the exploitation on a 50–50 basis, I have to recognize quite openly that considering the difficult circumstances this is a favourable solution, even though ... Austria ... wants to declare everything which was German to be state property.[8]

In short, the oil agreement was half a loaf instead of none. Renner added that a 50 per cent Austrian participation might be a 'good model' (*gutes Vorbild*) for dealings with Anglo-American oil companies. While Schärf was more dubious about the deal from the start, the trade minister (and later chancellor), Julius Raab, also saw some advantages, but all three expressed worries both about infringing the rights of Western interests (and thus becoming liable to compensate them later) and about going beyond the powers of a provisional government (KR 29, 5 September 1945). Whether as pretexts or not, these two points played an increasing role in arguments against the proposed agreement, and in the end stymied it.

In these discussions the communists were not simply a mouthpiece for Soviet claims. Admittedly they strongly urged the importance of concluding agreements on both trade and oil. Two weeks after Potsdam, Fischer stressed the importance of the trade talks and attacked what he alleged were attempts to sabotage them. But their support for nationalization was also, presumably knowingly, in conflict with Soviet claims. In forthright nationalist language, Koplenig called for the government to create a 'clear legal basis' (*klare rechtliche Grundlage*) and continued:

> In effect the Russians and the other occupation armies have the right to confiscate all German property and in law the Austrian state has no claim to this property as long as it does not pass a clear nationalization law. If we don't act quickly on this question, a lot of property will undoubtedly be traded and the government will be committing a sin of omission which is tantamount to a betrayal of the national interests of the Austrian people.[9]

Fischer even cited (in English) the principle of 'Right or wrong – my country' (KR 24, 15 August).

It is also interesting that neither Fischer nor Koplenig seem to have warned the Soviet Union of the government's planned nationalization. However, the Soviet veto clearly placed them in a difficult situation which they sought to evade by creating a diversion – attacking Western oil interests. At the beginning of October when the Red Army moved in to take over the oil under its physical supervision Fischer warned of the danger that the Soviet Union would unite with English and Dutch firms over the Austrians' heads, leaving only foreigners in control of Austrian resources (KR 35, 18 October).

In the end, Soviet actions exposed the difficulty of combining patriotism, communist ideology, anti-Nazism and blind admiration for the Soviet Union. While the communist leadership sometimes conceded not only the legal, but also the moral, right of the Soviet Union to take German assets they were committed to nationalization as an assertion of Austrian national interests (and, of course, socialist principles). In the end, here as elsewhere, the Soviet determination to pursue their own interests lost the communists the little popularity they had enjoyed and certainly contributed to their disastrous defeat in the November elections.

The Renner Government and the West

Discussions about Austrian sovereignty and the West in 1945 normally stress two aspects. One is diplomatic. It concerns the refusal of the West – and in particular the British government – to recognize the Renner government until the autumn of 1945, while the other makes larger claims about Western economic and geostrategic goals in Central Europe.

The reasons for the West's delay in recognizing the Renner government have been well covered (Stanley, 1975; Wagnleitner, 1986). As well as the objection to the Soviet *fait accompli*, which appeared to break the spirit – if not the letter – of the work of the European Advisory Commission, there was the fear of a repetition of Soviet moves in Poland and Rumania. Objections were made to the disproportionate weight of the communists in the government and, in particular, the appointment of Franz Honner as state secretary for the interior. Western fears may seem understandable in the light of events elsewhere in Eastern Europe but it is also clear that the West persisted in cold-shouldering Renner well after those fears had ceased to be reasonable. Indeed, they inflated the issue of recognition into a matter of prestige or used it as a pawn in the early Cold War. In the end the Americans and, more reluctantly, the British came to realize that their policy had taken them down a blind alley.

As both cabinet discussions and Josef Schöner's diary show, this slow transition was a frustrating experience for those Austrians in Vienna who were trying to rebuild the state and its administration (Schöner, 1992, pp.187, 208). To function at all, Renner needed to break through what he called the *Grenzkordon* (frontier cordon) to the West and extend the government's legitimacy by gaining the support of the provinces. He found it especially galling when the Western Allies came to Vienna at the start of June but left again soon afterwards without contacting the government (Protokolle, pp.186, 193). After the British elections Renner anticipated, with his usual optimism, that a 'a completely changed regime' would mean 'that we can hope for a much smoother confirmation of the government' (KR 20, 26 July). But this hope also soon evaporated. A week later Renner complained that the decrees issued by the British on their entry to Graz:

> ... reek of the filing cabinet. What they cooked up in England long ago without knowledge of the situation they are now publishing without observing what has happened in the meantime.[10]

Even more dangerously, the West's support of Austrian politicians in their own zones of occupation threatened to revive one ghost of the First Republic – the hostility of the provinces against the metropolis. When Karl Gruber, the provisional governor (*Landeshauptmann*) of Tyrol started to voice objections to the communist position in the government, Renner expressed this fear and, with it, the distaste of the traditional party politician for an unorthodox resistance leader:

> Now the point is not resistance but reconstruction, the three parties offer scope for every sort of belief. The members of the resistance movements and other movements will be recommended to enter one of the three parties.[11]

However, after a rearguard action at the Potsdam Conference, Western attempts to foster provincial resistance to Renner petered out. Once the Americans began to move away from it, the British had no option but to readjust their position as best they could. It was Renner who called the shots in summoning the provincial conference (*Länderkonferenz*) at the end of September. Shortly before it met, he rejected the British suggestion that the government should offer its resignation and, in general, stressed the importance of appearing neither defensive nor apologetic:

> I do not wish the state government to appear there with the feeling of a lack of legality, or even a bad conscience, or even with the feeling of sitting in the dock for having usurped a right, for which it is seeking to be covered. That would be a completely false point of view. We were convened by so called Reich parties, [*sic*] from all three of them, and not installed by a foreign power. The chairmen of these three Reich parties had the right, to act for the whole Reich [i.e.

> Austria]. So we did not lack in any way lack the legitimation as a state government.[12]

He was supported by the rest of the government. Gerö commented that resignation would be an act of hara-kiri which would lead posterity to conclude 'that we were usurpers' (KR 31, 19 September). In the event, although Renner did not dominate the conference to the same extent that he dominated his cabinet, the provincial conference was a success. Provincial objections to the government were more easily overcome, and provincial politicians more easily integrated than expected (Schöner, 1992, pp.392 ff). After some changes, which restored the provinces' constitutional powers, and an expansion rather than a reconstruction of the government, the way to national elections was clear.

Western slowness to adjust to the existence of the Renner government suggests an element of volatility, even irrationality, had entered their decision-making in the burgeoning Cold War. But was it also – as has been suggested – part of a broader Western strategy to extend its influence over Austria, and indeed Central Europe (Wagnleitner, 1986; Rauchensteiner, 1979)? One side of this argument can be traced back to the communist fears about Western capitalist interests which, as already outlined, were seen at the time as in conflict with Austria's national interests. Based on his observation of predatory US oil companies in South America and elsewhere (Rathkolb, 1985), Fischer saw the emergence of 'some mysterious English firm' (*irgendeine mysteriöse englische Firma*) as a sinister development and warned of 'speculative deals and deals of every sort' (*Spekulationenesgeschäfte und Schiebungen aller Art*) (KR 24, 15 August). He blamed these forces for sabotaging the negotiations with the Russians.

Predictably, the charge was rejected by Schärf who claimed that the socialists had been opposed to the treaty from the start, unless it took account of the government's provisional status. Renner supported him:

> On one point I am completely sure: that in the whole affair the intervention of foreign powers whether inside or outside our walls, has not had a significant influence, whether inside or outside the cabinet.[13]

The situation may not have been quite so clear-cut. There is no doubt that Western oil companies were expressing concern about their claims in Eastern Austria and that Western governments were warning against signing the oil agreement. But Western policy was not dictated by these claims. Even if the oil industry was a powerful lobby, in the case of Austria, its claims were seen by Western governments as little more than a lever to use against the

Soviet Union in order to relieve pressure on the Renner government. As for the socialists, whether Western claims were the reason or just an excuse to block the proposed treaty with the Russians is unclear. But there was no love lost between the Western oil companies and the socialists who, like the communists, were strongly committed to the principle of nationalization.

Quite apart from the differences between the Austrian politicians, it is worth noting that, contrary to Fischer's view, Western oil claims were not sheer invention. Before the *Anschluß* the oil companies had owned exploration options (although little actual exploration was done). After the *Anschluß* they were forced out by a discriminatory reallocation of these options to the benefit of German companies. Now they were in effect seeking to gain from the windfall which German investment in prospecting and exploration had produced. In short, their claims formed a third side of the triangle of claims for which, like the Austrian and the Soviet ones, some legal justification could be found.

The failure of the proposed oil deal and the Western role in it have sometimes been seen as part of a wider Western attempt to expand its influence into Central Europe (Rauchensteiner, 1979, Wagnleitner, 1986): Part of this view is based on the proposals put forward by Churchill in favour of making Austria the centre of a Danubian federation which would be Catholic, anti-communist and possibly ruled by the Habsburgs. Churchill's flights of fantasy on this point have often been taken too seriously. The serious point is that considerable doubts about Austria's economic 'viability' continued among Allied governments long after they had formally committed themselves to re-establishing the state (Keyserlingk, 1988). And these doubts did have a real economic basis – in 1945 Austria's future economic survival was far from self-evident. Nevertheless, by 1945 the West's commitment to re-establishing Austria was firmer than Robert Keyserlingk suggests (1988).

The Renner Government and the Establishment of Four-power Occupation

The 'Sanaphta' negotiations ground to a halt at about the same time as the four-power Allied Council met officially for the first time. It took another month before the government was given *de facto* recognition and, by then, it had become clear that four-power rule would mean more, rather than less, Allied involvement in the government's business. Renner had hopes that after the conference they would be in a position to demand of the four powers that they simply instructed the commanders in the provinces 'to follow what the state government lays down on this or that point' (*Ihr habt das zu machen, was die Staatsregierung euch in diesem oder jedem Punkte vorschreibt*)(KR 31, 19 September). This proved, once again, to be overoptimistic. Instead, it was his complaint, first applied to the British, that they were acting like an 'elephant into a row boat' (Rathkolb, 1985, p.133; Stanley, 1975, p.41) that now became generalized as a metaphor for the absurdity of four-power rule.

The higher level of Allied interference has led Gerald Stourzh and other historians to call the following period, lasting until the Second Control Agreement on June 1946, one of *'totale Kontrolle'* (Stourzh, 1966). While this probably overstates the Allies' ability to enforce measures within Austrian society it does convey the wide gulf which existed between Austrian and (some) Allied expectations. Sometimes the contrast contained elements of farce, such as the insistence of Lord Schuster, head of the British Legal Division, that Austria required a new constitution (KR 42, 12 December). Also, the delay caused by the need to go through the cumbersome quadripartite structures could be considerable.

In October Austrian resentment at four-power rule and impatience with the slowness of its bureaucracy surfaced in a series of heated discussions on currency. The inflationary impact of the enormous occupation armies (then estimated at around 200 000) came to a head at the end of the month. Once again, it was the communist ministers who voiced resentment in outspokenly nationalist terms. Ernst Fischer strongly opposed giving in to the Allies over the allocation of 2 million Schilling to the occupation funds. He described this and other Allied demands as 'shocking' (*empörend*) and meaning 'in effect a renunciation of Austria's independence' (*den faktischen Verzicht auf die Unabhängigkeit Östereichs*). He asked rhetorically if they 'wanted to move from being a liberated to a free country or to become a colony of foreign businesses' (*aus einem befreiten Lande eines freies Land werden oder ... eine Kolonie ausländischer Konzerne werden?*). The proposed law was a means of 'placing with our own consent, a noose around our neck, with which we will give up in future being a free independent state' (*mit dem wir mit unserer eigenen Zustimmung uns den Strich um den Hals legen mit dem wir darauf verzichten in Zukunft ein freier unabhängiger Staat zu sein*). The government should openly tell people 'what heavy burdens Austrian patriotism involves these days' (*welche schwere Aufgaben österreichischer Patriotismus heute bedeutet*) (KR 39, 23 November).

On this issue the socialists broadly agreed with the communists, while the finance minister, Georg Zimmermann, took a milder line. Renner wrote a letter to the Allied Council calling for a troop reduction and received a curt rebuff (Rauchensteiner, 1979). Long and complex negotiations with the Allies on the modalities of currency reform and the Allied allocation of 'occupation Schillings' followed. The currency reform at the end of the year brought no real resolution.

In considering these issues, which over the following years became a major symbol of Austria's sovereignty, it is useful to separate the politics from the economics. Currency, as a central aspect of both sovereignty and national emotion, can easily become exploited by demagogy. In the case of post-war Austria, this could obscure the basic point (which Zimmermann and others made) that, with or without the occupation, the re-establishment of an Austrian currency faced enormous obstacles. The devastation of the immediate post-war situation, the disruption of trade links and the shrinking of an export base which had always been weak meant that, in the short term, no currency had much chance of enjoying the confidence of the population – and certainly not enough to enable it to combat the black market.

The inflationary effect (and the black market impact) of the occupation armies naturally needs to be included in this equation. But so too does the countervailing importance of Austria gaining a Great Power commitment to keeping afloat. There was some truth in the response by the British commander-in-chief, McCreery, to the call for an end to the occupation that 'if the forces are withdrawn from Austria, there is very little likelihood of the country surviving' (Knight, 1986, p.29). In the medium term what mattered as much as the presence or absence of the occupation was that the Cold War led the United States to see Austria as a front-line state which could not be allowed to go under. In that sense it was not merely a matter of East–West tensions having 'repercussions in our little Austria' (*in unserem engen Österreich ihre Nachwirkungen*) (KR 34, 12 October), as Renner put it, but of those tensions creating the political conditions for Austria's survival.

Conclusion

In all the three perspectives discussed here, sovereignty was at the centre of consideration. In the first, the establishment of the Renner government is seen as a move towards its recovery, albeit one which could easily have gone wrong and led to Austria becoming a Soviet satellite with only the limited sovereignty allowed by the 'Brezhnev doctrine'. In the second, Austrian sovereignty is seen as under threat from the West, primarily due to the latter's refusal to recognize the government, but also because the West supposedly pursued economic and strategic goals incompatible with Austrian interests. In the third perspective, the belated recognition of the Renner government, instead of inaugurating a recovery of sovereignty, represented a false dawn. It led not to evacuation but to military bureaucracy, huge occupation forces and Great Power disagreements which were to keep Austria occupied for a decade. Some of the strengths and weaknesses of these perspectives have been discussed here.

A final point can be made about an assumption shared by all three: they take as their benchmark for evaluating sovereignty the commitment to independence made in the Moscow Declaration on the one hand, and the final restoration of sovereignty with the State Treaty in 1955 on the other. Although understandable, this surely takes insufficient account of the ambiguity of Austria's intermediate position between liberation and defeat. If the Moscow Declaration is seen less as an absolute promise of sovereignty which was then 'broken', but more as a propaganda instrument designed to stir up Austrian resistance (Keyserlingk, 1988), a less normative standard emerges. The lack of significant Austrian resistance in the following 18 months (at any rate when measured against these expectations) then points to a different, more relativist, measure of sovereignty for post-war Austria.

When the Renner government was set up, Austria was a partly defeated as well as a partly liberated country, and several aspects of Allied rule would have been unthinkable without this rationale. Not only denazification, but also the levying of occupation costs had to be justified under the rights of a victorious army under the Hague Convention. And Soviet seizures of German assets were related not just to Wehrmacht destruction in the Soviet Union but also to German investment in Austria for the purposes of waging war. In this sense, Renner was right to tell Kissilev that, as a result of Soviet policy, 'We don't feel that this expression "liberated country" quite conforms to the facts and our treatment' (*Wir empfinden diesen Ausdruck 'befreites Land' als eine den Tatsachen und unsere Behandlung nicht mehr ganz entsprechende Bezeichnung*) (KR 29, 5 September). Renner in particular was aware that a rigorous legal interpretation could bring Austria's treatment closer in line to that of Germany. His comments in the immediate post-war period frequently show his sense of the legal shakiness of Austria's claims to be a clearly liberated country. This applies both to Soviet claims (Protokolle, p.152) and to the Allied Commission which, he stated, was claiming 'full sovereignty over the territory based on the laws of war' (*nach kriegsrechtlichen Grundsätzen die volle Hoheit über das Gebiet*) (KR 25, 18 August). To Josef Schöner, Renner's 'begging and humble tones' were defensive and inept. He complained that Renner 'portrays us forcibly as a part of the defeated Germany, which simply happens to be in line for a bit better treatment (*stellte uns mit Gewalt als einen Teil des besiegten Deutschland dar, der halt zufällig ein bisserl anders behandelt werden soll!*) (Schöner, 1992, pp.227, 235). But Schöner himself feared that the establishment of the Allied Commission might lead to the disbanding of the fledgling government and the sacking of its civil servants (Schöner, 1992, pp.338–9).

Of course, such a policy would have been neither practicable or wise. But it is important to see the sovereignty which Austria had achieved at the end of 1945 against the full range of possibilities. It then becomes clear that the Renner government achieved a significant shift in the Allied position. After all, in the discussions of the European Advisory Commission, an Austrian government was planned only in the second phase – after the establishment of an Allied administration. This shift was due partly to chance, but also to the logic of the early Cold War and to self-confident lobbying despite the behind-the-scenes doubt, self-doubt and confusion suggested by the cabinet discussions. In the case of Renner himself it was reinforced by his sense that the *Anschluß* had in some sense been an expression of the right of self-determination, however misused, and perhaps even by an uneasy conscience about his own role. But Renner, the politician and the indefatigable optimist, also saw that the key to shifting Austria's treatment was Western public opinion. One example was the decision by the United Nations Relief and Rehabilitation Administration (UNRRA) in August to treat Austria as a liberated country, which led Renner to call for a step-by-step campaign to shift international public opinion in Austria's favour (Knight, 1994, p.186; Mähr, 1989, pp.30–31). Later in the year, with more confidence than before, Renner seems to have adopted the official 'victim thesis' that there could be no question of a peace treaty since 'in terms of national and international law we were not there' (*Wir waren staats- und völkerrechtlich nicht da*) (KR 39, 23 November).

By seeing the shift towards international acceptance of this view in less normative and more historical terms I do not, of course, want to argue that Austrian sovereignty should have been less than it was at the end of the period of the state government. Rather, I wish to argue that, under different circumstances, it might easily have been. In other words, in December 1945, Austria's sovereignty might be seen not as a glass which was half-empty but as one which was half – or at least a quarter – full.

Notes

1 Österreichische Gesellschaft für Quellenkunde (ed.), *Protokolle des Kabinettsrates der Provisorischen Regierung Karl Renner 1945, Band 1 29. April 1945 bis 10 Juli 1945*, Vienna: Berger 1995 (henceforth Protokolle); minutes of the remaining sessions, Osterreichisches Staatsarchiv, Archiv der Republik, Vienna are to be published shortly. They will be cited here as KR followed by the number of the session and the date. I am grateful to Austrian Federal Chancellory for permission to research into them.

2 'Für die Rote Armee sei das Wichtigste gewesen, das Land nicht ohne Verwaltung zu lassen ... wir wollen nichts als eine Verbesserung Ihrer Lage. Er lehne es ab, eine oder die andere Partei zu verteidigen' (KR 23, 7 August).

3 Renner's posthumously published account (1953, p.235), presumably edited by Schärf, refers to a communist insistence on the 1920 Constitution; Portisch (1986, p.162) sees the communist desire for a new constitution being blocked by the prior commitment (in

the *Unabhängigkeitserklärung*) to the 1920 Constitution; Rauscher (1995, pp.329–30) refers to communist objections to the centralised interim constitution (*vorläufige Verfassung*).

4 'Das Gesetz des Krieges ist: wer die Beute macht, nützt auch diese Beute aus ... Sie wissen alle, meine Herren, daß die sowjetische Union [*sic*] ihre ganze Industrie bis an die Wolga verloren hat und besonderes die Schwerindustrie' (Protokolle, p.135).

5 '... die Sowjetunion müsse auf Reparationen für alle Verluste, die sie erlitten habe, bestehen, und er sei überzeugt, daß alle Reparationen, die man ihr bieten wolle und könne, diese Verluste nicht gutmachen könne' (KR 29, 5 September).

6 'Deutschland hat von unseren Reichtümern vieles an sich gerissen, das nunmehr deutsches Eigentum ist, ihnen das wir jedoch in Österreich bei der eigentümlichen Lage unseres Landes nicht leben können' (KR 29, 5 September).

7 '... es genügt uns nicht, das zu besitzen, was als altösterreich nachweisbar ist. Wir müssen ein gewisses Maß von Industrien besitzen, um leben zu können, denn wir müssen exportieren, um zu leben. Wir müssen ein Drittel unseres Nahrungsbedarfs aus dem Auslande beziehen und können es nur kaufen. Aus diesem Grunde werden wir im Kabinett das beschließen, was wir als für die Existenz unseres Landes notwendig halten, auch wenn dies irgend einer Interpretation der Beschlüsse der Potsdamer ... Konferenz widerspricht' (KR 29, 5 September).

8 'Wenn nun Russland uns anstelle dessen einen Vertrag anbietet, durch den wir 50 zu 50 an der Ausbeutung mitwirken, so erkenne ich ganz offen an, daß das für Österreich in Anbetracht der schwierigen Umstände eine günstige Lösung ist wiewohl ... Österreich ... alles was da deutsch war, als Staatseigentum erklären [will]' (KR 29, 5 September).

9 '... faktisch haben die Russen und die anderen Besatzungsarmeen das Recht alles deutsche Eigentum zu beschlagnahmen, und rechtlich hat der österrreichische Staat auf dieses Eigentum keinen Aspruch, solange er nicht ein klares Gesetz über die Verstaatlichung beschließt. Wenn wir in dieser Frage nicht rasch handeln, wird zweifellos viel Vermögen verschleppt und verschoben und die Regierung begeht eine Unterlassung, die einem Verrat an den nationalen Interessen des österreichischen Volkes gleichkommt' (KR 24, 15 August).

10 '... riechen nach der Schublade. Was sie vorher in England längst ausgekocht haben ohne Kenntnis der Dinge, das publizieren sie und achten nicht darauf, was inzwischen geschehen ist' (KR 22, 31 July).

11 '... jetzt heißt es nicht Widerstand, sondern Wiederaufbau, die drei Parteien bieten für jede Art der Gesinnung Raum. Den Mitgliedern der Widerstandsbewegung und der anderen Bewegungen wird empfohlen, in eine der drei Partein einzutreten' (KRP 19, 24 July).

12 'Ich möchte nicht, daß die Staatsregierung dort mit dem Gefühl eines mangelnden Rechte oder gar eines schlechten Gewissens erscheint, vielleicht mit dem Gefühlt gar, auf der Anklagebank zu sitzen, weil man sich ein Recht usurpiert habe, wofür man hinterher Deckung suchen soll. Das wäre ein absolut falscher Gesichtspunkt. Wir sind von sog. Reichsparteien und zwar von allen drei Reichsparteien berufen und nicht durch eine auswärtige Macht eingesetzt worden. Die Vorsitzenden dieser drei Reichsparteien hatten das Recht, für die ganze Partei des Reiches zu handeln. Es hat uns also keineswegs die Legitimation als Staatsregierung gefehlt. ...' (KR 31, 19 September).

13 'In einem Punkt bin ich vollständig sicher, daß in der ganzen Angelegenheit die Einmischung auswärtiger Kapitalmächte weder intra noch extra muros, weder im Kabinett noch außerhalb des Kabinetts einen wesentlichen Einfluß genommen hat' (KR 30, 12 September).

Bibliography

Primary Sources

Fischer, E. (1973), *Das Ende Einer Illusion – Erinnerungen 1945–1955*, Vienna: Molden Knight, R. (1988) (ed.), *'Ich bin dafür, die Sache in die Länge zu ziehen'. Die Wortprotokolle der österreichischen Bundesregierung von 1945 bis 1952 über die Entschädigung der Juden*, Frankfurt/Main: Athenäum.

Österreichische Gesellschaft für Quellenkunde (ed.) (1995), *Protokolle des Kabinettsrates der Provisorischen Regierung Karl Renner 1945*, vol. 1 29. April 1945 bis 10 Juli 1945, Vienna: Berger.

Protokolle des Kabinettsrates der Provisorischen Staatsregierung, Österreichisches Staatsarchiv, Archiv der Republik, Vienna.

Rathkolb, O. (1985), *Gesellschaft und Politik am Beginn der Zweiten Republik, Vertrauliche Berichte der US Militäradministration aus Österreich 1945 in englischer Originalfassung*, Vienna Cologne Graz: Böhlau.

Renner, K. (1945), *Österreichs und die Einsetzung der Provisorischen Regierung der Republik*, Vienna. *Österreich über die Organisation der Zusammenarbeit der militärischen und zivilen Behörden, 1945*, Vienna: Staatsdruckerei.

Renner, K. (1945), *Denkschrift über die Geschichte der Unabhängigkeitserklärung Österreichs und die Einsetzung der Provisorischen Regierung der Republik*, Vienna: Staatsdruckerei.

Renner, K. (1945), *Drei Monate Aufbauarbeit der Provisorischen Staatsregierung der Republik Österreich*, Vienna: Staatsdruckerei.

Renner, K. (1953), *Österreich von der ersten zur zweiten Republik* (nachgelassene Werke Band II), Vienna: Staatsdruckerei.

Schärf, A. (1948), *April 1945 in Wien*, Vienna: Verlag der Wiener Volksbuchhandlung.

Schärf, Adolf (1950), *Zwischen Demokratie und Volksdemokratie. Österreichs Einigung und Wiederaufrichtung im Jahre 1945*, Vienna: Verlag der Wiener Volksbuchhandlung.

Schärf, A. (1955), *Österreichs Erneuerung 1945–1955. Das erste Jahrzehnt der zweiten Republik*, Vienna: Verlag der Wiener Volksbuchhandlung.

Schilcher, A. (1980), *Österreich und die Großmächte. Dokumente zur österreichischen Außenpolitik 1945–1955*, Vienna: Österreichische Geselleschaft für Zeitgeschichte.

Schöner, J. (1992), *Wiener Tagebuch 1944–1945*, ed. Eva-Marie Csáky, Franz Matscher, Gerald Stourzh, Vienna: Böhlau.

Secondary Sources

Ableitinger, Alfred (1992), 'Die innenpolitische Entwicklung' in Wolfgang Mantl (ed.), *Politik in Österreich: Die Zweite Republik: Bestand und Wandel*, Vienna: Böhlau.

Aichinger, W. (1977), *Sowjetische Österreichpolitik 1943–1945*, Vienna: Österreichische Geselleschaft für Zeitgeschichte.

Bader, W. (1966), *Austria between East and West 1945–1955*, Stanford: Stanford University Press.
Brook-Shepherd, G. (1957), *Austrian Odyssey*, London: Macmillan.
Barker, E. (1973), *Austria 1917–1972*, London: Macmillan.
Bischof, G. (1989), *Between Responsibility and Rehabilitation. Austria in International Politics, 1940–50*, Harvard PhD.
Herz, Martin (1982), 'The view from Austria' in Thomas T. Hammond (ed.), *Witnesses to the Cold War*, Seattle and London: University of Washington Press.
Keyserlingk, R. (1988), *Austria in World War Two: An Anglo-American Dilemma*, Kingston/Montreal: McGill-Queens University Press.
Knight, Robert (1986), 'British Policy towards Occupied Austria 1945–1951', London PhD thesis.
Knight, Robert (1994), 'Education and National Identity in Austria after the Second World War', in Ritchie Robertson and Edward Timms (eds), *The Habsburg Legacy, National Identity in Historical Perspective*, Edinburgh: Edinburgh University Press.
Knight, Robert (1996), 'Narratives in Post-war Austrian Historiography', in Anthony Bushell (ed.), *Studies in Political and Cultural Re-emergence 1945–1955*, University of Wales Press.
Kurth Cronin, A. (1986), *Great Power Politics and the Struggle over Austria 1945–1955*, Ithaca, NY: Cornell University Press.
Mähr,W. (1989), *Der Marshallplan in Österreich*, Vienna Graz Cologne: Styria.
Pelinka, A. (1989), *Karl Renner zur Einführung*, Hamburg: Junius.
Pelinka, Anton (1992), 'Karl Renner – A Man for all Seasons', *Austrian History Yearbook*, XXIII.
Portisch, H. (1986), *Österreich II: Die Wiedergeburt unseres Staates, Wien 1985*, vol. 2, Der lange Weg zur Freiheit, Vienna: Kremayr and Scheriau.
Rauchensteiner, M. (1979), *Der Sonderfall: Die Besatzungszeit in Österreich 1945 bis 1955*, Graz: Styria.
Rauscher, W. (1995), *Karl Renner: Ein österreichischer Mythos*, Vienna: Überreuther.
Stadler, K. (1982), *Adolf Schärf. Mensch. Politiker Staatsmann*, Vienna Munich Zürich: Europa.
Stanley, Guy, D (1975), 'Die britischen Vorbehalte gegenüber der provisorischen Regierung Renner 1945', *Zeitgeschichte*, **3**.
Stourzh, Gerald (1966), 'Die Regierung Renner, die Anfänge der Regierung Figl und die Alliierte Kommission für Österreich. September 1945 bis April 1946', in *Archiv für österreichische Geschichte*, **125**, 1966.
Stourzh, G. (1980), *Geschichte des Staatsvertrages 1945–1955 Österreichs Weg zur Neutralität*, Vienna: Styria.
Swain, G. and Swain, N. (1993), *Eastern Europe since 1945*, London: Macmillan.
Ucakar, K. (1987), *Demokratie und Wahlrecht in Österreich*, Vienna: Böhlau.
Wagnleitner, Reinhold (1978), 'Die Kontinuität der britischen Aussenpolitik nach dem Wahlsieg der Labour Party im Juli 1945', *Zeitgeschichte*, **5** (7).
Wagnleitner, Reinhold (1986), 'Die britische Österreichplanung' in Anton Pelinka and Rolf Steininger (eds), *Österreich und die Sieger*, Vienna: Braumüller.

3 Austrian Identity in a Schizophrenic Age: Hilde Spiel and the Literary Politics of Exile and Reintegration

Edward Timms

Introduction

In a speech delivered on 27 April 1995 at a special session of the Austrian parliament, Thomas Klestil found moving words to commemorate the 50th anniversary of the Second Republic:

> Hardly any other country in Europe has had more lessons to learn during this century than Austria. Hardly any country has had its sense of identity more profoundly disrupted, before so convincingly finding its way through a process involving great sacrifice to freedom and independence, democracy and prosperity. This deeply divided history presents itself to us when today, on the 50th birthday of the Second Republic, we draw up a balance and consider how we are to relate to that legacy from the past.[1]

Where President Klestil describes the political history of modern Austria as 'divided' (*zerklüftet*), it might be even more apposite to use the word 'schizophrenic', since it draws attention to the profound psychological tensions resulting from the traumas of the National Socialist period. The exiled Austrian author, Hilde Spiel, describing her impressions on returning to Vienna in 1946 as a British war correspondent, speaks of a 'schizophrenic spiritual condition' (*schizophrener Seelenzustand*) (Spiel, 1991a, p.226). Her writings, which will be analysed towards the end of this chapter, illuminate three main phases in the development of that condition: enthusiasm for the *Anschluß*, the Free Austria Movement, and the challenge of reintegration after 1945.

Enthusiasm for the *Anschluß*

When we consider how firmly established Austrian national identity is today, 50 years after the end of the Second World War, it is easy to forget how completely the First Republic was wiped off the map. In his history of the inter-war period, Hellmut Andics memorably described the First Austrian Republic as the 'State Which No One Wanted' (Andics, 1962). It is sometimes forgotten that, even under Nazi occupation, Austria was still the state which no one wanted. Initially, it was reduced to the status of the Ostmark – a province of the Greater German Reich. After 1942 even the name Ostmark disappeared, and all that was left was a collection of *Reichsgaue* (Figure 3.1). Worse still, the international community, after registering token protests, in practice accepted the annexation. In his book, *Austria in World War II: An Anglo-American Dilemma*, the diplomatic historian Robert H. Keyserlingk sums the situation up conclusively:

> In 1938 both the British and American governments recognized the Anschluß not only in fact but also in law, and they upheld this position throughout the war. ... Because the Anschluß was recognized, Austria was considered enemy territory throughout the war, and Austrians were placed in the category of German nationals and enemy aliens. (Keyserlingk, 1988, p.186)

Keyserlingk goes on to argue that Western statesmen consistently envisaged a 'federative solution' in Central Europe after the war, not the restoration of Austrian independence. Even the Moscow Declaration of 30 October 1943, he claims,

> ... did not represent serious Anglo-American planning, but formed part of a broader military strategy of fanning revolts ... . Active anti-Nazi resistance in Austria would seriously threaten Germany's war effort in a vital economic and military sector. The Moscow Declaration was meant to trigger an Austrian revolt. (Keyserlingk, 1988, p.189)

If we accept these conclusions, then the question arises: who, in the period around 1940, *was* committed to restoring the independence of Austria? In the Ostmark itself, there were, of course, numerous individuals opposed to the Nazi takeover. In the wake of the *Anschluß* nearly 20 000 Austrians were arrested and detained by the Gestapo (Luza, 1984, p.15). The threat of reprisals thus lay behind the *völkisch* propaganda of April 1938, which proclaimed that all German blood belonged together (Figure 3.2). In the referendum of 10 April 1938, 99.7 per cent of the votes cast were in favour of the *Anschluß* – an astonishingly high figure, even allowing for widespread intimidation. Chancellor Schuschnigg and the leaders of the

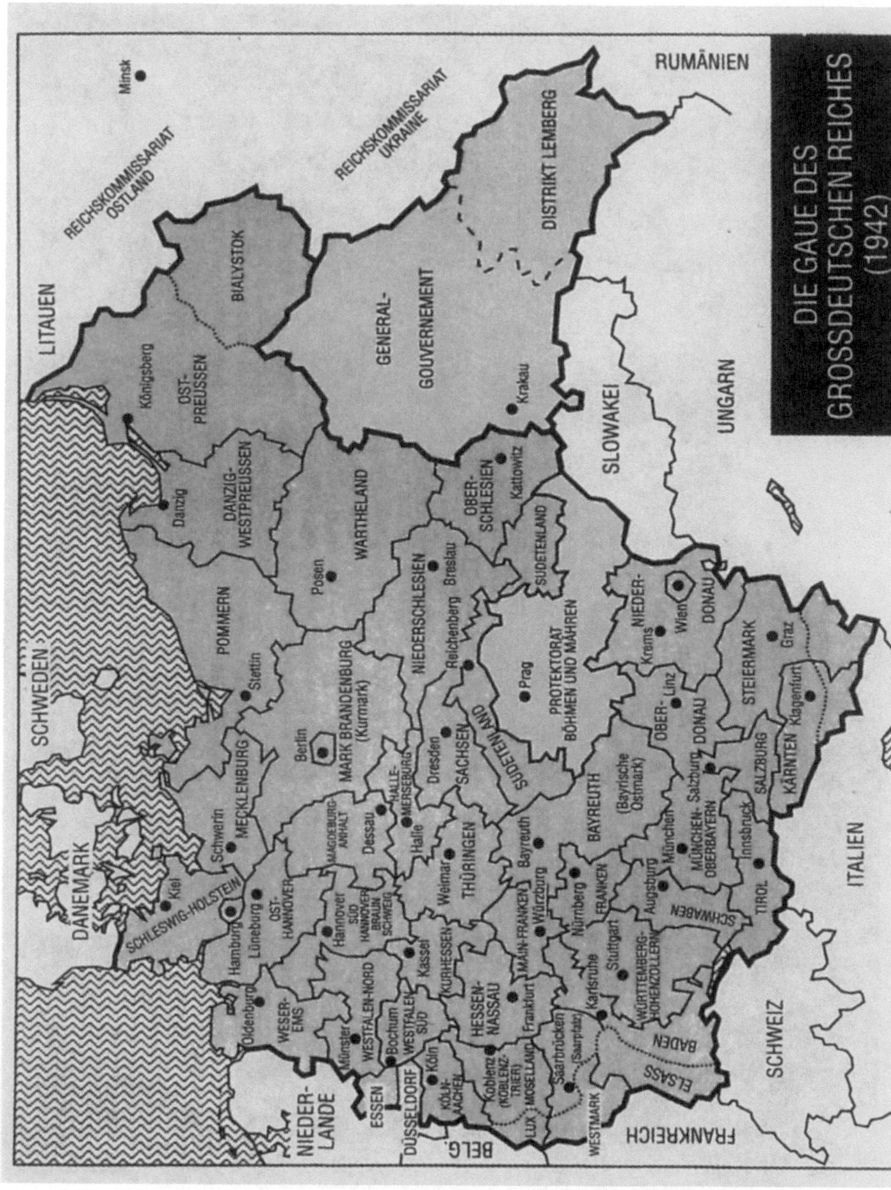

Figure 3.1 Map of Germany (1942) showing how Austria was absorbed into 'Die Gaue des Großdeutschen Reiches'
Reproduced from *Atlas Zeitgeschichte* by Manfred Scheuch by kind permission of Verlag Christian Brandstätter, Vienna.

Figure 3.2 Nazi propaganda display in Vienna, April 1938
Reproduced from *Anna & Anna* by Hilde Spiel by kind permission of Verlag Kremayr & Schierau, Vienna.

Ständestaat were all in prison or in concentration camps, so there was no conservative leader who might have rallied some resistance. To make matters worse, Karl Renner, founding father of the Republic, openly supported the *Anschluß*. After 1945 it was argued that Renner, like many others, acted under duress, but this claim is hard to reconcile with the extraordinary euphoria which seized Austria in the spring of 1938. It was not simply fear of the Nazis that led so many Austrians to welcome the destruction of the First Republic, but enthusiasm for the *Anschluß*. Austrian independence was undermined by what President Klestil describes as 'the lack of a positive attitude towards the state'.[2]

The key figure in this collapse of faith in Austria was Karl Renner. It is often assumed that, after the *Anschluß*, Renner withdrew into private life. In fact, during the summer and autumn of 1938 he devoted himself to writing one of the most revealing political documents of this period – the 80-page pamphlet entitled *Die Gründung der Republik Deutschösterreich, der Anschluß und die Sudetendeutschen* (The Founding of the Republic of German-Austria, the *Anschluß* and the Sudeten Germans). Attempts have sometimes been made to deny the authenticity of this document which survives in the form of page proofs corrected in Renner's hand (Figure 3.3). In fact, the pamphlet shows that Renner supported the *Anschluß* as a longstanding political commitment, not merely a matter of expediency. Indeed, as he repeatedly emphasizes, the absorption of Austria into the German Reich was something for which he had campaigned ever since November 1918.

In *Die Gründung der Republik Deutschösterreich* Renner repeatedly disparages the independence of Austria. He insists that all the provinces of Austria (with the exception of Styria) were overwhelmingly in favour of the *Anschluß* throughout the period of the First Republic, at least until Dollfuß began to exercise his seductive influence:

> It was only in much later years, when people increasingly began to doubt whether *Anschluß* was achieveable, that the [Christian-Social] leaders allowed themselves to be seduced by Engelbert Dollfuß into regarding the Austrian part of the German *Volk* not merely as a branch of the German nation, but as a nation in its own right, and to praise the independence of Austria, that harsh shackle imposed by Saint-Germain, as if it were an absolute panacea![3]

In a further passage Renner even expresses an aversion to the very name of Austria. In preference to *Österreich* he had apparently proposed the adoption of the name *Die Ostalpenlande*:

> That the German Alpine lands should become an independent state on their own appeared equally inconceivable and intolerable to all factions at the time when the state was being reconstituted. That was simply not on the table! The Austrian

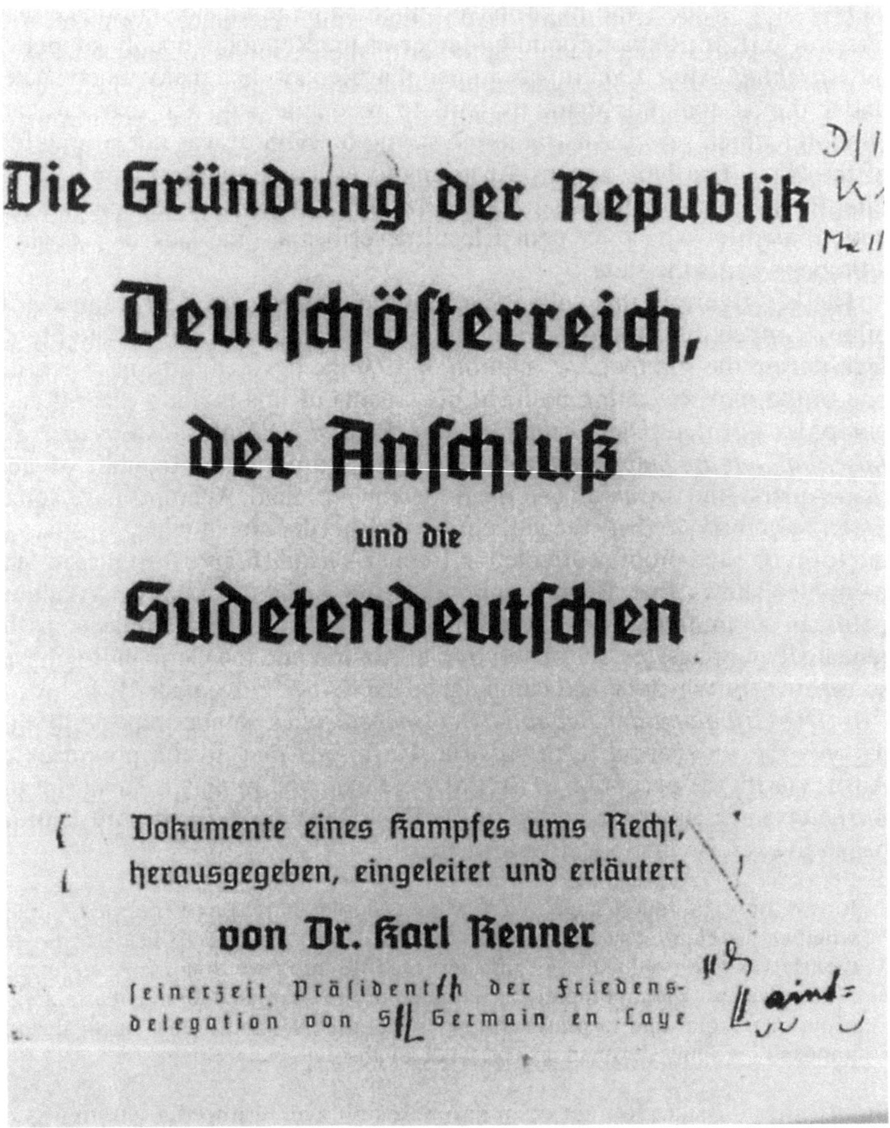

Die Gründung der Republik

Deutschösterreich,

der Anschluß

und die

Sudetendeutschen

Dokumente eines Kampfes ums Recht,
herausgegeben, eingeleitet und erläutert

von Dr. Karl Renner

seinerzeit Präsident der Friedens-
delegation von St. Germain en Laye

Figure 3.3 Title page of *Die Gründung der Republik Deutschösterreich* – the pamphlet written by Karl Renner in summer 1938 to justify the *Anschluß*

Reproduced from *Karl Renner, der Anschluß und die Sudentendeutschen*, ed. Eduard Rabofsky by kind permission of Globus Verlag, Vienna.

> Alpine lands were basically nothing more than the Ostmark of the Babenbergs. .... When the Peace Treaty did bring this about, I proposed to a circle of leading men that we should choose the name 'The Eastern Alpine Lands', in place of the name Austria, which was the name of the great power that had collapsed. And that was the name which I incorporated in the national anthem.[4]

For Renner, writing in the summer of 1938, the Austrians, like the population of the Sudetenland, are essentially Germans. In an even more tendentious passage, written just as Nazi Germany was intensifying the military threat to Czechoslovakia, he argues that it is legitimate to reunite these 'divided' nations by all possible means, if necessary 'by war'. The peace treaties of 1919, which denied the Austrians and the Sudetenlanders the right to self-determination, were imposed by force:

> ... hence it must now and also in the future be legitimate for those nations which are still divided or indeed were divided for the first time in 1919 to become united by all possible means, if necessary even by means of war.[5]

Renner's argument was designed to justify not simply the *Anschluß* but also the German annexation of the Sudetenland 'through the threat of war and if necessary through war' (Renner, 1990, p.78). However, his pamphlet had only reached the proof stage when it was overtaken by events – specifically by the Munich Agreement – which rendered his arguments in favour of war redundant. Fortunately for Renner's subsequent reputation, this pamphlet defending German military expansion and denigrating the existence of Austria was not published during his lifetime (it did not appear until 1990).[6]

The fact that the Social Democratic leadership, from Karl Renner in Gloggnitz to Otto Bauer and Oskar Pollak in exile, showed so little interest in Austria's independence, helps us to understand a further significant factor: the weakness of the Austrian resistance during the Second World War. Austria – as President Klestil acknowledged in his speech of 27 April – was a country in which there was 'no military and only limited political resistance' (Klestil, 1995). However, this is not to devalue the numerous individual acts of resistance against the Nazi regime. The study, *The Resistance in Austria 1938–1945*, by Radomir V. Luza leaves us filled with admiration for the courageous efforts of individuals, ranging from Catholic priests and Jehovah's Witnesses to Communists and Revolutionary Socialists. But this does not alter the fact that there was no cohesive Austrian resistance or partisan movement comparable to that in France or Poland. Luza himself emphasizes in his conclusion that the Austrian resistance 'lacked a coordinated centrally organized leadership' and that 'left to themselves, the clandestine forces were individually weak and incapable of than more than scattered and merely local actions'. The principal exception was the

Austrian Communist Party. Through an analysis of the ideological affiliations of 2795 Austrians involved in resistance activities, Luza discovered that approximately 45 per cent had links with the Communist Party. However, according to his calculations, only 5 per cent were associated with the Social Democrats or Revolutionary Socialists. The Social Democrats did not succeed in organizing a strong or cohesive resistance movement, although Adolf Schärf gained considerable respect through his attempts to coordinate underground activities (Luza, 1984, pp.83, 218–19, 276–7 and 292–3).

The scattered resistance groups that did develop in Austria were brutally crushed by the Gestapo, and the losses endured by the Austrian people should certainly not be underestimated. The figures given by Luza show that more than 2700 Austrians were executed between 1938 and 1945 for resistance-related activities, while a further 16 000 died in concentration camps, in addition to the 65 000 Austrians of Jewish origin who were murdered by the Nazis. But it was only towards the end of the war, when the German army was retreating on all fronts, that an organized Austrian resistance movement, known as 05, finally emerged (Luza, 1984, pp.160–64 and 274–5). So strong was the Nazi stranglehold that it was almost inevitable that the campaign to restore Austria's independence would have to be conducted from exile. We are all familiar with the importance of the Czech, Polish, Dutch and Belgian governments in exile, not to mention the Free French movement led by General de Gaulle. What, one might ask, was the role of the Austrian government in exile?

The answer, of course, is that there was no Austrian government in exile. Austria after 1938 was technically a province of Greater Germany, and most Austrians held German passports, including those who escaped into exile after 1938. It would thus have been impossible under international law to establish such a government. Those who might conceivably have represented an independent Austria were treated as 'enemy aliens', if not interned as potential German spies. Moreover, even in exile there was a lack of political leadership. There was no Austrian de Gaulle nor any statesman of stature dedicated to the defence of the Republic. On the conservative wing, Kurt von Schuschnigg was too compromised by the anti-democratic policies of the *Ständestaat* to be acceptable as leader of any government in exile. The second key figure in the conservative camp, Sir George Franckenstein, long-serving Austrian ambassador in London, did provide a rallying point for Austrian patriots. But when Franckenstein opted to become a British citizen, this reinforced the impression that Austria was a lost cause.

In the United States the head of the conservative Free Austria Movement could also claim to have resisted Nazism, since he had been a member of the Schuschnigg cabinet. But the political role he played was so ineffective that few people will be familiar with his name – Hans Rott. In autumn 1943, after the Moscow Declaration, Rott did make an attempt to persuade the American State Department to consider setting up an Austrian government in exile but he was told in no uncertain terms that the position of Austria was *not* analogous to that of countries that were genuinely under foreign military occupation, such as Norway or Belgium (Keyserlingk, 1988, p.171). The only Austrian leader in the United States who enjoyed the confidence of President Roosevelt was Otto von Habsburg. But Otto and the legitimists showed little interest in the Austrian Republic, since they were dreaming of recreating 'a postwar Danubian federation under Habsburg rule' (Keyserlingk, 1988, p.63).

The Free Austria Movement

Who did believe in an independent Austria? For an answer to this question we must turn to the groups of artists and writers who formed the Free Austria Movement in exile. One of the traditional functions of imaginative literature is to sustain a concept of the nation which has been politically suppressed by autocratic regimes or foreign invaders. We only need to think of the great patriotic poets who, during the nineteenth century, sustained Polish or Czech national identity or the *samizdat* writers of Eastern Europe who kept alive the spirit of national resistance under Soviet domination. In the case of Austria between 1938 and 1945, however, the situation was different – indeed, profoundly schizophrenic. The principal Austrian patriots were rootless cosmopolitans such as Joseph Roth in Paris, Oskar Kokoschka in London or Stefan Zweig in Bath. Austrian authors who remained in the Ostmark, with few exceptions, vociferously declared themselves to be Germans.

The bibliography of Austrian literature in the Nazi period, *Handbuch der Österreichischen Literatur im Nationalsozialismus*, which is being prepared by Professor Uwe Baur, sets out this depressing story. The list of pan-German and pro-Nazi anthologies of writings by Austrian authors published between 1933 and 1945 includes well over 100 volumes, with titles like *Gesänge der Ostmark*, *Heim ins Reich* and *Volk auf dem Marsch*. The great names of conservative Austrian writing are all there: Rudolf Hans Bartsch, Richard Billinger, Bruno Brehm, Franz Karl Ginzkey, Paula Grogger, Robert Hohlbaum, Heinz Kindermann, Mirko Jelusich, Alexander Lernet-Holenia, Max Mell, Franz Nabl, Friedrich Schreyvogel, Karl Hans Strobl, Franz Tumler, Karl Heinrich Waggerl, Hans Watzlik and Josef Weinheber (Baur, forthcoming). After the *Anschluß* there was a stampede by Austrian writers to declare that they were Germans. Many of them, like Strobl and

Schreyvogel, were not simply patriotically pro-German but fanatically pro-Nazi. Their presiding genius was Baldur von Schirach, the Nazi youth leader who as *Reichsstatthalter* in Vienna effectively controlled Austrian cultural life. Insofar as there was any significant attempt to sustain a separate Austrian identity, it was not national or political, but regional and folkloristic, like Weinheber's poems about Vienna or Max Mell's evocation of Styria in *Steirische Heimat* (1943). Unlike Germany itself, Austria does not seem, during the Nazi period, to have produced a significant literature of 'inner emigration'. Were there really no devout Austrians who wrote diaries during the night, recording their revulsion at the Nazi regime and their faith in a national rebirth, as did Theodor Haecker, Luise Rinser and Viktor Klemperer in Germany?

During that profoundly schizophrenic period between 1938 and 1945 the concept of a 'Free Austria' was largely sustained by writers, artists and intellectuals in exile. 'AUSTRIA SHALL BE FREE' declared a poster that was displayed not on the Ringstrasse but in Piccadilly Circus (Figure 3.4). The achievement of these Austrian exile groups is summed up in the preface to a volume of essays published in 1995 to mark the 50th anniversary of the liberation of Austria under the title *Austrian Exodus: The Creative Achievements of Refugees from National Socialism*:

> Politically, the *Anschluß* had in effect been accepted by the international community, at least until the Moscow Declaration of 1943 proclaimed that the Allies would re-establish the Austrian Republic. Culturally, it thus became even more important for the exiles to sustain through their artistic activities the concept of a 'Free Austria'. Since there was no Austrian government in exile, the poets had to take over the role of leadership normally played by politicians. The reaffirmation of Austrian independence during the years 1938–45 was essentially the task of small groups of poets and painters, actors, musicians and cabaret performers in Hampstead, Swiss Cottage and Golders Green (parallelled by similar groups in the United States). (Timms and Robertson, 1995, p.xii)

Perhaps it is misleading to speak of 'small groups' of poets and artists. It should be remembered that, by the end of 1943, no less than 27 organizations, representing more than 7000 members, had joined the Free Austria Movement in London (Muchitsch, 1995, p.31).

These groups were, of course, extremely diverse, representing the whole political spectrum from Communists and Revolutionary Socialists on the Left to Christian-Socials and monarchists on the Right. Given the failures of the traditional leadership in both the conservative and socialist camps, it was perhaps inevitable that the well organized communist cadres should have exerted a disproportionate influence. There have been many accounts of the infighting between the different factions and the personality clashes within

Figure 3.4 'Austria Shall Be Free': poster for an exhibition in London, summer 1943
Reproduced from *Österreicher im Exil: Grossbritannien 1938–1945*, ed. Wolfgang Muchitsch by kind permission of Österreichischer Bundesverlag, Vienna.

their leadership. It is nevertheless possible to discern within this diversity an overriding unity of purpose: to defy Hitler's attempt to erase Austria from the map. The one principle to which all groups subscribed – even (after some hestitation) the Social Democrats – was the independence of Austria.

After the Moscow Declaration, this political goal naturally became more explicit. But, even in earlier publications, the insistence that Austria is essentially *different* from Germany forms a *leitmotif*. The Free Austria exhibition in Piccadilly Circus dates from the summer of 1943, several months before the Moscow Declaration. There was a plethora of smaller organizations, including associations of Austrian lawyers, doctors, musicians, engineers, chemists, architects, technicians and scientific workers. However, the cultural activities of the exiles were notable for their quality as well as their quantity. The programme of the Austrian Academy in Great Britain during the months of May and June 1940 is particularly impressive:

8 May	Sir George Franckenstein: The Essence of Austrian Culture
9 May	Dr Felix Braun: Austrian Literature
14 May	Dr Wilhelm Stekel: Austria's Contribution to the Problems of Psycho-Therapy
16 May	Prof. Dr Friedrich Hertz: The Austrian Idea
23 May	Dr Karl Geiringer: Haydn's Operas. Arias accompanied by a Chamber Orchestra
30 May	Prof. Dr Ernst Freund: Austria's Contribution to the Solution of Cancer Problems
4 June	Otto Erich Deutsch: Franz Schubert and England
6 June	Dr Ernst H. Buschbeck: The Austrian Character of Austrian Baroque
11 June	Dr Egon Wellesz: The Spirit of Austrian Music
13 June	Erich A. Blackall: Franz Grillparzer and Austrian Drama
18 June	Prof. Dr F. A. Hayek: The Austrian School of Economics
20 June	Dr Otto Benesch: The Landscape in the Austrian School of Painting at the Beginning of the 16th Century
25 June	Prof. Dr Max Neuburger: The Contribution of the Vienna Medical School
27 June	Dr Hans Redlich: Anton Bruckner, the Austrian Symphonist

The programme added that Elisabeth Bergner and Stefan Zweig had consented to give two special lectures in June (Muchitsch, 1992, p.381). In 1940, to judge from this distinguished list of speakers, the cultural capital of Austria was London. An almost equally impressive series of names is included on the list of Austrian delegates to the international PEN Congress of September 1941. It includes Elias Canetti, Theodor Kramer, Anna Mahler, Karl Mannheim, Robert Neumann, Otto Neurath, Arthur Koestler and Hilde Spiel (Muchitsch, 1992, pp.409–10).

As the war drew towards a close, the activities of these exile groups shifted from a defensive stance (affirming that Austria still existed) towards a constructive programme – planning the revival of cultural life in Austria after the war. The problem, after 1945, was how to bring about some form of reintegration between the two dimensions of Austria's divided cultural identity – between the Free Austria Movement in exile and the Austria of the Ostmark. There have been many accounts of this painful process of reconstruction. Among the most illuminating is the testimony of Hilde Spiel, whose career combines the most signifiicant features of both exile and reintegration.

The Challenge of Reintegration

Hilde Spiel, who was born in Vienna in 1911 as the child of converted Jews, was fortunate in being able to settle in Britain as early as 1936 with her husband Peter de Mendelssohn. She adapted rather successfully to life in London, achieving considerable fluency in English and making a name for herself as a contributor to progressive journals such as the *New Statesman*.[7] When she returned to her native Vienna early in 1946, as a war correspondent in British uniform, she was dismayed by what she found – not simply a city in ruins and under military occupation, but a political culture which appeared to promise little hope of democratic reconstruction. Her judgement, expressed in a letter from Vienna, was extremely pessimistic:

> I am sure that the last thing in the world I would wish to be is a woman of Vienna. That might be tolerable for someone like my mother, who is content with the infinite charms of that familiar and much loved atmosphere, with the familiar streets and the Vienna Woods and the beautiful churches and the splendid weather. But for someone who needs a little more than that, first and foremost the Western way of thinking, it would be intolerable. Staying in Vienna would be completely impossible for me if it were not in conjunction with the British, to whom one belongs and with whom one associates. Here everything is delightful apart from the attitude of the Viennese, who are either Nazis (whose sting has admittedly been completely drawn), or charming, politically absurd members of the Volkspartei, or prosaic bourgeois Social Democrats, or doctrinaire Communists, or charming but absurd Communists. That is roughly the extent of it. They are either corrupt or exhausted or politically obtuse or fanatical, but one thing does speak in their favour: their great love of art ... I am convinced that the only chance for the Austrians lies in their enormous talent for all art forms, their exceptionally good taste and their artistic sensitivity. If they learn to restrain themselves and to leave politics to others, they will have a future in Europe.[8]

It is clear to us that she underestimated the resourcefulness of the Austrian political leadership, including Karl Renner. But the main conclusion she draws was nevertheless to prove prophetic. The development of an active *Kulturpolitik* has indeed made an exceptionally important contribution to the restoration of Austria's international prestige.

What makes the case of Hilde Spiel so instructive is not merely her autobiographical writings, which record the problems of reintegration so vividly, but also her play, *Anna & Anna*, which gives definitive expression to the 'schizophrenic spiritual condition' of Austria. This text, originally conceived as a novel and later rewritten as a film script, was not actually performed as a play until 1988, only two years before Spiel's death (it has since been shown on television). The aim of the play is to balance against each other the two dimensions of Austria's divided identity in the years 1938–45, using an ingenious Doppelgänger technique, facilitated by fluid scenic transformations.

The heroine Anna, a partly Jewish woman with a job in the Austrian State Theatre Administration, finds herself torn into two halves by the *Anschluß*. Anna 1 remains in Vienna through the war, painfully struggling to maintain her integrity under Nazi rule; Anna 2 emigrates to London, becoming first a domestic servant and later an announcer for the Austrian service of the BBC, thus helping to create an alternative Austrian identity in exile. The primary quality of the play lies in its avoidance of black-and-white characterization. Anna 1 represents Austria under the German occupation, but the Austrian values which she embodies still retain, even under Nazi domination, elements of a cultivated and humane tradition (there is even a sub-plot about a resistance group in a factory, which Anna 1 intermittently supports). However, we are shown that the values of those who remained in Vienna under the Nazi regime, however worthy their intentions, are inevitably corrupted by shameful compromises. The journalist Stefan, a close friend of Anna 1, is forced to churn out propaganda in support of the Nazi regime and even expresses his admiration for Baldur von Schirach.

Anna 2, representing Austria in exile, is clearly portrayed as the more sympathetic figure. The scenes set in London, written partly in English, emphasize her courage, adaptability and resilience under pressure, not least during the Blitz, when the house in which she is working is virtually destroyed. The play achieves its finest effects through ironic documentary juxtapositions reminiscent of Karl Kraus. For example, the productions of the Nazi-controlled Burgtheater are juxtaposed against the programme of the Austrian exile theatre in Swiss Cottage, the Laterndl (Figure 3.5). In London the Free Austria Movement is being built up around a concept of Austria associated with Nestroy's comedies and Hofmannsthal's conception of the 'spiritual realm of the nation'. Meanwhile, in the Burgtheater the

"The Lantern"

THE LITTLE THEATRE FROM VIENNA

153, FINCHLEY ROAD,
SWISS COTTAGE, N.W.3.

Telephone: PRImrose 5548.

Every Monday 7.15 p.m.
THE WORLD'S LITTLE STAGE:
March 4th, 11th, 18th, 25th.
"Der Talisman", a Comedy by JOHANN NESTROY.
Music: Kurt Manschinger. Admission 1/-, 1/6, 2/6.

Every Saturday 4.30 p.m.
MUSIC AND LITERATURE, Matinees of the Lantern.

March 2nd
Bert Brecht: Songs from "Dreigroschenoper", "Mahagonny" poems and prose (Evelyn Barring, Marianne Walla, Martin Miller, Georg Knepler). Admission 1/-.

March 9th
Songs and Marches from Old Vienna (Evelyn Barring, Franz Marischka, Peter Preses, Fritz Schrecker). Admission 1/-.

March 16th
Alice Schäffer — Dr. Fritz Berend
Schubert's Winterreise". Admission from 1/-.

March 30th
Second Concert "Contemporary Music". Chamber Music and Lyric by Schoenberg and his pupils. Admission from 1/-.

Every Sunday 4.30 p.m.
THE LANTERN AT HOME (Tea and Dance)
Admission 1/- (incl. tea and sandwiches).

From March 1st to 21st every night (excl. Mondays) 7.15 p.m. our 3rd programme: "FROM ADAM TO ADOLF".
March 23rd, 7.15 p.m.
First night of our 4th programme: "THE ETERNAL SCHWEJK"
March 24th and following weeks (excl. Mondays) 7.15 p.m.
"THE ETERNAL SCHWEJK"

All performances and lectures in German language.
Admission to members only.
Annual subscription for English Members 5/-;
Refugee Members 1/-

Figure 3.5 'The Lantern': programme of the Austrian exile theatre in London

Reproduced from *Anna & Anna* by Hilde Spiel by kind permission of Verlag Kremayr & Schierau, Vienna.

values of Prussian militarism are being celebrated under the patronage of Gauleiter Bürckel.

The problem for Spiel, as a dramatist, is is how to reintegrate the two Annas – the two Austrias – at the end of the play. Unfortunately, the solution she adopts is both dramatically and historically unconvincing. First, in April 1945, we are shown members of the Austrian resistance, with Anna 1 among them, assembling at the Palais Auersperg and declaring that it is they who will reconstruct Austria. Then Anna 2 flies into Vienna in a Dakota, as a correspondent for the Austrian Service of the BBC, to write a report on post-war conditions. Returning to her flat in the suburb of Vienna where the original division of the heroine's personality had occurred, Anna 2 is miraculously reintegrated with Anna 1 into a single person (Spiel, 1989, pp.173–4). The gritty documentary drama ends with characteristically Viennese insouciance, as if it were a Raimund fantasy in which all problems miraculously vanish when the good fairy waves a magic wand!

We know that it wasn't really like that. When Spiel herself returned to Vienna as a war correspondent in 1946, she kept a diary describing her impressions, originally written in English and later published in German under the title *Rückkehr nach Wien*. In this diary she does record the hopeful signs of an Austrian cultural reawakening, particularly the new spirit in the *Rathaus* generated by Viktor Matejka, a Catholic whose concentration camp experiences had converted him to communism. Her admiration for Ernst Fischer, another communist who was briefly minister of education, is also clear. But she also emphasizes that the process of re-education was proving extremely difficult, not least because of the weakness of the Socialist Party and the fact that so few socialist intellectuals had returned to Austria: 'Of that "coming generation" of twelve years ago only a very few have returned from exile'.[9] Those who did return found little scope for realizing their dream of a 'Free Austria' – a radical socialist democracy in which they would themselves have been welcomed back to provide a new style of intellectual leadership. The very fact that the anti-Nazi exiles had been proved right and the fellow travellers of Nazism proved so terribly wrong resulted in a groundswell of resentment. Hilde Spiel records how former acquaintances in Vienna kept telling her how lucky she was to have been in London, and hence to have escaped the horrors which the Viennese had had to endure. They were blissfully unaware that she and her children had narrowly escaped death during the Blitz.

Further complicating factors arose as a result of the four-power occupation and the Cold War. It soon became clear that exiles in London such as Hilde Spiel, who were wrestling with their consciences about whether or not to return to Austria, had to face multiple forms of hostility – not just the traditional groundswell of anti-Semitism but also the new orthodoxy of anticommunism. Ernst Fischer and Viktor Matejka soon found themselves excluded from positions of influence as a result of the anti-communist backlash. And Friedrich Torberg, returning from exile in the United States with an almost McCarthyite suspicion of crypto-communists, became the cultural arbiter whose aim it was to exclude anyone with alleged left-wing sympathies from the theatres and editorial offices of Vienna. Torberg, together with the equally fervent anti-communist Hans Weigel, in effect colluded with the restoration of a conservative cultural and political consensus which left little scope for radicalism in literature and the arts during the 1950s.

Hilde Spiel describes in the second volume of her autobiography how she herself was denounced by Torberg as a communist fellow traveller. She had good reason to feel that there would be no welcome in Vienna for her conception of 'the western way of thinking' – that of a radical democrat with socialist sympathies, who felt intellectually at home with the *New Statesman*. Not surprisingly, her return to Vienna was delayed for a further 17 years. The fact that it was not until 1963 that she finally took the plunge shows how difficult the reintegration process was. Shortly after her return, however, she became a key figure in Viennese cultural life, as general secretary of the Austrian PEN Club and, through her personal commitment, she did help to bring about a synthesis between the values of the two Austrias. Paradoxically, what most attracted her back were those literary friends whose conservative humanism she viewed as complementing her own liberal humanism. Her literary allies in Austria after 1963 included prominent writers with a Nazi past, such as Doderer and Lernet-Holenia, in whose work she could nevertheless recognize a vision of Austria with which it was possible to identify.

When Spiel, working closely with Lernet-Holenia, became secretary-general of Austrian PEN, she was in effect taking a symbolic, as well as practical, step to bring together the two dimensions of Austria's 'schizophrenic spiritual condition'. The fact that she ultimately believed her efforts to have failed does not undermine her considerable achievement. Her efforts to liberalize the Austrian PEN Club were finally frustrated by her adversary, Friedrich Torberg. In one of the most ludicrous episodes in recent Austrian cultural history, she was ousted from her position in the Club by Lernet-Holenia and a conservative clique which regarded the award of the Nobel Prize for Literature to Heinrich Böll as some kind of a communist plot! It was not until the early 1970s, when the *Grazer Literaturversammlung* was formed in opposition to the conservative establishment in Vienna, that a more radical 'Western way of thinking' began to shape Austrian writing.

Nevertheless, Spiel did make a significant contribution to Austrian public life, helping to fulfil the programme which she had sketched in her letter of

1946: that Austria should be revalidated through the arts. From her experiences in exile she brought back with her the conviction that a reaffirmation of Austrian culture was essential to legitimize the processes of social and eonomic reconstruction. And in her own most ambitious contribution to literary history, the volume in the *Kindlers Literaturgeschichte der Gegenwart* series which she edited on contemporary Austrian literature, *Die zeitgenössische Literatur Österreichs* (1976), she showed how a distinctive literary tradition may contribute to an authentic concept of nationhood.

Conclusion

The outside observer, surveying the evolution of the Second Republic, can hardly fail to be impressed not simply by social stability and economic achievement, but also by a *Kulturpolitik* that has successfully recreated the idea of an independent Austria. Should this be dismissed as merely a myth, an elaborate confidence trick using the values of Mozart or Hofmannsthal to justify the policies of Kreisky or the equivocations of Waldheim? It is clear that, after the trauma of National Socialism, the rebuilding of national self-confidence did require the acceptance of certain sustaining myths, including a willingness to forget the sins of the past. That process was certainly carried too far, and it was not until the Waldheim years that the myth of Austria as the 'first free country to fall victim of Hitlerite aggression', propagated by the Moscow Declaration, was fundamentally challenged. Despite all these difficulties, however, the process has ultimately been successful. In short, if schizophrenia is an appropriate metaphor for the traumatic situation of Austria at the end of the Second World War, then we can only conclude that the patient – after protracted therapy – has finally made a remarkable recovery.

Notes

1 'Kaum ein anderes Land in Europa hat in diesem Jahrhundert mehr Lehren erhalten als Österreich. Kaum ein Land ist in seinem Selbstverständnis schwerer erschüttert worden, bis es aus diesem opferreichen Prozeß so überzeugend zu Freiheit und Unhabhängigkeit, zu Demokratie und Wohlstand gefunden hat. Diese tief zerklüftete Geschichte steht vor uns, wenn wir heute, am 50. Geburtstag der 2. Republik, Bilanz ziehen – und uns die Frage stellen, wie wir mit dem Vermächtnis von damals umgehen' (Klestil, 1995).

2 'Die größte Schwäche der 1. Republik war das Fehlen einer positiven Staatsgesinnung' (Klestil, 1995).

3 'Erst in viel späteren Jahren, als man immer mehr an der Durchführbarkeit des Anschlußes zu zweifeln begann, ließen sich diese [christlichsozialen] Führer durch Engelbert Dollfuß verführen, den österreichischen Teil des deutschen Volkes nicht bloß als einen Stamm

der deutschen, sondern als besondere Nation anzusehen und die Unabhängigkeit Österreichs, diese harte Fessel aus Saint-Germain, geradezu als Panazee zu preisen!' (Renner, 1990, p.40).

4 'Daß die deutschen Alpenländer allein ein selbständiger Staat werden sollten, das erschien zur Zeit der Konstituierung allen Richtungen gleich undenkbar und unerträglich, das kam erst gar nicht in Frage! Die österreichischen Alpenländer waren im Grunde nicht viel mehr als die Ostmark der Babenberger ... Als es durch den Freidensvertrag doch dazu kam, schlug ich im Kreise führender Männer vor, statt dem Namen Österreich, dem Namen der untergegangenen Großmacht, den Namen "Die Ostalpenlande" zu wählen, den ich auch in die Staatshymne aufnahm' (Renner, 1990, p.36).

5 '... so muß es jetzt und auch in Hinkunft recht sein, daß jene Nationen, die noch geteilt sind oder gar erst 1919 geteilt wurden, mit allen Mitteln, im Notfall auch mit dem Mittel des Krieges, sich einigen' (Renner, 1990, p.85).

6 For an overview of Renner's career, which emphasizes his opportunism, see Pelinka (1989).

7 For a perceptive account of Spiel's attitude towards writing in English, see Fliedl (1995, pp.78–93).

8 'Ich bin sicher, daß ich um nichts in der Welt eine Wienerin sein möchte. Das mag für jemanden wie meine Mutter hingehen, die sich mit den unendlichen Reizen der wohlbekannten und geliebten Atmosphäre begnügt, mit dem vertrauten Straßen und dem Wienerwald und den wunderschönen Kirchen und dem herrlichen Wetter. Aber für jemanden, der ein bißchen mehr braucht als das, fürs erste schon einmal die westliche Art zu denken, wäre es unerträglich. Mir wäre ein Aufenthalt in Wien vollkommen unmöglich, wenn es nicht im Verein mit den Briten wäre, zu denen man gehört und mit denen man umgeht. Alles ist hier liebenswert außer der Haltung der Wiener, die entweder Nazis sind (denen der Stachel freilich völlig genommen wurde), oder reizende, politisch unsinnige Volksparteiler, oder prosaische, bourgeoise Sozialdemokraten, oder doktrinäre Kommunisten, oder reizende, aber unsinnige Kommunisten. Das ist so ungefähr der Aufriß. Sie sind entweder korrupt oder ausgelaugt oder politisch verdummt oder fanatisch, aber etwas spricht für sie: ihre große Liebe zur Kunst. ... Ich bin überzeugt, daß die einzige Chance der Österreicher in ihrem ungeheuren Talent für alle Künste liegt, ihrem außerordentlich guten Geschmack und ihrer künstlerischen Sensitivität. Wenn sie lernen, sich zurückzuhalten und die Politik anderen zu überlassen, haben sie eine Zukunft in Europa' (Spiel, 1991, pp.235–6).

9 'Von jener "kommenden Generation" von vor zwölf Jahren sind die wenigsten aus dem Exil zurückgekehrt' (Spiel, 1991a, p.98).

Bibliography

Andics, H. (1962), *Der Staat, den keiner wollte: Österreich 1918–1938*, Vienna: Herder.

Baur, U. *et al.* (forthcoming), *Handbuch der österreichischen Literatur im Nationalsozialismus*, vol.2, Liste der erfaßten Anthologien und Sammelschriften, (work in progress).

Fliedl, Konstanze (1995), 'Hilde Spiel's Linguistic Rights of Residence' in E. Timms and R. Robertson (eds), *Austrian Exodus: The Creative Achievements of Refugees from National Socialism*, Edinburgh: Edinburgh University Press.

Keyserlingk, R. H. (1988), *Austria in World War II: An Anglo-American Dilemma*, Kingston/Montreal: McGill-Queens University Press.

Klestil, T. (1995), 'Die historischen Wahrheiten nicht ausblenden' in *Wiener Zeitung*, 28 April.

Luza, R.V. (1984), *The Resistance in Austria, 1938–1945*, Minneapolis: University of Minnesota Press.

Muchitsch, W. (ed.) (1992), *Österreicher im Exil – Großbritannien 1938–1945: Eine Dokumentation*, Vienna: Bundesverlag.

Muchitsch, Wolfgang (1995), 'The Cultural Policy of Austrian Refugee Organisations in Great Britain', in E. Timms and R. Robertson (eds), *Austrian Exodus: The Creative Achievements of Refugees from National Socialism*, Edinburgh: Edinburgh University Press.

Pelinka, A. (1989), *Karl Renner: Zur Einführung*, Hamburg: Junius.

Renner, K. (1990), *Die Gründung der Republik Deutschösterreich, der Anschluß und die Sudetendeutschen*, photographically reproduced corrected proof, edited by Eduard Rabofsky, Vienna.

Spiel, Hilde (1989), *Anna & Anna*, Vienna: Kremayr & Scheriau.

Spiel, Hilde (1991a), *Die hellen und die finsteren Zeiten: Erinnerungen 1911–1946*, Reinbek bei Hamburg: Rowohlt.

Spiel, Hilde (1991b), *Rückkehr nach Wien: Ein Tagebuch*, Frankfurt-am-Main: Fischer.

Timms, E. and Robertson, R. (eds) (1995), *Austrian Exodus: The Creative Achievements of Refugees from National Socialism*, Edinburgh: Edinburgh University Press.

4 Superpower Perceptions of Austrian Neutrality Post-1955

Oliver Rathkolb

Introduction

The secondary literature on the history of the Austrian State Treaty of 1955 and Austrian neutrality primarily focuses on the analysis of the historical antecedents (Stourzh, 1985, pp.326–32; Stourzh, 1997), on legal interpretations (Verdroß, 1977; Rotter, 1981; Zemanek, 1991; Neuhold, 1992), and on political science perspectives (Schlesinger, 1972), although economic aspects sometimes also play a role in the research debate (Butschek, 1993). This chapter concentrates on the superpower assessments of the geopolitical and economic context of Austria's position and compares these external 'floating' geostrategic perspectives with domestic views. The chapter will be limited to the periods 1955–59 and 1960–63. The first case study deals with the Western powers' 'negative forecasts' for Austrian neutrality. The second underlines the acceptance by the Kennedy administration of an active and positive role for Austria, as well as the conflicting interpretations of the role of neutrals in the European Economic Community (EEC).

Austrian Neutrality as a 'Contained' Secret Alliance with the West, 1955–59

The declassification of internal documents from the US, British, Russian and Austrian primary sources mean that the period immediately after 1955 is the best documented. The Austrian solution of 1955 was regarded by the Eisenhower administration (both by the president himself and by Secretary of State John Foster Dulles) as a major success from the US geostrategic point of view. Eisenhower, in particular, was fascinated by the 'Swiss model', but not because there was a strict neutrality policy strictly applied. What appealed to him was Switzerland's high level of military defence expenditure. West Germany had been militarily integrated into NATO, and the military vacuum in Austria – where, since the early 1950s, only a rather symbolic number of Western combat troops faced a conventional Soviet force that amounted to some 30 000 soldiers located in Eastern Austria (Rathkolb, 1995b, p.28; McIntosh, 1996, pp.245–8) – was to be closed after the Allied withdrawal by an Austrian army comprising 65 000 soldiers under arms. Furthermore, the Soviet army had to pull back from Austria and also lost the right to retain its lines of communication in eastern Central Europe (Hungary, Rumania) based on the 1946 peace treaties (Rauchensteiner, 1979, p.332).

The new Austrian army could draw on the nucleus of the US- and British-trained B-Gendarmerie (*Gendarmerie-(Sonder-)Schulen*), which numbered 6102 persons in October 1954 and was to be equipped from US military sources in Italy already earmarked for this purpose (Stifter, 1977, pp.164f). According to evidence in recently declassified primary sources, the new Austrian army, based on compulsory military service, was established not only to prevent a possible communist *coup d'état*, but also to assist in defending the NATO north–south line in case of all-out war and aggression by the Warsaw Pact (Rathkolb, 1995b, p.29). Defence meant primarily inhibiting and delaying a 'communist' advance aimed at Northern Italy or at Southern Germany through Carinthia. There is, however, still no evidence that the US key decision-makers planned at the time to guarantee the sovereignty of Eastern Austria (including the capital, Vienna) and pinning down NATO to the automatic defence of the eastern border of Austria by conventional forces or nuclear weapons. The US wanted to react 'automatically' only if direct NATO interests were involved. Leaving aside rumours from Austrian sources, there is, to date, no evidence that the US and/or NATO had developed a *de facto* nuclear shield over Austria and had thereby taken over Austrian defence tasks.

The US therefore not only declined to guarantee Austrian neutrality, but in the early post-1955 years also executed a policy of 'split neutrality', ignoring the neutral status of Western Austria, which was located along NATO's north–south line. This included constant rail transportation of NATO ammunition through the Tyrol (with secret Austrian permission and the assistance of the Austrian Federal Railways) and the absence of Austrian sovereignty over that part of its airspace which covered the air corridor from Germany to Italy. The rearmament of Austria's army by the US led to US military attachés developing close contacts with Austrian army officers in important positions, with whom they drew up a clear strategic plan. This stipulated that, in the event of an all-out confrontation, Austrian military forces would join NATO in the western territories and not defend Eastern

Austria. This was accepted by still unidentified members of the higher Austrian officers corps. On the political level, however, both Chancellor Julius Raab of the People's Party and the socialist members of his cabinet, Vice-Chancellor Adolf Schärf and Under-Secretary of State for Foreign Affairs Bruno Kreisky, opposed this course. Yet it was not until the Lebanon crisis of July 1958 that there was an acceptance of split NATO integration – not only in case of war. When US fighter planes continued violating Austrian sovereignty by crossing the Tyrol without permission, Chancellor Raab issued a sharp public protest during an official visit in Moscow which happened to coincide with the overflights (McIntosh, 1996, p.254). These incidents caused considerable turmoil in the US–Austrian relations, but fostered a stronger Austrian emancipation from the US and NATO subsequently.

Western non-observance of Austrian neutrality in the early years was even greater in the CIA and the British MI6 than within the State and Defence Departments. As early as 1949, the CIA had been authorized by the National Security Council to plan undercover 'stay behind operations' in Europe and to plant arms caches containing rifles, ammunition, explosives and the like to equip a very small guerrilla army to fight against the Soviets and their communist 'comrades'.[1] According to documents that have still not been declassified, between 1950 and 1954 the CIA planted 79 such caches in Austria without informing the Austrian government. They were located primarily in Salzburg (27) and Upper Austria (33), but also in Styria (5). Some 65 of these caches were still in place in 1996 and contained a total of more than 300 pistols, 250 rifles, 270 sub-machine guns, 65 machine guns, ammunition and explosives (*Die Presse*, 24 September 1996, p.12). The main documentary evidence has still not been released to the public. The British MI6 built 33 caches in Styria and Carinthia – most of them turned over to the Austrian army as late as 1965, when one was plundered and its contents sold on the black market (*Die Presse*, 14 April 1996, p.3). The CIA caches were kept secret until early 1996, when the *Boston Globe* published a report based on information supplied by a member of the CIA. Both the CIA and MI6 planned these guerrilla operations because they feared that the Red Army would overrun Europe and reach the Atlantic and that this would involve nuclear warfare from both sides. According to the planning, it would take more than six months to strike back with 'effective aerial attacks … intensifying political, psychological and warfare'.[2] During this operation, parachutists were to be sent into Austria, where they would open a guerrilla front in Western Austria – presumably by recruiting earmarked Austrians. The US had obviously gained all the necessary information from the Austrian bureaucracy. The list of Austrian soldiers and officers between the ages of 20 and 40 who could be drafted had been compiled as early as 1952–53. It included those with experience in the German Wehrmacht during the Second World War, of which 30 000 were in Upper Austria and 12 600 in Salzburg (Stifter, 1977, p.165).

Despite these undercover activities and the 'official' US military doctrine immediately after 1955 treating Western Austria as a secret ally in case of an all-out war, US decision-makers have never been prepared to guarantee the territorial integrity of Austria by guaranteeing its neutrality status. This position was already quite clear in 1953, when the debate about a neutral status for Austria began. The State Department was only prepared to reduce Austrian pressures for a territorial guarantee and to hinder a unilateral Soviet guarantee by declaring:

> ... that the United States should be prepared to treat any violation of the integrity of Austrian territory or neutrality as a grave threat to the peace, without however guaranteeing its territory or neutrality, except within the framework of the UN.[3]

The National Security Council discussed another option – a declaration by the three Western allies 'supporting, not guaranteeing, Austria's political and territorial integrity'.[4] President Eisenhower accepted this option, which was similar to a statement issued in the Arab–Israeli conflict in 1950.

Immediately before the signing of the Austrian State Treaty, Secretary of State Dulles informed his NATO ministerial colleagues that the US could never support a territorial guarantee for Austria and that, in the event of such a guarantee becoming a precondition of the treaty, the latter could not be signed.[5] Although, soon after 1955, Austria tried to reopen the discussion on guaranteeing neutrality, the Eisenhower administration firmly blocked their efforts. Even during the Hungarian crisis, when Italy tried to sound out a territorial guarantee for Austria to prevent a Soviet attack on the Italian border, the US rejected these efforts.[6] The US ambassador in Austria, Llewellyn Thompson, opposed attempts by the Austrian Foreign Ministry to use the Soviet intervention in Hungary to press a declaration of guarantee from the US, stating that it was 'extremely foolish to even start discussion'.[7] Austria gave up these efforts in the late 1950s, although a guarantee of Austrian neutrality along the lines of the Swiss model was a central component of the original Austrian understanding of neutrality (Stourzh, 1985, p.205).

The guarantee issue was not the only means by which the State Department and Secretary of State John Foster Dulles tried to isolate the Austrian example. Austria's peculiar position was also to remain an exception in Europe. When Soviet Foreign Minister Molotov tried to persuade Dulles in May 1955 to nominate Vienna as the summit venue, the US secretary of state vigorously opposed this suggestion, since he feared that the Austrian example could weaken the Western ideological defence line in Europe and other parts of the world (Rauchensteiner, 1987, p.181). It is, however, interesting to note that Gallup public opinion polls have shown that, since 1952, there has been a growing tendency throughout Europe to favour a neutral position vis-à-vis the Cold War if it threatened to become 'hot'. (The exception has been Great Britain, where people were inclined to side with the US even in case of nuclear war.)[8]

When Chancellor Raab tried, in 1958, to develop a 'bridge-building' role for Austria between East and West and proposed concrete measures concerning disarmament and détente, Dulles bluntly refused to take up this Austrian initiative. The establishment of the International Atomic Energy Agency (IAEA) in Vienna in 1957 should not therefore be regarded as indicating a reversal of the policy of 'containing neutrality', but rather as a compromise whereby the US accepted the Soviet proposal concerning the geographical location of the IAEA headquarters in return for the Soviets acceding to the US proposals on key IAEA personnel. It should be mentioned that the Eisenhower administration's opposition to Raab's 'bridge-building' was, as David McIntosh's findings have shown, in keeping with a specific policy which the US then had concerning the role of small nations (including, for example, Costa Rica and the Lebanon) in great power politics (McIntosh, 1996, p.259).

In Austria, the Eisenhower administration favoured the split-neutrality/ secret NATO ally concept, but never feared that Austria would be satellized and drawn into the communist orbit – even when fighting the 'Soviet–Austrian honeymoon' in 1958.[9] At that time, Chancellor Raab had, while in Moscow, criticized the overflights in the Tyrol during the Lebanon crisis; he had simultaneously successfully negotiated a reduction of the reparations shipments and Austria dragged her feet on the claims of US, British, Canadian and Dutch oil firms ('Vienna memorandum'). Despite this short-term conflict, the US perception of a firm Western integration of Austria on political, ideological, economic, cultural and (under cover) even military levels, did not change. On the other hand, British foreign policy experts had developed a different perception of the future of Austria's neutrality after 1955. In his review for 1955, the British ambassador in Vienna, Sir George Wallinger, suggested that 'Austrian neutrality might well be only the first step to satellization … in brief, neutral Austria would become not an honest broker but a double agent'.[10] In his closing remarks he even stated that:

> The step from timid compliant neutralism to a Communist or even a rightist coup d'état in Vienna need not be a long one. Yet, Austria's bootstraps are strong enough: it remains to be seen whether she has it in her (with such help as she can get) to pull herself up by them.

Colleagues in the Foreign Office, however, were not so negative in their interpretation and compared the 'hesitant' Austrian foreign policy towards the Soviet Union with the 'dependence of the Latin-American States from the United States, which in return was quite a strong picture of dependence'.

Both perceptions very soon proved to be wrong. The Hungarian crisis caused the British ambassador in Vienna to reverse his interpretation as early as October–November 1956. In his review of the first months of 1956, Sir George had criticized 'Austrian muddleheadedness about their neutrality. Chancellor Raab in particular does not appear to understand the difference between neutrality and neutralism.' Yet, particularly in light of the Austrian government's very open official protest against the Soviet intervention in Hungary and the role which the government took in taking care of all refugees, it soon became quite clear that Austria's foreign policy was prepared to relinquish any form of ideological and political neutrality and to express clear pro-Western, anti-communist and anti-Soviet positions. It should be noted that much of the care of the refugees was presented in the context of a clearly anti-communist media and public opinion campaign and not just as the duty of a neutral state. The Soviets were not really irritated by the Austrian attitude, since they were already well aware of the strong pro-Western integration preferences within the Austrian decision-making elite. Even when a Soviet soldier was killed by an Austrian gendarme, the Soviet Union reacted within diplomatic limits. This was part of a general line of accepting the pro-Western tendencies as long as they did not constitute any form of a new *Anschluß* with Germany. The Soviet Foreign Ministry was instructed to 'answer' even Austria's membership in the Council of Europe in 1956 only with newspaper articles protesting against this decision.

It is interesting to note that the original British views corresponded with the Socialist Vice-Chancellor Adolf Schärf's strong criticisms of Raab's Ostpolitik, which he interpreted in the same way as Sir George Wallinger.[11] In the 1956 review, Ambassador Wallinger acknowledged for the first time that, during the Hungarian crisis, 'Austria has converted a dangerous lack of direction in her policy into a positive concept of neutrality that has been seen to have attractions in the satellite lands'.[12] John Foster Dulles, in return, disliked this 'attraction' of Austrian neutrality for communist Eastern European states, when Governor Stassen proposed, at a National Security Council meeting at the end of October 1956, letting 'the Russians know that we would accept for the satellites some neutralised status like that of Austria'.[13] While Dulles objected, it is not quite clear whether he feared an escalation of the Hungarian crisis or whether he disliked the idea of accepting a status quo in the Cold War over eastern Central Europe through 'neutralization'.

Throughout the 1950s, the Eisenhower administration continued to dispute Austria's role between East and West, since it was seen to be 'too weak to play the role of a bridge'[14] in policies vis à vis eastern Central Europe and the Soviet Union.

The Austrian government, on the one hand, continued to advocate an extremely close relationship with the West (which led, for example, to the expulsion of communist-front organizations from Vienna, the decline of a Soviet offer to accept a Schilling loan for Lower Austria, or Austria's becoming a member of the Council of Europe), and, on the other hand, pursued a distinct Ostpolitik, which started under Chancellor Raab and was continued by Foreign Minister Kreisky after 1959 with his 'near abroad policy' (*Nachbarschaftspolitik*) (Rathkolb, 1995a). Raab especially tried very hard to improve Austria's relationship with the Soviet Union, whereas the socialists were extremely pro-American, or at least anti-communist and anti-Soviet. Under-Secretary of State Kreisky and a large number of socialist functionaries even organized, together with Catholic organizations, an anti-communist counter-festival in 1958–59 – partly with CIA funds – to demonstrate against the World Youth Festival. Raab wanted to play down the whole affair and decided that People's Party organizations should not take part in these anti-communist activities (Rathkolb, 1994, p.132).

The Soviet Union at the time accepted these open pro-Western tendencies.[15] Only after 1959 – when Austria sounded out the possibilities of becoming at least an associate member of the EEC – did Soviet pressures increase considerably (Rathkolb, 1993, p.51). Although the Soviet Union always argued that the State Treaty and the Neutrality Law would be by association with the EEC, the Soviet leadership primarily feared that Austria would strengthen Germany within the EEC, thereby creating a 'new *Anschluß*'. Soviet experts knew very well that Austrian neutrality policy was basically pro-Western, despite efforts by Raab to counter this trend by policies towards the East (Rathkolb, 1995a, pp.113f). The Soviet Union even argued that an associate or full membership would justify reviving the Allied Commission for a period, since this act would be interpreted as an open violation of the *Anschluß-Verbot* of the Austrian State Treaty (Kreisky, 1988, p.176).

Because economic integration had always been an important component within the Cold War, US diplomats applied some mild pressure on the Austrian government against pushing forward a neutral economic policy and in favour of staying within the limits of the economic cold warfare. This meant that Austrian firms were obliged to observe the rules of the Co-ordinating Committee (COCOM) in Paris which drafted lists of goods and services which were not to be exported into the communist orbit.

Permission for a large number of goods had to be obtained via Washington (Breuss, 1983, pp.124ff). Austria continued to observe the COCOM-embargo rules, a policy which had started during the Korean war (Rathkolb,

1990, p.136). This continuity resulted in additional business problems for the firms formerly under Soviet administration in Austria, which were returned in 1955 – the USIA firms. They were not allowed to continue all their business contacts with the East. US and Western pressure was so strong that even Switzerland was not able to carry out an independent and neutral foreign trade policy and had accepted in the Hotz–Linder agreement of 23 July 1951 the COCOM embargo against the Eastern bloc (Schaller, 1987). The US was well aware of the problems which the Austrian economy faced. After the end of Marshall Plan aid and the signing of the State Treaty the US therefore continued to offer economic assistance to strengthen the Western integration in Austria:

> The next few years will be decisive in influencing the orientation of Austrian 'neutrality'. It seems important, therefore, that US activities will be accepted by Austria as not infringing on her neutrality, and which will provide a basis for transmitting American ideas and influence should be pressed forward to the maximum extent.[16]

To summarize the perceptions of the late 1950s, it can be noted that, despite a clear pro-Western connotation, Austrian neutrality did not play any role in the East–West confrontation, but was seen as an exception which should certainly not be repeated. The West, and the US in particular, generally distrusted the concept as such – even when proposed as a means for transforming the communist sphere of influence. A number of projects involving close military cooperation, linked to the rebuilding of an Austrian army and the joining of Austrian forces in the Western provinces in case of all-out conflict between NATO and the Warsaw Pact, caused this distrust to recede. However, it revived as soon as Austrian political decision-makers tried to carry out a strict neutrality policy (for example, during the overflights of US aircraft in connection with the Lebanon crisis) and to reverse this concept of 'split neutrality'. The Soviet Union had no real problems with the Westernization of Austrian neutrality (even on the military level), but strictly opposed any possible close moves towards the Federal Republic of Germany through economic integration.

Preferring Contained Active Neutrality (1960–67)

As US Secretary of State Dean Rusk pointed out, 'Kennedy, different from J.F. Dulles, positively assessed Austria's neutrality and the function of the neutrals'.[17] The new president even proposed Vienna (together with Stockholm) as possible sites for the first summit with Khrushchev, thereby accepting a positive function for a 'new' neutral in the East–West détente efforts. This acceptance marked an important change in the external response to Austrian foreign policy since, under Raab, the efforts of the small neutral state to play a role in the East–West-détente negotiations had been rejected by Dulles.

Dean Rusk even proposed using the Austrian example of neutrality as a means towards conflict resolution for Laos in March 1961.[18] Austrian diplomats did not really like this idea, since they feared that the US was guiding Austrian neutrality towards the Finnish model, which implied stronger Soviet influence.

However, the neutrals in Europe were to be contained in a new way, especially since Kennedy's Under-Secretary of State George W. Ball had developed a new strategy for a strong and united Western Europe. He feared that a close association of the EEC with the three neutrals – Austria, Sweden and Switzerland – would destroy the prospects of a strong European political, and maybe even military, union following the success of economic integration. Ball urged the Austrians to observe the Soviet concerns about neutrality in the debate on how to be integrated into the EEC, (for example, by associate membership) (Ball, 1982, p.219). The Kennedy administration was well aware of Austria's economic dependence on the EEC, compared with Sweden and Switzerland, but tried to lead the politicians towards a special bilateral agreement with the Community. As a neutral, Austria should stay out of the European political integration process.

President Kennedy himself had spoken out against weakening the political aims of the European Community by including the neutrals:

> The Commission argued, as it had during the Maudling negotiations, that the Common Market's Treaty of Rome should not be weakened to give the neutrals the Common Market's economic benefits without accepting its political responsibilities of supranationalism. (Taber, 1969, p.54)

Kennedy and Ball wanted Great Britain to join the EEC as soon as possible and had a certain dislike for all policies and institutions which could hinder this aim. Sweden and Switzerland, however, were under much heavier attack than Austria. George Ball explains this different treatment thus:

> My impatience with the Swiss and Swedes, who hid behind neutrality for their own benefit, did not extend to Austria, which was not a free agent. Austria's neutrality was required by the 1955 Austrian State Treaty... . The effect of Austrian participation in the Common Market would amount, so Pravda argued on December 1, 1961, to economic and political union with West Germany, which the Treaty forbade.

This preferential treatment of Austria in the political debate was – though not in its concrete consequences – a result of Edward Heath's meeting with Ball in January 1962 in which Heath pleaded for an association of the neutrals with the EEC, since they were an integral part of Europe.[19]

In the summer of 1962 the US stopped her anti-neutrals campaign, partly because of Great Britain's insistence on loyalty towards the European Free Trade Association and Commonwealth concerns. It is interesting to see that the Kennedy administration and the Soviet leadership had reached – without direct contacts – tacit agreement over the perception of Austria's neutrality and both backed the primacy of neutrality over economic considerations. At the same time, the Kennedy administration acceded to the strong representations of the Austrian government to liberate its trade with Eastern Europe from strict compliance with COCOM, an instrument which the Eisenhower administration used in tight economic warfare against the Soviet Union and the Eastern bloc.

It is worth noting that Ball's original concept of accepting, even re-evaluating, neutrality but containing it in favour of stronger political union in Europe was reintroduced by France in 1967. From 1964 onwards, the Austrian Chancellor Josef Klaus reinforced the efforts at working out a special agreement with the EEC, suppressing the previous concerns articulated by the socialists around Foreign Minister Kreisky that the Soviet Union would not accept a close formal arrangement with the EEC. During a visit by Couve de Murville to Vienna, the French foreign minister underlined a new trend in his country's perception of détente in Europe, favouring a strictly neutral Austria, outside the EEC (Toncic-Sorinj, 1982, p.379). During 1960 and 1962, President de Gaulle was inclined to favour a unilateral association of Austria with the EEC, provided that Austrian neutrality was not thereby affected (Rathkolb, 1991, p.87). However, in the end, France was primarily interested in stability in East-Central Europe in the framework of de Gaulle's policy of détente. At the same time, Couve de Murville stated that France then favoured the non-integration for Austria not only to take into account the Soviet Union's security interests, but also to contain the growing German influence in the area (Toncic-Sorinj, 1982, p.379). Due to the strong economic influence of the German economy on Austria and the historical interactions between the two countries, France feared that Austria would strengthen German power within the EEC, thus weakening French power.

Conclusions

Austrian neutrality was never seen by the superpowers as a concept of free-riding within the economic and military Western integration trends of the 1950s and 1960s. Today, some analysts try to interpret Austrian neutral status as a policy of staying away from the West, while obtaining all the economic and security benefits of association with it. Historical facts prove that Austrian neutrality was never protected by NATO, despite the fact that Austria sided with the West in the economic and ideological cold warfare. In contrast to Finnish neutrality, Austrian neutrality policy was, from the outset, a clearly 'Western' biased one and, as early as 1946, the pro-Western trend was dominant in decision-making at the government level. Notwithstanding its propaganda campaigns, the Soviet Union accepted this trend of Western integration on the ideological and economic level and even on a military level as far as all-out war planning preparations were concerned. The break-even point of the Soviet perception of Austrian neutrality, however, was the German question, meaning that the Western integration of Austria could not be allowed to result in a strengthening of (West) German capabilities within the EEC. The Eisenhower administration did not want an active neutrality policy, a perspective the Austrians tried to fuel into their position right in between the two bloc systems. Despite Raab's efforts to establish relatively close relations with the Soviet Union, he never went so far as to implement a *Schauckelpolitik* between East and West. The clearly anti-communist attitudes in Austrian public opinion and within the People's Party's coalition partner, the socialists, would never have allowed a 'Finnish model'. British fears that Austria was on the way to becoming a communist satellite were based on a misinterpretation of signals which Raab sent to Moscow in order to develop a positive atmosphere for political negotiation. From Kennedy onwards, the very limited interpretation of neutrality changed into a broader concept, accepting Austrian efforts at encouraging détente policies and carrying out an active Ostpolitik designed to develop a relatively good relationship with Austria's communist neighbours. But this concept, too, was to be contained from the US point of view in the early Kennedy years, meaning that European political integration via the EEC was not to include the neutrals.

Notes

1 Stifter (1997, pp.129f), based on documents from the National Archives, College Park by Christopher Simpson, Gladio-type Guerilla Operations in Austria: a report, Washington DC 1990.

2 National Archives (=NA), Washington, DC, Record Group (=RG) 218, Box 11, CCS 004.04 (11-4-46), Report by the Joint Intelligence Committee to JCS, 30 November 1950 and JSPC 891/25/ 18 August 1950, Joint Strategic Planning Committee, Strategic Guidance for Mobilization Planning 'Straightedge', p.703, and § 47, p.50.
3 Telegram State and Embassy, Vienna, NSC Action 28 April NA, RG 59, 663.001/4-2955.
4 Telegram State and Embassy, Vienna, NSC Action 28 April. NA, RG 59, 663.001/4-2955, p.39.
5 Foreign Relations of the United States 1955–1957, Vol. V, (1988), Washington, DC, Government Printing Office, p.91.
6 Memo of Conversation, 13 November 1956. NA, RG 59, 763.00/11-1356, Box 3577.
7 Telegram, 10 November 1956. NA, RG 59, 763.00/11-956.
8 Neutralism in Europe Summary Report, drafted by the Department of State, June 1955, The Declassified Documents 1992, Frame 0236.
9 Matthews to C. Douglas Dillon, 7 November 1958, NA, RG 59, 763.5-MSP/11-758, 2.
10 George Wallinger to Macmillan, 4 November, 1955, Public Record Office, Foreign Office, 371/117780 163512.
11 Adolf Schärf, *Geschichte*, pp.1f, Verein für Geschichte der Arbeiterbewegung, Vienna, Nachlaß Schärf, old number Pa 28. Schärf, however, did not include the criticism of Ostpolitik in his unpublished manuscript, *Österreich wieder in der Freiheit, 1955–1957* (revised 1959), a copy of which has been obtained from Dr Herbert Lackner, Vienna.
12 George Wallinger to Selwyn Lloyd, Annual Report for 1956, 24 January, 1957, Public Record Office, Foreign Office, 371/130273 162343.
13 John Foster Dulles, Memo of Conversation, 26 October 1956, NA, John Foster Dulles Papers, General Correspondence, Box 1 (on microfiche in The Declassified Documents 1988/301). Stassen had already proposed on 18 January 1956 during a NSC meeting to use 'neutralization' as a vehicle for an evolutionary transformation of communism in eastern Central Europe (*The Foreign Relations of the United States 1955–57, Vol. XXVI* (1992), Washington, DC: Government Printing Office, p.31).
14 Wallinger to Selwyn Lloyd, Annual Report for 1956, 24 January 1957. Public Record Office, Kew, Foreign Office 371/130273 162343.
15 A selection of diplomatic reports from the Soviet embassy and from the Foreign Ministry in Moscow underline this thesis (copies of the originals in the Bruno Kreisky Archives, Vienna, Collection Documents from the Russian Foreign Ministry, 1945–1961).
16 Message, 17 October 1955, NA, RG 59, 763.5-MSAP/10-1755,p.3.
17 Martin Fuchs, *Diaries*, 3 June 1961, Austrian Institute for Contemporary History, Collection Martin Fuchs.
18 Ibid., 31 March 1961.
19 Public Record Office, Foreign Office 371, vol. 164698 (615/11), Memorandum on Lord Privy Seal's talks in Washington (undated).

Bibliography

Primary Sources

Austrian Institute for Contemporary History, Martin Fuchs Collection, *Diaries*, Bruno Kreisky Archives Vienna (Collection Documents from the Russian Foreign Ministry).

National Archives Washington, DC Record Groups 59 and 218.

Public Record Office, Kew, Foreign Office.

Verein für Geschichte der Arbeiterbewegung Wien, Nachlaß Adolf Schärf.

Secondary Sources

Ball, G.W. (1982), *The Past Has Another Pattern*, New York: W.W. Northon & Co.

Breuss, Fritz (1983), *Österreichs Außenwirtschaft 1945–1982*, Vienna: Signum Verlag.

Butschek, F. (1993), 'EC Membership and the "Velvet" Revolution: The Impact of Recent Political Changes on Austria's Economic Position' in Günter Bischof and Anton Pelinka (eds), *Austria in the New Europe*, Contemporary Austrian Studies 1, New Brunswick: Transaction Publishers, pp.62–80.

Kreisky, Bruno (1988), *Im Strom der Politik. Der Memoiren zweiter Teil*, Vienna: Kremayr & Scheriau.

McIntosh, David (1996), 'In the Shadow of the Giants: U.S. Policy Toward Small Nations: The Cases of Lebanon, Costa Rica, and Austria in the Eisenhower Years' in Günter Bischof and Anton Pelinka (eds), *Austro-Corporatism Past – Present – Future*, Contemporary Austrian Studies 4, New Brunswick: Transaction Publishers, pp.222–79.

Neuhold, Hanspeter (ed.) (1992), *The European Neutrals in the 1990s: New Challenges and Opportunities*, Boulder, Colorado: Westview Press.

Rathkolb, Oliver (1990), 'Historische Bewärungsproben des Neutralitätsgesetzes 1955. Am Beispiel der US-amerikanischen Österreich-Politik 1955–1959' in Niklaus Dimmel, Alfred-Johannes Noll (eds), *Verfassung. Juristisch-politische und sozialwissenschaftliche Beiträge anläßlich des 70–Jahr-Jubliläums des Bundes-Verfassungsgesetzes*, Vienna: Verlag der Österreichischen Staatsdruckerei.

Rathkolb, Oliver (1991), 'De Gaulle im Spiegel österreichischer Außenpolitik und Diplomatie 1958/59–1965', *Jahrbuch für Zeitgeschichte 1990/91*, Vienna-Salzburg: Geyer Edition.

Rathkolb, Oliver (1993), 'Austria and the European Integration after World War II' in Günter Bischof and Anton Pelinka (eds), *Austria in the New Europe*, Contemporary Austrian Studies 1, New Brunswick: Transaction Publishers, pp.42–61.

Rathkolb, Oliver (1994), 'Bruno Kreisky: Perspectives of Top-Level U.S. Foreign Policy Decision Makers, 1959–1983' in Günter Bischof and Anton Peklinka (eds), *The Kreisky Era in Austria*, Contemporary Austrian Studies 2, New Brunswick: Transaction Publishers, pp.130–51.

Rathkolb, Oliver (1995a), 'Austria's "Ostpolitik" in the 1950s and 1960s: Honest Broker or Double Agent?', *Austrian History Yearbook*, **25**, pp.129–45.

Rathkolb, Oliver (1995b), 'The Foreign Relations between the USA and Austria in the late 1950s' in Günter Bischof and Anton Pelinka (eds), *Austria in the Nineteen Fifties*, Contemporary Austrian Studies 3, New Brunswick: Transaction Publishers, pp.24–38 .

Rauchensteiner, M. (1979), *Der Sonderfall: Die Besatzungszeit in Österreich 1945–1955*, Graz: Styria Verlag.

Rauchensteiner, M. (1987), *Die Zwei. Die Große Koalition in Österreich 1945–1966*, Vienna: Österreichischer Bundesverlag.

Rotter, M. (1981), *Die dauernde Neutralität*, Berlin: Duncker & Humblot.

Schaller, A. (1987), *Schweizer Neutralität im West-Ost-Handel. Das Hotz-Linder-Agreement vom 23. Juli 1951*, Bern: St. Gallener Studien zur Politikwissenschaft.

Schlesinger, T.O. (1972), *Austrian Neutrality in Postwar Europe. The Domestic Roots of a Foreign Policy*, Vienna: Wilhelm Braumüller.

Stifter, C. (1997), *Die Wiederaufrüstung Österreichs. Die geheime Remilitarisierung der westlichen Besatzungszonen Österreichs 1945–1955*, Innsbruck: Studienverlag.

Stourzh, G. (1985), *Geschichte des Staatsvertrages 1945–1955. Österreichs Weg zur Neutralität*, Graz: Styria Verlag.

Stourzh, G. (1997), *Geschichte des Staatsvertrages 1945–1955. Österreichs Weg zur Neutralität*, Vienna: Böhlau Verlag.

Taber, G.M. (1969), *John F. Kennedy and the United States of Europe*, Brussels: College of Europe.

Toncic-Sorinj, L. (1982), *Erfüllte Träume: Kroatien-Österreich-Europa*, Vienna: Amalthea Verlag.

Verdroß, A. (1977), *Die immerwährende Neutralität Österreichs*, Vienna: Verlag für Geschichte und Politik.

Zemanek, Karl (1991), 'The Changing International System: A New Look at Collective Security and Permanent Neutrality', *Österreichische Zeitschrift für Öffentliches Recht und Völkerrecht, neue Folge*, **42**, pp.277–94.

PART II
SOCIETY AND POLITICS

5 The Development of Austrian National Identity

*Ernst Bruckmüller**

Introduction – of Anniversaries

In 1995 Austria celebrated two anniversaries: 50 years of the Second Republic and 40 years of the State Treaty. There were few reports of great celebrations. The 'grumpy republic' (*grantige Republik*) clearly had difficulties in conceiving of festivities capable of promoting collective remembrance (Wilflinger, 1995, pp.9f). Even an Anniversary Office especially opened for 1995–96 was closed down before the ideas it had generated could be brought to fruition.[1] Is this inability to celebrate a republican, or democratic peculiarity? That can hardly be the case, for most other European democracies celebrate their national holidays with considerable gusto. Is it an Austrian peculiarity? In view of Austria's countless local festivals and celebrations, ceremonies held to mark the anniversaries and founders' days of fire brigades and other associations, as well as provincial holidays and the honouring of provincial patron saints, that also appears unlikely. Festivals and commemorative days are obviously enjoyed frequently and without any great problems.

However, Austria's recent history offers few dates which the whole population could unhesitatingly interpret as memorable successes or as formative experiences (*Ursprungserlebnis*). Austrian armies lost the wars of 1859, 1866 and 1914–18. Even those Austrians who regarded Hitler's war as their own returned home defeated. The democratic principles of the existing Constitution are not supported by reference to a successful revolution. In 1919 the independent Republic of Austria seemed to have been forced upon the people, rather than having been freely chosen by them. Things were

*Translated by Kurt Richard Luther and Anne-Maria Bruckmüller from a manuscript largely drawn from Bruckmüller (1996).

different in 1945, but the following decade was still associated with the experience of occupation, which might help explain why the 50th anniversary of the end of war gave rise to silent reflection rather than to loud cries of joy (Jagschitz and Karner, 1995). The twentieth century is a period which, through the recollections of our parents and grandparents, we can to some extent still reconstruct as real-life histories. However, its 'great' political events mainly offer material that makes for controversial common remembrance: For the 'reds', 1918 meant revolution, social legislation, democracy and proletarian rule. For the 'blacks' and the middle classes, the same year meant defeat, the collapse of the monarchy, the threat of 'Bolshevism' and material deprivation. In 1934 the 'blacks' 'won', whilst the 'reds' and 'browns' experienced a painful defeat in two short, but bloody, civil wars. But 1938 was a triumph for the National Socialists and German nationalists, whose dream of becoming a part of Germany seemed to have been fulfilled. Along with the mentally handicapped, people now stigmatized as 'Jews', 'gypsies' or as 'antisocial' suffered persecution, expulsion and murder. Political enemies from the ranks of the Catholics as well as the Left were disciplined, imprisoned, carted off to concentration camps and killed. For all these people, the year 1938 was a catastrophe. In 1945, on the other hand, National Socialists and German nationalists were on the losing side and, with Germany's defeat, the 'blacks' and 'reds' won. These completely contradictory memories clearly militated against the development of a culture of collective celebration. Matters were exacerbated by the fact that many of the older generation were emotionally at home in their '*Lager* religion' (that is, the political identity of their subculture), which was often more important for their individual identity than being 'Austrian' (Hanisch, 1995; Lehnert, 1995).

The first time all Austrians were able to experience a common, unifying success was on 15 May 1955, when the State Treaty was signed. There certainly seems much to be said for those survey results that locate the genesis of Austrian national identity in the Second Republic and especially in the period after 1955 (Bruckmüller, 1994, p.18). The second pillar of Austrian national identity is permanent neutrality, approved by parliament on 26 October 1955. Although it was from the 1970s the object of greater public attachment than the State Treaty, permanent neutrality has since become somewhat tarnished and lost part of its youthful lustre. It is still accepted, but is no longer as central to Austrian national consciousness as it was in the Kreisky period (Bruckmüller, 1994, pp.134ff). Nonetheless, at the end of 1990, 82 per cent of respondents stated they would prefer foregoing EU-membership to renouncing neutrality and in the summer of 1993 that view was still held by 68 per cent (Plasser, Ulram, Sommer and Vretscha, 1993, p.41). In the spring of 1995, some 78 per cent of respondents in a youth survey were 'proud' of neutrality (Plasser, Ulram, Sommer and Vretscha, 1993, p.41).[2]

The 15 May was rejected as Austria's national day in favour of 26 October, a date with much weaker emotional connotations and, indeed, much less susceptible to emotional loading. Accordingly, there is in effect no date which outshines all others as the day of Austrian national identity. The debate in politics, the media and the arts presents us with a picture of a society full of contradiction and repression, in which guilt is freely ascribed. There appears to be no unifying 'Austrian myth'. As the mythological inventory is so empty (or, alternatively, so contradictory and rich), one could simply forget such anniversaries. But what actually happens is exactly the opposite. The whole culture industry – theatres, museums, publishers, writers, exhibitors and historically aware journalists – finds one anniversary after another and one justification after another for performances, exhibitions and scandals. This shows that even a secularized society has a profound need to reflect on its origins, to search for the roots from which the present might possibly derive and to satisfy itself of its own identity by embedding its own individual origins and history in the great tide of human history (Schmidt-Dengler 1994).

As I have already tried to point out, this is quite difficult in Austria. Immediately after its re-establishment in 1945, the young Second Republic, faced with many other urgent problems, was confronted with the difficulty of finding a new spiritual and symbolic foundation on which to build a solid new statehood (*Staatlichkeit*). For all that, the Second Republic immediately opted for the traditions of the First, whose Constitution and state symbols, such as the flag and coat of arms, were immediately adopted, albeit with minor variations. This is all the more surprising in view of the fact that the First Republic was hardly regarded as a success story. It was only because of Austria's negative experiences after 1938 that its first experiment at surviving as a small state could, in retrospect, be seen in a much more positive light (Stourzh, 1990, pp.49f). But what else could have served as a symbol? To be sure, certain traditions relating to Austria's cultural self-image and its image of outsiders could be taken over from the corporatist state dictatorship (*Ständestaat*) and the monarchy, especially as a means of distinguishing Austrians from the Germans. Thus 'the Austrian' of 1933–38, divested of his or her markedly 'corporate' (*ständische*) and 'German' elements, was restored to favour (Reiterer, 1986). Yet the political Left remained sceptical about Austria. In 1946 the Socialist Party's central secretary, Erwin Scharf, remarked that from 1934–38, *Österreich* had had the same meaning as *Volksgemeinschaft* during the time of National Socialism (Kriechbaumer, 1990, p.182).

Political Controversies – between German and Austrian Nationalism

Immediately after Austria's restoration in 1945 there were considerable differences in how the 'national issue' was addressed in the programmes of the three parties originally licensed by the Allies. Whilst the Austrian People's Party (ÖVP) demanded 'the most intensive effort aimed at building up the Austrian nation' and the Communist Party of Austria (KPÖ) also declared itself as Austrian-national, the Socialist Party of Austria (SPÖ) still had no opinion on the matter. There is nothing to be found on this issue in its first party programmes, save for the comment that one should not stigmatize the whole German nation with collective guilt for the Nazis' crimes (Kriechbaumer, 1990, pp.679 and 840). It was especially after 1955 that German national interests were again reinforced. In 1956 the paper *Die Aktion* published an article about the 'fictitious idea (*Geflunker*) of the Austrian nation', which appears 'to thrive only among weeds' (Torberg, 1964, p.296). On the occasion of the Schiller festivities in 1959, about 3000 members of 'national youth organizations', which Friedrich Torberg (1964, pp.296f; also Kreissler, 1984, p.433) bluntly referred to as 'Nazi faces', marched from Vienna Town Hall to the *Heldenplatz* where Hitler had addressed the crowds on the occasion of the *Anschluß* in March 1938. On 23 December 1961, the newspaper *Die Presse* was obliged to publish a rebuttal statement by the *Turnerbund* (Austrian Association of Gymnasts), in which it wrote that 'beyond loyalty to the German *Volkstum*' the *Turnerbund* sought also to educate the youth to have 'love of their fatherland Austria'. In response, Torberg (1964, p.297) wrote a commentary which included the following statement: 'it would be best if the young people really were educated *beyond* loyalty to the German *Volkstum* and *in* loyalty to the Austrian. Unfortunately, that is far from what is happening … .'

At that time, the spectacular acquittals of Austrian members of the Nazi extermination machinery began. In 1963 the acquittal, by an Austrian jury, of Franz Murer, the 'Lord of the Vilnius Ghetto', was greeted with public approval (Torberg, 1964, pp.299f). Institutions such as the *Institut für Österreichkunde*, which were intended to strengthen a decidedly Austrian consciousness, were only able to mitigate this trend.

Whilst the ÖVP and the KPÖ were the only real 'Austrian' parties immediately after the war, it is possible to detect the development of national consciousness within the SPÖ from about 1957 onwards. In that year Felix Butschek was the first to speak of an Austrian national identity being anchored in Austrians' minds. In 1962 Hermann Mörth stated in the *Zukunft* that this national identity was 'underdeveloped' but, in general, the SPÖ appears, from this point in time, to have overcome its difficulties with the notion of an independent Austrian nation (Kreissler, 1984, pp.454ff.). Within the Catholic part of the political spectrum, it was in particular the journal *Die Furche* which around 1960 tried to intensify the debate about the Austrians' national consciousness (Kreissler, 1984, pp.457f).

Göbhart and Borodajkewicz

The 'Göbhart affair' caused the controversy about Austrian national identity to reach a previously unknown intensity and breadth, spreading, for the first time, beyond the relatively small circle of politicians and intellectuals. Dr Franz Göbhart was the head teacher of the pedagogic academy in Graz, a committed Catholic and member of the ÖVP. In January 1964 he received from the *Deutsches Kulturwerk europäischen Geistes* (German Cultural Institution of European Spirit) an invitation to attend a film presentation. In reply, Göbhart wrote to the organizers that German national machinations had no business in Austrian schools. The *Kulturwerk* thereupon started proceedings against him for defamation. Through an MP of the Freiheitliche Partei Österreichs (FPÖ), it also tabled a question to the minister of education, with the aim of getting the latter to issue an official admonishment of Göbhart. As the reaction was at first quite limited, German national organisations concerned to promote *deutsche Volkheit* announced that a lecture on the topic 'Are we Austrians Germans?' was to be held on 9 April 1964 (the eve of the 26th anniversary of Hitler's Austrian referendum). The speakers were to be the well known German national author Fritz Stüber and the former Nazi professor, Hellfried Pfeifer. In Graz, a counter-front was established, which called for the speeches to be banned. Sixteen out of Graz's 18 headteachers declared their support for Göbhart. In the end the *Kulturwerk*'s Neo-Nazi rally was banned, though a counter-demonstration did take place, at which Göbhart stated, 'I am glad that Graz is not the city in which the *Volk* arises (*Stadt der Volkserhebung*), but the city in which Austria arises'. Neo-Nazi agitation was now also widely denounced in the media.

Around 1964–65, public discussions about national identity became more frequent and, for the first time, they also took place on television. Thus, for example, the FPÖ's Tassilo Broesigke confronted the ÖVP's Heinrich Drimmel, or Bruno Kreisky (SPÖ). The well known thesis of Austrians' membership of the German nation (*deutsches Volkstum*) were countered by those arguing in favour of a specific Austrian identity, in support of which they cited the consolidation of Austrian consciousness since 1945 (Kreissler, 1984, p.452).

This political debate was given a new and tragic twist through events surrounding Taras Borodajkewicz, professor of Economic History at the *Hochschule für Welthandel*. Much loved by his students for his minimal demands as an examiner, he tended to spice up his lectures with parenthetic comments that were openly anti-Semitic and German nationalist. In 1964–65, students rebelled against this and there were demonstrations for and against Borodajkewicz. During the course of one such demonstration in 1965, a pensioner named Ernst Kirchweger was killed by a Neo-Nazi demonstrator (Bailer-Galanda, Lasek and Neugebauer, 1992, p.287). In the end, the professor was dismissed.

All these events finally led key political actors to conclude that it was necessary to strengthen Austrian national consciousness and to find some additional symbolism which would help realize that goal. The 1965 decision to establish an Austrian national holiday can only be understood in light of this background (Spann, nd, p.31).

The Austrian Nation as a 'Congenital Ideological Abnormality'

It is, of course, possible that anyone who believed the Austrians to be part of another (that is, the German) nation could come to regard the newly constituted 'Austrian nation' as an ideological construct or, in the harsher language of former Carinthian Governor Dr Jörg Haider, as a 'congenital ideological abnormality' (*ideologische Mißgeburt*). Haider's 1988 choice of words[3] unleashed an intense controversy and is indicative of the strength of German nationalism in the FPÖ under his leadership. This terminology did not, of course, make the FPÖ very attractive and so it was necessary for the party's 'national' position to be revised. The FPÖ's traditional pan-Germanism has been manifested on a number of occasions and was still apparent in 1989 during German unification. Its new German–Austrian orientation has proved much more successful, but is only Austrian national in a very limited sense.

The 'Austrian Nation' as a Product of Forgetfulness?

During the course of the Second Republic, growing self-awareness gradually gave rise to an Austrian national identity, but was criticized from both the left and the right of the political spectrum. That criticism always focused upon the widespread tendency for collective 'forgetfulness' regarding the formation of the Austrian nation after 1945: right-wingers committed to the notion of *Volkstum* have continued to reproach adherents to an Austrian national identity for having, for example, abandoned the common 'house of German history', or repressed the common *Volkstum*. For their part, the 'progressives' have pilloried those who have forgotten, or repressed, Austria's part in the crimes of National Socialism. These critics believe that the pernicious fiction of Austria having been a 'victim of fascism' has been predicated upon this lapse of memory. According to this frequently repeated charge, the role of victim (*Opferrolle*) was in turn the prerequisite for the establishment of Austria's contemporary national identity. Ernest Renan (1992, pp.41f) has pointed to the great importance of not only collective memory, but also collective forgetfulness:

> Forgetfulness and … historical errors are essential factors in the creation of a nation and it is for this reason that advances in historical investigation are often a danger for nationalism. … the essence of a nation lies in all individuals having many matters in common and also in their having forgotten much. No French citizen knows whether he is a Burgundian, an Alans, a Taifales, or a Visigoth; each must have forgotten Saint Bartholomew and the Midi massacres of the middle of the thirteenth century.

The Findings of Empirical Social Research

National Identity

More or less comparable data on this question are available for the period since 1956.[4] In 1956 the Fessel Institut organized a poll entitled 'Austrians' national identity' (*Nationalbewußtein der Österreicher*). When asked 'Do you personally think we are a group of the German people, or are we a distinct Austrian people?', 49 per cent replied that Austrians were a distinct people, 46 per cent opted for being a part of the German people and 5 per cent remained undecided. Women exhibited stronger Austrian nationalism, with 54 per cent answering that Austrians were a distinct people, whilst only 46 per cent of men did so. Austrian nationalism was most intense in the region of Vienna, followed by the Tyrol, Vorarlberg, Lower Austria and the Burgenland.

A poll conducted in 1964–65 by the *Sozialwissenschaftliche Studiengesellschaft* (SWS) found that 47.4 per cent of the sample responded positively to the proposition that 'The Austrians constitute a nation', 23 per cent agreed 'they are slowly beginning to feel that they are a nation', whereas 15.3 per cent believed 'Austrians are not a nation'. At 15 per cent, the proportion of undecided was quite high. Divided on the basis of party preferences, the 1964–65 findings are as in Table 5.1.

The results of a 1966 Gallup Institut poll for William T. Bluhm (1973, pp.226ff) are interesting, although his more differentiated questionnaire makes it difficult to compare fully his study with others presented here. His findings

Table 5.1 National identity and party identification in 1964–65 (%)

	FPÖ	KPÖ	ÖVP	SPÖ	None	Total
Austrians are a nation	22.0	50.0	52.5	55.7	37.5	47.4
Austrians are not a nation	53.0	22.0	11.4	8.7	16.7	15.3
Austrians are slowly beginning to feel like a nation	20.4	17.0	22.0	23.8	24.8	23.0
Don't know	4.6	11.0	14.1	11.8	21.0	14.0

Source: Wagner (1982, pp.124ff).

Table 5.2 National identity and party identification in 1966 (%)

	ÖVP	SPÖ	FPÖ	None	Total
Austria is a completely distinct nation	30	44	16	36	35
Although Austria belongs to the realm of German language and culture, Austria is a distinct nation	31	30	21	38	29
Although Austria is an independent state, Austria belongs to the German nation	12	6	30	7	11
Although Austrians are a political nation and stand up for independence, they belong to the German nation	10	8	23	7	9
Although Austrians belong to the realm of German language and culture, they are slowly starting to feel like a nation	13	7	6	6	8

Note: The 'missing' figures denote 'don't knows'.
Source: Bluhm (1973, pp.226ff).

in terms of party identification are given in Table 5.2. National consciousness is clearly related to age. The first proposition was approved by 40 per cent of those aged up to 30, by merely 30 per cent of those aged 31–50 and by 36 per cent of those over 50. Occupational status is also important, with the first question being answered in the affirmative by 39 per cent of blue-collar workers, 33 per cent of farmers and 31 per cent of the self-employed and professionals, but by only 16 per cent of civil servants. On the other hand, the third question was answered positively by only 8 per cent of workers, 12 per cent of farmers, 13 per cent of the self-employed, but by 19 per cent of civil servants. Amongst those who approved of proposition four, civil servants and the self-employed were again overrepresented (12 per cent) when compared to blue-collar workers (9 per cent) and farmers (8 per cent).

These findings are largely compatible with those of 1956, when workers and farmers were also overrepresented amongst those who held Austrians to be a distinct nation: 62 per cent of workers and 56 per cent of farmers, but only 32 per cent of the self-employed and entrepreneurs held this view (the average was 49 per cent). Overall, the 1966 poll showed that, despite clear differences related to age, occupation, region and status, a sense of Austrian identity was becoming increasingly firmly rooted in the population.

Notwithstanding the fact that its prime focus was the federal army, a 1973 IFES poll was more comparable to the surveys discussed above than Bluhm's 1966 investigation. This poll found that 62 per cent of Austrians thought Austria was a nation, 12 per cent believed Austria was slowly beginning to think of itself as a nation, whilst 19 per cent had no opinion at all and only 7 per cent clearly rejected the notion of distinct Austrian nationhood. Analogous questions were posed in a 1977 SWS study, the results of which were very similar. Some 62 per cent of respondents again said that Austria was a distinct nation and 16 per cent thought it was on the way to becoming one. However, the proportion not expressing an opinion fell from 19 to 11 per cent and the percentage who clearly rejected the existence of an Austrian nation grew from 7 to 11 per cent. Even the answers to questions about the period during which an independent national identity had allegedly developed were similar, although respondents were more inclined to accord significance to the post-1945 period (see Table 5.3). Also worthy of note is the fact that even amongst FPÖ supporters there was a strong decline in the view that Austria was not a distinct nation (only 22 per cent, as opposed to 53 per cent in 1964–65).

Table 5.3 The period to which the development of Austrian national identity was ascribed in 1977 (%)

Before 1918	15	1938–1945	4	In recent years	3
After 1918	14	1945–1955	29		
1934–1938	2	after 1955	26	Don't know	6

Source: Wagner (1982, pp.124ff).

The figures of a 1979 SWS poll were quite similar. Some 68 per cent stated that Austrians constituted a nation, 14 per cent said they were on the way to becoming one and only 6 per cent decidedly rejected the nation. If one divides up the figures on the basis of party supporters, one finds that, in 1979, FPÖ sympathizers took the position which adherents of other parties had taken in 1965 (see Table 5.4).

Table 5.4 National identity and party identification in 1979 (%)

	FPÖ	KPÖ	ÖVP	SPÖ	None
Austrian are a nation	49	60	66	75	59
Austrians are beginning to feel like a nation	24	13	14	12	17
Austrians are not a nation	23	17	7	3	8
Don't know	4	10	13	10	16

Source: Wagner (1982, pp.124ff).

The *Paul-Lazarsfeld-Gesellschaft für Sozialforschung*'s 1980 study (Paul-Lazarsfeld, 1980)[5] is close both in time and in its findings to the 1979 poll. Thus, 67 per cent regarded Austria as a distinct nation, 19 per cent said it was developing in that direction, 11 per cent clearly rejected the existence of an Austrian nation and 3 per cent had no opinion.

During the 1980s FPÖ supporters became surprisingly Austrian nationalist, although in 1993 they again exhibited more German nationalist tendencies. From Table 5.5[6] one can clearly see that, whilst Austrian national identity has been consolidated amongst supporters of the SPÖ, ÖVP and Greens, in the case of FPÖ supporters it is prone to certain fluctuations. Indeed, the high national identity values of 1987 may be related to the party's government participation between 1983 and 1986.

Over time, therefore, the proportion of those who regard Austria as a nation has stabilized at about 80 per cent (see Table 5.6): Since the 1960s the consciousness of being Austrian has become increasingly pronounced and one can now detect a definite Austrian national identity. In 1987 this was underscored by a survey which asked people how they might respond if they were asked 'Are you German?' whilst abroad: 87 per cent said they would have declared themselves to be Austrians; 2 per cent would have described themselves in terms of their regional, or *Land*, identity; 3 per cent would reply 'Austrian Germans'; 6 per cent 'German'; and 3 per cent would

Table 5.5 National identity and party identification in 1987 and 1993 (%)

	Party Identification				
	1987				1993
	SPÖ	ÖVP	Greens	FPÖ	FPÖ
National identity					
German	6	6	1	5	
German-Austrian	2	3	–	2	
Regional Austrian	1	2	–	3	
National identity					
Austria not a nation	4	3	6	7	13
Austria developing into a nation	12	18	19	16	14
Austria a nation	82	75	73	77	71
Concept of a nation (*Nationsbegriff*):					
Linguistic nation (*Sprachnation*)	22	21	11	18	28
Nation state (*Staatsnation*)	73	76	87	81	68

Sources: 1987: Stourzh and Ulram (1987 p.6); FPÖ 1993: Fessel+GfK.

Table 5.6 The development of Austrian national identity, 1964–93 (%)

	1964	1970	1977	1980	1987	1989	1990	1992	1993
Austrians are a nation	47	66	62	67	75	79	74	78	80
Austrians are slowly beginning to feel like a nation	23	16	16	19	16	15	20	15	12
Austrians are not a nation	15	8	11	11	5	4	5	5	6
No response	14	10	12	3	3	3	1	2	2

not, or could not, answer (Stourzh and Ulram, 1987, p.4). It is very likely that analogous questions would not have been answered in the same way before 1945, nor before 1938 or 1934.

All polls undertaken during the last 15 years or so on the question of the age of Austrian national identity agree that it is predominantly interpreted as a product of the Second Republic. Whilst in 1965 some 38 per cent claimed it developed in the period before 1938, by 1980 only 23 per cent and, in 1987, a mere 18 per cent did so. Conversely, in 1965, 40 per cent argued for the period between 1945 and 1955; in 1980 it was 58 per cent and in 1987 61 per cent. Meanwhile, the proportion of those citing the period after 1955 increased by 8 per cent in 1980 and by 9 per cent in 1987. In this sense, Austria is a 'young' nation (Stourzh and Ulram, 1987, p.12).

This national identity clearly refers to the territory of today's Republic of Austria (Kreissler, 1984; Wagner, 1982 pp.109ff; Stourzh and Ulram, 1987, *passim*; Stourzh, 1990, pp.99ff). When speaking of an Austrian national identity, a little less than three-quarters of Austrians had in mind the idea of a 'nation-state' (*Staatsnation*) – that is, a concept of nation predicated upon the people's consent to the state in which they live. A fifth to one quarter (in 1993, 27 per cent) had in mind the idea of 'linguistic nationalism' (*Sprachnation*) – that is a nation based on a common language (Stourzh and Ulram, 1987 p.4; re: 1993, Fessel+GfK). Similar results were obtained by Reiterer *et al.* in a poll from 1984 (n=1999), although there are slight variations due to the questionnaire not being quite comparable. Here again, statist and consensual answers predominated. Thus the first concept that 14 per cent of respondents associated with 'nation' was 'state', whilst for 34 per cent, 'nation' was primarily associated with 'a consensual community based on the desire to live together economically and politically'. By contrast, linguistic and cultural definitions were prioritized by only 16 and 10 per cent respectively, and a mere 6 per cent approved of the historically important credo that a nation comprised a 'community of origin/descent' (*Abstammungsgemeinschaft*) (Reiterer, 1988, p.5). If one examines orientations using occupational and educational criteria, there appears to be a positive correlation between membership of the upper educational classes and the idea that a nation comprises a voluntary political community (*politische Willensgemeinschaft*). According to this study, the idea that 'language' constitutes the defining criterion of the nation was very much overrepresented amongst FPÖ supporters (Reiterer, 1988, pp.6f). One could, very tentatively, interpret this as indicating a reversal of traditional attributes: Austria's 'classic' educated middle classes (*Bildungsbürgertum*) often used to combine more or less pronounced Austrian patriotism with a clear commitment to the German *Kulturnation*. Such patterns of identification have lost much of their former strength (Lepsius, 1990, pp.203ff). On the other hand, the somewhat stronger 'German' tone of the FPÖ, the clientele of which has undergone enormous change since 1986 (*Die Presse*, September 1995), points to a stronger persistence of more German nationalist orientations amongst those classes into which such attitudes only penetrated relatively late.

National Identity and Provincial Identity (Landesbewußtsein)

The 1987 investigation of Austrian identity was the first also to ask which regional entity was the bearer of primary identification. Translated into ethnological or ethnohistorical terms, the question would be: which tribal entity do people feel they belong to? The following answers were possible: the *Heimatort*, (the native place – an indicator of local patriotism); the respondent's own *Land* (regional or *Land* patriotism); Austria (this could be either statist, or national patriotism); Germany (primarily 'a German' – German nationalism); (Central) Europe ('European' – European patriotism), the world ('cosmopolitan' – cosmopolitanism). As shown in Table 5.7, the answers in the individual *Länder* varied considerably.

Table 5.7 Territorial objects of emotional attachment in 1987 (%)

	Vienna	LA	B	Tyrol	Car	Vlbg	Styria	UA	Szbg	Austria
Locality	38	30	31	16	23	21	25	35	24	29
Region	8	16	24	58	53	44	39	23	33	27
Austrian	46	55	44	19	24	28	32	27	25	39
German	1	0		1			2	1	2	1
(Central) European	4	1		1		4	2	1	4	2
Cosmopolitan	4		1	2		3	1	2		2
Other	2	0			1		0	0	3	1

Note: LA: Lower Austria; B: Burgenland; Car: Carinthia; Vlbg: Vorarlberg; UA: Upper Austria; Szbg: Salzburg.
Source: Stourzh and Ulram (1987, p.23).

The Viennese, Lower Austrians and Burgenlanders were quite strong local patriots, had a less well developed sense of *Land* identity, but were nonetheless still disproportionately 'Austrian'. By contrast, the Tyrolese, Vorarlbergers and Carinthians proved to be the most fervent *Land* patriots with a less pronounced sense of local and national patriotism, especially in the Tyrol. In Styria, Upper Austria and Salzburg, the territorial orientation of affective identities seemed much more evenly distributed, although Styrians seemed most closely related to the second group.

'European' and 'cosmopolitan' orientations were less well developed. They centred on Vienna and Vorarlberg, where they correlated well with levels of economic development, but were to some extent also present in Salzburg. The survey revealed no clear correlation between territorial affective orientation and political partisanship, with slight exception in the case of Green supporters, amongst whom there was a clear underrepresentation of local patriotism and an overrepresentation of European or cosmopolitan orientations. The distribution of *Land* and Austrian identifiers among Green supporters fell within the normal range.

Austrian nationalists usually reside within their own *Land*. However, when asked to identify the 'typical' Austrian, the sample most frequently cited Tyrolese, Viennese and Salzburgers, whilst the Burgenlanders and Vorarlbergers were regarded as the least 'Austrian'. Even the Vorarlbergers themselves shared this perception and again held the Tyrolese and the Viennese to be typically Austrian. In other words, the Vorarlbergers are least inclined to consider themselves to be 'typically Austrian' and their *Land* identity seems to be characterized by a certain distance from the 'typically Austrian' *Länder* (Diem, 1988, pp.30f).

In many ways, national identity and *Land* identity are interconnected, as illustrated by answers to questions about national and *Land* symbols. As long as the questions are not concerned with specific local peculiarities, there is considerable overlap in what is identified (for example, 'mountains', 'countryside', 'lifestyle', 'political system' and so on). What is 'typically Austrian' also tends to be associated with specific cities, regions and *Länder*. According to the 1988 survey results, the Tyrolese appear to be the 'most typical' Austrians (Diem, 1988, pp.10f).

National Pride

National and *Land* identity are relatively diffuse expressions of certain common aspects, and perhaps more differentiated expressions of Austrians' collective feelings can be obtained if one enquires about their national pride. The findings of empirical social research concerning Austrians' national pride are reflected in Table 5.8.

Research from the early 1990s (see Table 5.9) has shown that, relative to other countries, Austrian national pride is quite pronounced. Compared to Austria, the levels of national pride amongst even the allegedly very chauvinistic French and Swiss, who supposedly hold a high opinion of themselves, are modest. This is all the more surprising in view of the massive distrust which Austrians express vis-à-vis their own political institutions (see below). Moreover, the object of collective Austrian pride has been subject to considerable variation. In 1980 the beauty of Austria's countryside was already the prime object of identification, followed by social and political peace which were also held in high esteem. However, if one

Table 5.8 National pride, 1973–90

Proud to be Austrian	1973 %	1982 %	1985 %	1987(1) %	1987(2) %	1988(1) %	1988(2) %	1989 %	1993 %
Very	56	69	65	53	57	51	63	53	61
Quite	34	24	26	34	32	35	27	35	31
Not very	2	1	3	5	3	4	5	7	4
Not at all	1	1	1	1	1	2	1	1	1

Sources: 1973–88: IMAS, *Bundesweite Repräsentativumfragen 1989*; 1993: Fessel+GfK, *Bundesweite Repräsentativumfragen*.

Table 5.9 Strong national pride in international comparison

Country	Year	% 'Very proud' of their National Affiliation
USA	1985	87
Great Britain	1985	58
Austria	1989	53
France	1985	42
Switzerland	1989	31
Federal Republic of Germany	1990	21

Source: Plasser and Ulram (1993a, p.40).

Table 5.10 Important objects of Austrian national pride in 1980 (%)

	All	Minimal Education	(Qualified for) Higher Education
Beautiful countryside	97	96	96
Political and social peace	96	95	96
Family and friends live here	94	95	92
Pleasant people	94	95	90
Common language	93	94	89
Neutrality	87	85	82
Many good musicians and poets	79	77	79
Satisfaction with government policy	74	78	62
Good food	74	78	53

Source: Gerlich (1988, p.259).

examines not general objects of identification, but pride in Austrian achievements, numerous changes between 1980 and 1987 become apparent (see Table 5.11). There has been nothing short of a collapse in support for national policy (*Staatspolitik*). The very positive evaluation it received in 1980 was attributable to Bruno Kreisky's capacity to convey to Austrians a sense of their importance in the international arena. Between then and 1987, there were numerous greater and lesser scandals, peaking in Waldheim's presidential election campaign of 1986, which was presumably more damaging to Austrians' self-image than it was to the country's image abroad. By 1987 Austrians showed an increased tendency (already visible in Table 5.10) to be proud of their cultural heritage – a legacy which the Austrians of today have, of course, merely inherited, rather than actively contributed towards. Another area of activity that could possibly promote identity formation is sport, which at the time of the surveys, however, was experiencing a low point.

Table 5.11 Personal pride in areas of Austrian achievement

% personally proud of Austrian achievements in the respect of	Ranking 1980	Ranking 1987	% 1980	% 1987	+/–
Popular music (waltzes, etc.)	3	1	81	83	+2
Medicine	2	2	82	74	–8
Classical music	7	3	60	71	+11
The performing arts	4	4	73	67	–6
Science and research	5	5	73	66	–7
Sport	1	6	90	66	–24
The fine arts	9	7	57	57	0
Literature	7	8	58	55	–3
National policy	6	9	72	27	–45

Source: Stourzh and Ulram (1987, p.28).

In the areas of economics and politics, which impact on everyone's lives, levels of pride are, again, high only in respect of activities that relate in some way to the beauty of Austria's countryside or to its cultural heritage. As can be seen from Table 5.12, what is striking is the low level of pride in what is objectively one of the most noteworthy facts of post-war economic history – namely, the remarkable development of Austrian industry since 1945. This has transformed the small state (*Kleinstaat*) from a rather unviable,

Table 5.12 Pride in Austrian economic and political achievements

	% Proud	% Not Proud
Austria as a tourist destination	91	6
Internal security, low rates of crime	75	18
Social security	72	23
Vienna as a congress venue	69	23
Sozialpartnerschaft (corporatism)	63	28
Austria's role in the world	56	37
Modern technological development	46	44
The position of Austria's economy in the global market (exports)	42	49
Overcoming environmental problems	23	69

Source: Stourzh and Ulram (1987 p.29).

semi-agrarian exporter of raw materials into a highly industrialized economy (albeit one inclined to excessive consumption), whose economic strength is on a par with other European states of a similar size. Conversely, the survey finds that tourism is rated very highly, despite the fact that the per capita wealth it generates is associated with not inconsiderable costs in respect of, for example, the countryside and cultural assets. What we have here are astonishing examples of cognitive dissonance (Nowotny and Schuberth, 1993).

Attitudes to the Political System

In general, Austrians are democrats. Only amongst FPÖ supporters is there a widespread desire for a 'strong man' (see Table 5.13). An overwhelming majority (over 90 per cent) of Austrians are of the opinion that democracy is always better than dictatorship. (The figures for Germany, Italy and Spain are 90, 70 and 68 per cent respectively.) It may help our understanding of Austrians' collective identity if we compare their political identity with that of the Germans. As shown by Table 5.14, Austrians appear to interpret their republic very much as a (positive) welfare state. It is associated much less frequently than in Germany with concepts such as 'Constitution', and there is thus no Austrian equivalent of the 'constitutional patriotism' (*Verfassungspatriotismus*) as has developed in the Federal Republic – possibly something to do with the carefree manner in which Austria's political elite deal with the Constitution.[7] Austrians are significantly less likely to mention such notions as 'liberty' or

Table 5.13 The desire for a 'strong man' 1980 and 1993 (%)

	(Tend to) Agree*	(Tend to) Disagree
Austrian average 1980	24	74
Austrian average 1993	19	76
Occupation 1993		
Unskilled blue-collar	35	50
Self-employed	31	66
Farmers	24	59
Pupils/students	9	88
Party identification 1993		
FPÖ	59	36
ÖVP	21	74
LIF	14	79
SPÖ	13	83
Greens	8	91
Regular newspaper 1993		
Kronen-Zeitung	24	69
No newspaper	21	73
Täglich Alles	21	70
Kurier	10	88
Presse	9	86
Standard	7	89

*Percentage agreeing with the proposition: 'Actually, we do not need a parliament at all, but a strong man who can implement decisions quickly.'
Source: Composite from diagrams 483 and 484 of Sozialwissenschaftliche Studiengesellschaft (1993).

'justice' (1989). In addition, the state still tends to be regarded (again positively) as a functioning bureaucratic state.

Central institutions of modern democracies, such as parliament, parties or the media, are much less highly valued in Austria than in Germany and Switzerland (see Table 5.15). That is not the case, however, in respect of the bureaucratic apparatus. In October 1993 a study was conducted into Austrians' perceptions of their parliament (SWS, 1993). Some 37 per cent of those polled reported that, in the preceding two to three years, their personal

Table 5.14 State image (*Staatsbild*) in Austria and the FRG

% who associate 'state' with	Austria 1976	Austria 1989	Germany 1989
Social security	64	55	56
Constitution	24	32	39
Bureaucracy	16	30	
Order	33	30	30
Liberty	33	28	37
Justice	29	28	37
Tax burdens	27	25	24
Economic planning	24	24	19
Being patronized (*Bevormundung*)	2	10	6
Subject status (*Untertanen*)	3	6	7
Excessive egalitarianism (*Gleichmacherei*)	3	5	7
Anonymity	2	4	4

Source: Bretschneider and Ulram (1992, p.321).

Table 5.15 Confidence in various institutions

% expressing great confidence in ...	Austria	FRG	Switzerland
Police	56	63	55
Courts	53	58	52
Government departments	46	49	45
Army	37	54	49
Government and parliament	27	48	51
Media	23	44	–
Parties	17	36	–

Source: Plasser and Ulram (1993, p.35).

assessment of the parliament had deteriorated, 45 per cent said it had remained the same and only 7 per cent thought there had been improvements (12 per cent had no opinion on this matter).

The Austrians even have a considerably lower opinion of their political system than the Swiss do of theirs (see Table 5.16). All in all, when one compares Austria with other European countries, it appears to be more

Table 5.16 Assessment of the political order in Austria and Switzerland

'Looking at things as a whole, is our political order in ... good, or is it not good?'	Austria %	Switzerland %
Very good	2	10
Good	26	55
On the whole positive	**28**	**65**
Just right	**33**	**28**
Bad	25	3
Very bad	5	0
On the whole negative	**30**	**3**
Undecided	8	3

Source: Plasser and Ulram (1993a, p.35, table 13).

Table 5.17 International comparison of subjective competence

Country	Year	% disagreeing that 'People like me have no influence on what the government does'
USA	1988	58
Switzerland	1991	46
Australia	1987	42
Netherlands	1988	38
Germany	1989	32
Austria	1989	24
Czech Republic	1993	23
Slovak Republic	1993	22
Hungary	1992	10
Poland	1992	8

Source: Plasser and Ulram (1993b, p.44).

'eastern'. Austria's level of democratic subjective competence is quite far removed from that of established Western democracies and is closer to those of post-socialist states (see Table 5.17).

When compared internationally, the few dimensions of political identity which we have been able to consider here provide grounds for some concern. On the one hand, there is a strong preference for democracy; on the other hand, there is enormous political dissatisfaction (*Politikverdrossenheit*). There are quite high levels of political satisfaction, but also emotional distrust of those who classically embody the public face of democracy. There is scepticism about one's own competence and a comparatively high level of positive evaluation of National Socialism. And all this is overlayed by a strongly developed sense of national pride.

Historical Consciousness

Austria's historical identity was investigated in some detail as part of the large Austrian study conducted in 1987 (Stourzh and Ulram, 1987, pp.35–43). In a nutshell, the findings were as follows: with the exception of the Maria-Theresian and Josephinian periods, what happened before 1914 is lost in the mists of time; interest in the Bamberger period and the years preceding the 1848 March Revolution (the *Vormärz*) is particularly low; and people are most interested in the World Wars, the First Republic, the *Anschluß* to National Socialist Germany and in the whole history of the Second Republic. The corporate dictatorship (*Ständestaat*) tends to be repressed. The grand reign of Maria Theresa, who appears to have become something of a semi-mythical mother figure, ranks very highly in Austrians' collective consciousness. That apart, however, there is no historical consciousness that reaches back very far in time. But even the relatively short period in which people are more interested is not very well understood:

> Only 56 per cent were able to identify correctly the political camps which fought each other in the civil war of February 1934; 25 per cent answered incorrectly, 22 per cent did not answer at all. As far as the murder of Dollfuß in July 1934 is concerned, only 43 per cent answered correctly, '…' a third (32 per cent) wrongly and a quarter (25 per cent) did not answer at all. (Stourzh and Ulram, 1987, p.43; cf. Stourzh, 1990, p.110)

Despite their alleged interest in contemporary history, Austrians do not hold a very honourable position as far as the acceptance of positive sides of National Socialism is concerned (see Table 5.18). At 43 per cent, the proportion of those who attributed both negative *and* positive sides to National Socialism is unusually high. This helps to explain how it is possible, in a late twentieth-century European democracy, a politician making positive statements about National Socialism can generate not only abhorrence but also political attention, resonance and support (Scharsach, 1992, pp.97ff; Bailer and Neugebauer, 1993, pp.378f).

It must, of course, be acknowledged that historical understanding is constantly undergoing change. It is, above all, members of the younger

Table 5.18 Evaluation of National Socialism in Austria and Germany, 1989 and 1990

% who believe that National Soclialism had ...	FRG 1989	Western Germany 1990	Eastern Germany 1990	Austria 1989
only bad sides	29	21	18	16
more bad sides	34	36	37	34
on the whole negative	**63**	**57**	**55**	**55**
good and bad sides	35	41	40	43
more good sides	1	1	1	1

Source: Plasser and Ulram (1993a, p.39).

generation who demand a more profound debate about matters such as Austria's complicity in and during National Socialism.[8] We can only hope that this will provide more detailed knowledge of events, which in turn will lead in the first place to the questioning of all oversimplified historical accounts, but above all to greater tolerance towards other people and a gentler historiographical discourse that uses knowledge of the tragic past to generate responsibility for the future.

European Identity

> Both absolutely and in comparison to other western European countries, the European identity of the Austrian population is exceedingly weak. The identity of only 21 per cent of Austrians has at least some European component (i.e. they consider themselves to be not only Austrians, but also Europeans). In contrast to Switzerland, for instance, generation-specific differences are extremely small; the orientation of the young generation is also directed towards the nation-state and is not supranational. (Plasser, Ulram, Sommer and Vretscha, 1993, p.41)

This statement is based on poll data from 1991–93, which show only a very slow development towards a supranational identity. According to a more recent study of foreign policy awareness (Neuhold and Luif, 1992), Austrians' evaluations hardly differ from those of experts working in the media. Most Austrians are thus sceptical about the possibility of rapid change in formerly socialist countries, with some exceptions such as the Czech and Slovak Republics and Hungary. The overwhelming majority considered relations to the new, enlarged Germany to be unproblematic.

Almost nine out of ten welcomed German reunification and hardly anyone perceived in it any dangers for Europe or for Germany's neighbours. The new Germany is, however, a large external factor (*Außengröße*): 92 per cent of Austrians rejected an *Anschluß* with Germany. This corresponds to many other poll results, according to which Germany may well be regarded as a 'relative', but with no desire for a fusion of the two states.

In 1990–91 the Austrians believed that the European Community would, in future, remain loosely associated. Its development towards a genuine 'union' was hardly noticed, although it is of course impossible to establish whether this means that Austrians lacked awareness of the actual dynamics of the integration process or, alternatively, were engaged in wishful thinking. At that time, a small majority perceived EC-membership as positive. Were there to be a clear choice between neutrality and EC-membership (that is, if membership were to be possible only at the price of relinquishing neutrality), neutrality would be the preferred option. In respect of attitudes to individual large states, the survey showed, above all, declining sympathy towards the USA. In 1978 58 per cent of those polled had stated that Austria should maintain especially close and good relations with the USA, but by 1987, the figure was down to 38 per cent.[9] The Third World was given little attention; a majority was of the opinion that the extent of Austrian foreign aid (regrettably small in international comparison) was just right. Moreover, the response of three-quarters of those polled to the question about accepting asylum-seekers and refugees was that 'the boat is full'.

One can have some sympathy for Austrian fears of the big wide world, since young nations are understandably more anxious about their identity than old, large and internally consolidated nations. Notwithstanding the various millennial celebrations, Austria is a young nation, in the sense that it has only relatively recently had to stand by itself on the world stage for the first time. For until 1918 (and again from 1938 to 1945) the country was incorporated into much larger entities. After the errors of 1918–45 the Austrians finally achieved an accepted, independent existence that endowed them with an identity. They then raised that independence, together with neutrality, which served as a symbol for its acceptance, on to their altars and now do not wish to bid farewell to them. After all, European integration promises a constant preoccupation not only with one's own worries – large or small – but also with all those which the European Union will have to face, from Ireland to Greece. And pan-European concerns regarding formerly socialist Europe will also be shared by the Austrians.

Notes

1 The 'Büro 95/96' was run by Heinz Rögl. See *Wiener Journal*, no. 153, June 1993, pp.24f and nos. 159–60, pp.25f.
2 For the poll of spring 1995, see *'Die Presse'*, 9 April 1995, Supplement, *50 Jahre Zweite Republik*, pp.I and V.
3 On Austrian television's *'Inlandsreport'* (home report) of 18 August 1988. Compare Bailer and Neugebauer (1993, pp.373 f).
4 Thankfully, they are collated in Wagner (1982, pp.124ff), from which, unless otherwise indictated, all the following data up to and including 1980 are drawn.
5 This volume contains both an evaluation of the data (which were published separately) and contributions by Gunter Falk, Norbert Leser, Anton Pelinka, Otto Schulmeister, Gerald Stourzh and Hans Strotzka.
6 This survey was part of a project entitled *Österreichbewußtsein in den achtziger Jahren*, which was financed by the Austrian National Bank's Jubilee Fund (No. 3072) and directed by Gerhard Stourzh and Peter Ulram. It will henceforth be referred to as Stourzh and Ulram, 1987.
7 Compare the very critical article by Funk (1992), who argues that the Constitution (*Bundesverfassungsgesetz*) has been inappropriately used and points to the over 8000 amendments which have resulted in the Constitution becoming 'bloated'. The second president of the National Assembly, Heinrich Neisser (ÖVP), maintains that the Austrians have been unable to develop an 'emotional attachment' to the Constitution analogous to that which, for example, the Americans have to theirs (*Die Presse*, 12 September 1995, p.6).
8 The desire to make people conscious of the disastrous events of the Third Reich was shared by an average of 52 per cent of respondents, whilst 47 per cent preferred to 'let the grass grow over it'. Amongst those aged under 30, some 61 per cent supported greater publicity and only 35 per cent opted for the grass and thus repression (Stourzh and Ulram, 1987, p.83).
9 Bretschneider (1978), cited in Neuhold (1992). See also a poll published in *Die Presse*, 22 July 1987.

Bibliography

Bailer, Brigitte and Neugebauer, Wolfgang (1993), 'Die FPÖ: Vom Liberalismus zum Rechtsextremismus' in *Handbuch des österreichischen Rechtsextremismus*, 2nd edn, Vienna: Wiener Verlag, pp.327–428.

Bailer-Galanda, Brigitte, Lasek, Wilhelm and Neugebauer, Wolfgang (1992), 'Politischer Extremismus (Rechtsextremismus)' in Herbert Dachs *et al.* (eds), *Handbuch des politischen Systems Österreichs*, 2nd edn, Vienna: Manz, pp.286–95.

Bluhm, William T. (1973), *Building an Austrian Nation. The Political Integration of a Western State*, New Haven and London: Yale University Press.

Bretschneider, Rudolf (1978), 'Das außenpolitische Bewußtsein des Österreichers' in *Österreichische Zeitschrift für Außenpolitik, Sonderheft 1979*, pp.37–48.

Bretschneider, Rudolf and Ulram, Peter (1992), 'Anmerkungen zur politischen

Kultur Österreichs' in Wolfgang Mantl (ed.), *Politik in Österreich. Die zweite Republik: Bestand und Wandel*, Vienna: Böhlau, pp.316–24.

Bruckmüller, Ernst (1994), *Österreichbewußtsein im Wandel. Identität und Selbstverständnis in den 90er Jahren*, Vienna: Signum.

Bruckmüller, Ernst (1996), *Nation Österreich. Kulturelles Bewußtsein und gesellschaftpolitische Prozesse*, revised and extended edn, Vienna: Böhlau.

Dachs, Herbert, Gerlich, Peter, Gottweis, Herbert, Horner, Franz, Kramer, Helmut, Lauber, Volkmar, Müller, Wolfgang C. and Tálos, Emmerich (eds) (1992), *Handbuch des politischen Systems Österreichs*, 2nd edn, Vienna: Manz.

Diem, Peter (Anon) (1988), *Integrative und desintegrative Phänomene in Österreich unter besonderer Berücksichtigung der Rolle der Massenmedien*, duplicated ms Vienna.

Funk, Bernd-Christian (1992), 'Die Entwicklung des Verfassungsrechtes' in Wolfgang Mantl (ed.), *Politik in Österreich. Die zweite Republik: Bestand und Wandel*, Vienna: Böhlau, pp.683–706.

Gerlich, Peter (1988), 'Nationalbewußtsein und nationale Identität in Österreich. Ein Beitrag zur politischen Kultur des Parteiensystems' in Anton Pelinka and Fritz Plasser (eds), *Das österreichische Parteiensystem*, Vienna: Böhlau, pp.235–70.

Hanisch, Ernst (1995), 'Politische Symbole und Gedächtnisorte' in Emmerich Tálos *et al.* (eds), *Handbuch des politischen Systems Österreichs. Erste Republik 1918–1933*, Vienna: Manz, pp.421–30.

Jagschitz, Gerhard and Karner, Stefan, (eds) (1995), *Menschen nach dem Krieg, Schicksale 1945–1955* (Katalog der Ausstellung Schallaburg 1995), Vienna: Kat. d. NÖ Landesmuseums NF 367.

Kreissler, Felix (1984), *Der Österreicher und seine Nation. Ein Lernpropzeß mit Hindernissen*, Vienna, Cologne and Graz: Böhlau.

Kriechbaumer, Robert (1990), *Parteiprogramme im Widerstreit der Interessen. Die Programmdiskussionen und die Programme von ÖVP und SPÖ 1945–1966*, Vienna: Verlag für Geschichte und Politik.

Lehnert, Detlef (1995), 'Politisch–kulturelle Integrationsmilieus und Orientierungslager in einer polarisierten Massengesellschaft' in Emmerich Tálos *et al.* (eds), *Handbuch des politischen Systems Österreichs. Erste Republik 1918–1933*, Vienna: Manz, pp.431–43.

Lepsius, M. Rainer (1993), 'Nation und Nationalismus in Deutschland' in Rainer M. Lepsius, *Interessen, Ideen und Institutionen*, Opladen 1990, reprinted in Michael Jeismann and Henning Ritter (eds), *Grenzfälle. Über neuen und alten Nationalismus*. Leipzig: Reclam, pp.193–214.

Neuhold, Hanspeter (1992), 'Zusammenfassung' in Hanspeter Neuhold and Paul Luif (eds), *Das außenpolitische Bewußtsein der Österreicher. Aktuelle internationale Probleme im Spiegel der Meinungsforschung*, Vienna: Braumüller, pp.171–8.

Neuhold, Hanspeter and Luif, Paul (eds) (1992), *Das außenpolitische Bewußtsein der Österreicher. Aktuelle internationale Probleme im Spiegel der Meinungsforschung*, Vienna: Braumüler.

Nowotny, Ewald and Schuberth, Helene (eds) (1993), *Österreichs Wirtschaft im Wandel. Entwicklungstendenzen 1970–2010*, Vienna: Service Fachverlag.

Paul-Lazarsfeld Gesellschaft für Sozialforschung (ed.) (1980), *Das österreichische Nationalbewußtsein in der öffentlichen Meinung und im Urteil der Experten*, Vienna: Paul Lazersfeld Gesellschaft für Sozialforschung.

Plasser, Fritz and Ulram, Peter A. (1993a), 'Politischer Kulturvergleich: Deutschland, Österreich, Schweiz' in F. Plasser and Peter A. Ulram (eds), *Staatsbürger oder Untertanen? Politische Kultur Deutschlands, Österreichs und der Schweiz im Vergleich*, Frankfurt-am-Main: Peter Lang.

Plasser, Fritz and Ulram, Peter A. (1993b), 'Zum Stand der Demokratisierung in Ost-Mitteleuropa' in Fritz Plasser and Peter A. Ulram (eds), *Transformation oder Stagnation? Aktuelle politische Trends in Osteuropa (Schriftenreihe des Zentrums für angewandte Politikforschung)*, vol. 2, Vienna: Signum, pp.9–88.

Plasser, Fritz, Ulram, Peter, Sommer, Franz and Vretscha, Andreas (1993), *Gesellschaftspolitischer Monitor 1993*, duplicated ms, November 1993.

Reiterer, Alfred F. (1986), 'Vom Scheitern eines politischen Entwurfes. "Der österreichische Mensch" – ein konservatives Nationalprojekt der Zwischenkriegszeit' in *Österreich in Geschichte und Literatur*, vol. 30, pp.19–36.

Reiterer, Albert (ed.) (1988), *Nation und nationales Bewußtsein in Österreich. Ergebnisse einer empirischen Untersuchung*, Vienna: Verband Wiss.Ges. Österreichs.

Renan, Ernest (1992), *Qu'est-ce qu'une nation? Et autres essais politiques. Textes choisis et présentés par Joel Roman*, Paris: Presses Pocket.

Scharsach, Hans-Henning (1992), *Haiders Kampf*, 12th edn, Vienna: Orac.

Schmidt-Dengler, Wendelin (ed.) (1994), 'Der literarische Umgang der Österreicher mit Jahres- und Gedenktagen', *Schriften des Instituts für Österreichkunde*, no. 59, Vienna.

Sozialwissenschaftliche Studiengesellschaft (1993), 'Parlamentsverständnis in Österreich' in *SWS-Rundschau*, vol. 33 (4), pp.474–88 (n = 1514).

Spann, Gustav (nd), 'Zur Geschichte des österreichischen Nationalfeiertages' in Bundesministerium für Unterricht, Kunst und Sport (ed.), *26. Oktober. Zur Geschichte des österreichischen Nationalfeiertages*, Vienna, pp.27–34.

Stourzh, Gerhard and Ulram, Peter A. (1988), *Österreichbewußtsein 1987*, duplicated manuscript, part of a project (no. 3072) entitled '*Österreichbewußtsein in den achtziger Jahren*', supported by the Austrian National Bank's Jubilee Fund.

Stourzh, Gerald (1990), *Vom Reich zur Republik. Studien zum Österreichbewußtsein im 20. Jahrhundert*, Vienna: Edition Atelier.

Tálos, Emmerich, Dachs, Herbert, Hanisch, Ernst and Staudinger, Anton (eds) (1990), *Handbuch des politischen Systems Österreichs. Erste Republik 1918–1933*, Vienna: Manz.

Torberg, Friedrich (1964), *Pamphlete – Parodien – Postscripta*, Munich and Vienna: Albert Langen–George Müller.

Wagner, Georg (ed.) (1982), *Österreich. Von der Staatsidee zum Nationalbewußtsein. Studien und Ansprachen*, Vienna: Verlag der österreichischen Staatsdruckerei.

Wilflinger, Gerhard (1995), 'Die grantige Republik', *Wiener Journal*, (175), April.

6 Austrian Political Culture: From Subject to Participant Orientation

Anton Pelinka

Consociational Democracy: Learning from History

Austria's political culture has been analysed from the approach developed in the late 1960s and early 1970s by the Almond/Verba/Powell school. An especially clear picture of how Austria's political culture developed from centrifugal to consociational democracy has been provided by Kurt Steiner (1972).

Consociationalism is based on the degree of social fragmentation and the trends of elitist behaviour. Deep fragmentation between the *Lager* (camps, pillars) was a characteristic of both the First and the Second Republic. However, the transition from the First to the Second Republic witnessed a clear change in the attitude of the socialist and Catholic-conservative elites. The behaviour of these two major political elites has shifted from conflict orientation towards the predominance of compromise, the background to these changes being their historical experience of the collapse of the First Republic, the civil war of 1934, the authoritarian *Ständestaat*, German occupation and Nazi rule. The socialist and the Catholic-conservative elites had seen the results of centrifugal democracy and, by learning from history, they changed their attitude towards compromise.

The characteristic fragmentation of Austrian society dates from the end of the nineteenth century and resulted from specific cleavages which helped shape Austrians' political identity. Thus the class cleavage created the political identity of the socialist camp, the intellectual representation of which took the form of Austro-Marxism. Religion was the creative force of the Catholic-conservative camp, intellectually represented by political

Catholicism. For its part, ethnicity was the underlying factor creating the pan-German camp, intellectually represented by pan-Germanism.

The consequences of identity being generated along cleavage lines and through *Lager* structures were to be both profound and enduring. Political loyalties were constructed by, and primarily existed, within, the rival *Lager* – that is, within extremely well organized, highly disciplined and almost perfectly closed subsocieties, or 'political subcultures'. Political mobility between the subcultures was virtually non-existent, as indicated by extremely stable electoral behaviour – a stability which had one remarkable exception: the rise of the (Austrian) Nazi party, the NSDAP. Finally, political conflicts between the subsocieties followed the pattern of international conflicts – that is, there was no generally accepted authority with a power monopoly, and there was militarization beneath the national level in the form of party militia.

This was the kind of fragmented society on which the fate of the First Republic depended. Moreover, this kind of fragmented society, or political culture, still existed in 1945, when the socialist and the Catholic-conservative elites tried to overcome centrifugal democracy. Consensus instead of competition was the recipe that fostered consociational democracy (Luther and Müller, 1992).

Accordingly, the political culture of the first three or four decades after 1945 indicated continuity as well as a new beginning: Society was still the same – fragmented according to the cleavages of the turn of the century. However, by significantly changing their political orientation and behaviour, the elites started a new chapter of Austrian political culture.

Aspects of 'Subject Orientation'

Fragmentation is a precondition for consociational democracy. The general rule of this type of political culture is elite power-sharing by means of mutual guarantees. Thus any elite considered to be important participates in an elite cartel, defined by the reduction of, and exemptions from, the political market. Any participating elite also has the right to veto any decision. Mutual veto is one of the central rules of consociational democracy (Lijphart, 1977; Luther, 1992).

Underpinning such a political culture has to be the self-evident dominance of consensus and compromise among the political elites. The acceptance of this rule in post-Second World War Austria tended to militate in favour of an Austrian national identity. The latter was different from the traditional pan-Germanism that was deeply rooted within, albeit not completely restricted to, the third, pan-German, *Lager*. Consensus and compromise also tended to favour general political moderation and thus contrasted sharply to the highly ideological and emotional style of the First Republic.

The institutionalization of consensus and compromise has been (and still is) the Austrian system of *Proporz* (Lehmbruch, 1967). *Proporz* denotes the extension of power-sharing guarantees to almost all spheres of society, including those elsewhere normally beyond traditional politics. Proportional representation for the two major *Lager* was implemented not only in parliament, but also at the level of the federal cabinet (*Bundesregierung*); in provincial cabinets (*Landesregierungen*); in the Constitutional Court (*Verfassungsgerichtshof*) and throughout the educational system (and especially at the provincial level, where the *Landesschulräte* were very important). Post-war nationalization meant that proportionality was also extended to industry and banking. The effect of *Proporz* was to create the dual system of the 'two empires'. The 'black' empire was that of the conservative *Lager* controlled by the *Österreichische Volkspartei*, or ÖVP, whilst the 'red', socialist empire was headed by the *Sozialistische Partei Österreichs*, or SPÖ. Not only the political system, but Austrian society itself became more or less divided between those two pillars.

A very special aspect of Austrian consociationalism was (and still is) the system of 'social partnership' – the Austrian version of corporatism (Bischoff and Pelinka, 1995). This institutionalized cooperation between government, employers and employees was developed as a kind of subsidiary government after 1945. The political elites of the two major camps established a decision-making process specifically designed to deal with social and economic matters in a non-competitive way. The Joint Commission on Wages and Prices (*Paritätische Kommission für Lohn- und Preisfragen*), founded in 1957, became the heart of a complex network, the operational principle of which was not majority rule, but consensus. This became a perfect example of mutual veto, since both partners ('black' capital and 'red' labour') had the right to block any decision.

The importance of social partnership as a form of subsidiary government became especially important after the 1966 transition from grand coalition to single-party government. Notwithstanding the existence in parliament of a Westminster-like confrontation between the governing party and opposition parties, social partnership not only prevailed, but acquired a new significance. It in effect constituted a continuation of the grand coalition by different means. All important decisions in the sphere of social relations and economic development were agreed upon between employers (especially the Federal Chamber of Commerce) and employees (especially the Austrian Federation of Trade Unions – the *Österreichischer Gewerkschaftsbund*, or ÖGB).

A good example of the heightened impact which social partnership had on the political decision-making process after 1966 is the Labour Relations

Act (*Arbeitsverfassungsgesetz*) of 1973. Despite the SPÖ's overall parliamentary majority and its clear and indisputable programmatic tradition in support of parity in codetermination (*paritätische Mitbestimmung*), the SPÖ and ÖGB did not react to the veto which the employers used within social partnership, by trying to force a majority decision in parliament. Instead, informal talks between the social partners in the pre-parliamentary arena led to the development of a compromise agreed upon by the votes of both the ruling SPÖ and the opposition ÖVP. That compromise established a system of codetermination that favoured the owners and thus fell short of the majority governing party's strong preference for parity (Atzmüller, 1984).

Although social partnership is an elitist arrangement which overshadows the parliamentary process, it was nevertheless very popular amongst Austrians. Various public opinion polls even indicated that, when asked to choose between social partnership and parliament, a majority of Austrians opted for social partnership (Gerlich and Ucakar, 1981). Moreover, the regular elections to the various 'chambers' repeatedly demonstrated the broad popular acceptance of social partnership, since the overwhelming majority of the vote at chamber elections went to the party groups responsible for this compromise orientation. Thus the constituent parties of the ÖVP dominated the chambers of commerce and agriculture, whilst the SPÖ faction (*Fraktion*) dominated the chamber of labour (as well as the ÖGB).

The Austrian system of consociationalism was at its peak in the 1970s when more than 90 per cent of the electorate voted for either the SPÖ or the ÖVP. Together with a turnout of over 90 per cent, this gave a high degree of legitimacy to a system that had the distinct flavour of an elite cartel. Austria was at this time characterized by an almost perfect two party-system and by a perfect corporatist system in which power-sharing was undertaken by almost identical actors. This system could correctly claim an almost perfect correspondence to the public's wishes, as expressed by elections and by public opinion polls.

The system had one deficit: the proportionality of Austria's electoral system. In the 1970s a proportional electoral system was thought to foster clear parliamentary majorities and the proportionality of the system was thus further reinforced. The design of the revised electoral law favoured new and small parties. From 1986 the proportionality of the electoral system was to become an important factor promoting the decline of party concentration and of consociationalism in general.

Aspects of Change

In the 1980s the winds of change began to have an impact on this well developed set of political decision-making. The electorate began to turn away from the two major parties, and subcultural loyalties (*Lagermentalität*) declined (Plasser, Ulram and Grausgruber, 1992).

The first and most visible indicator was the deconcentration of the party system. Between 1975 and 1994, the traditional major parties' combined share of the vote went down from 93 to 63 per cent. In addition, electoral turnout declined from over 90 to just over 80 per cent. At the general election of 10 October 1994, only 50 per cent of those entitled to vote decided to support either the SPÖ or the ÖVP. The other half of the electorate abstained or voted for one of the other parties (Müller, Plasser and Ulram, 1995). Even though the election of 17 December 1995 reversed this trend a little, the breakdown in the 1980s and early 1990s of the previously extremely concentrated party system was an astonishing signal, demonstrating a dramatic change in Austria's political culture.

In many regional or sectoral elections deconcentration went even further: The turnout at the 1994 elections to the Chambers of Labour was just over 30 per cent, whilst in many local elections an overall majority of young voters abstained too.

The trend towards deconcentration was accompanied by a trend towards a remarkable degree of flexibility. Thus the proportion of 'late-deciders' in the electorate rose sharply and their decisions last became increasingly decisive for the outcome of elections (Plasser and Ulram, 1995).

This decline in the ability of SPÖ and ÖVP to mobilize voters was part of a crisis that shook other aspects of the Second Republic identified with stabilising effects. In 1990 a debate on the legal status of the Austrian chambers started. It attacked not social partnership itself but the institutional and procedural prerequisites of the Austrian form of corporatism. Social partnership as a principle was (and still is) regarded positively (Bruckmüller, 1994),[1] but its rigid organization and legalistic structure has increasingly been subjected to criticism from significant sectors of public opinion.

A similar crisis challenged the Roman Catholic Church. Although Austria is statistically still a predominantly Catholic country, with about 80 per cent of Austrians being Catholic, the active part of the Church constitutes only a minority. Moreover, this minority has lost its integrative force. Open conflicts between different wings of the Church, plebiscitarian protests against some of the bishops and a decline of the traditional linkage between Church and politics – characterized by the very existence of a Catholic-conservative camp – all indicate a high degree of secularization.

Even the popular doctrine of permanent neutrality, widely considered to be part of the Second Republic's success within a fragmented Europe, has lost some, or even most, of its meaning. The 1989 decision of the SPÖ/ÖVP government to apply for European Union membership and the Austrian referendum of 12 June 1994, which resulted in a surprisingly high degree of acceptance of Austria's entry into the EU, were not considered to mark a break with the Austrian interpretation of neutrality. However, they demonstrated that Austrian foreign policy is no longer significantly influenced by neutrality.[2]

The winds of change influenced Austria's political culture especially by reducing the mobilizing capacity of the political parties. Party membership went down in the case of the SPÖ from about 700 000 at the end of the 1970s to about 450 000 by the mid-1990s (Ucakar, 1997). In the case of the ÖVP, this trend is similar (Nick and Pelinka, 1996; Müller, 1997).

Austria witnessed the rise of new political parties such as the Greens which entered parliament in 1986; and the Liberal Forum which was founded in 1993. In addition, the Freedom Party (*Freiheitliche Partei Österreichs*, or FPÖ) has achieved sensational electoral successes since 1986, when it had acquired a 'new-old' profile. However, none of these parties could translate their increasing voting share into organized party members. The Greens and the Liberals did not even start a membership organization in the traditional sense, whilst the FPÖ reformed its membership organization in 1995 (Luther, 1997, pp.287–94).

The new mobility did not exchange old loyalties for new ones; it was, and is, characterized by a decline of loyalties in general. The Austrians did not change *Lager*, but instead began to leave their respective camps for the openness of flexible pluralism. Increasing numbers of Austrians started to abandon the traditional pattern of inherited and lifelong political partisanship and electoral discipline.

Explanations for the New Mobility

The most visible explanation for the decline of loyalties typical of consociationalism is the generation gap. All analyses of the 1994 and 1995 elections (Müller *et al.*, 1995; Plasser and Ulram, 1995) demonstrate the importance of generation. Within the group of voters below the age of 30, there is a five-party system, with the SPÖ and FPÖ competing for the pole position. Within the group of voters above the age of 60, there is still the traditional post-1945 system: two major parties and a middle-sized party, but no other party of any significance.

This generation gap indicates the breakdown of the party system's ability to recreate itself. Political loyalties, which for decades have been smoothly transferred from one generation to the next, are no longer susceptible to such hereditary succession. Political socialization has changed dramatically. The new pattern of socialization emphasizes individualization instead of a collective, *Lager*-oriented perception of politics.

Among the younger generation, another gap is visible – the education gap. The probability of a young Austrian qualified to enter university, or who is a graduate, preferring the FPÖ is extremely low. Better-educated young Austrians have a strong preference for the Liberals, as well as for the Greens. But the young generation of blue-collar workers has a strong preference for the FPÖ. Education does not work in the FPÖ's favour.

The education cleavage stands for 'postmaterialism vs materialism' (Inglehart, 1977; 1990). The better educated, economically and culturally privileged Austrians stand against the lesser educated, underprivileged: the modernisation losers. This implies a new class conflict. Paradoxically, the FPÖ which, for good reasons, is considered a party of the extreme Right, is also the party of the underprivileged workers and working class and competes with the SPÖ (the old working-class party) for the same segment of the electorate.

There is also a gender gap. Among the younger generation, male voters demonstrate a significantly higher preference for the FPÖ, whilst females prefer the Liberals and the Greens. Notwithstanding the fact that women make up a majority of the electorate, in 1994 and 1995, the ratio of males to females among FPÖ voters was about 60 to 40 (Plasser and Ulram, 1995). The gender gap can be explained by the bias that extremist parties usually enjoy among male voters. If this explanation is accepted, this would indicate that the FPÖ is the only party in Austria's parliament which is perceived not as moderate, but as extremist.

Extrapolating the Trends

According to a technique of comparative scenarios applied by Peter Ulram to the Austrian political system in 1990, current Austrian trends can be internationalized in the following way (Ulram, 1990).

- *Italianization.* Despite the reassuring message that the SPÖ and ÖVP may perceive in the outcome of the 1995 election, it is still possible that there may be a complete breakdown of the party system and a realignment along new cleavages. The political development of Italy in the early 1990s offers an interesting case study of how a rather well developed 'civil society' can survive the collapse of key political structures. Italy constitutes a possible example of how Austria may develop, since the two countries share interesting similarities in respect of their political cultures. These include parallels between the *correnti* system of the Italian Christian Democrats and the constituent Leagues (*Bünde*) of the ÖVP; as well as the *parantela* relationship between Italian political parties and economic interest groups which, in many respects, reflects the sophisticated way that Austrian parties are synchronized with economic interest groups by means of auxiliary associations such as the SPÖ's Faction of Socialist Trades Unionists (*Fraktion sozialdemokratischer Gewerkschafter)*, or the Austrian Farmers' League (*Österreichischer Bauernbund)* of the ÖVP.

- *Netherlandization.* Another possibility is the decomposition of the party system through the establishment of breakaway parties, as happened in the Netherlands in the 1970s as a result of the decline of the traditional loyalties underpinning Dutch 'pillarization'. The cleavages responsible for the Catholic–Protestant conflict had been overcome and other cleavages diminished. The consequence was a decline in corporatist structures and decreasing parliamentary predictability, majority-building and cabinet stability. Netherlandization can be called 'a gentler version of Italianization'.
- *Switzerlandization.* The Swiss system is still stable, but crumbling at its fringes. Despite the outcome of the 1995 Swiss general election, the long-term trend of declining party concentration remains and holds out the potential for a step-by-step undermining of the dominance of Switzerland's permanent government coalition. There is also a tendency towards political abstentionism, as expressed in extremely low electoral turnouts. This has been, and still is, explained by the Swiss plebiscitarian formula but nevertheless the decline of *Porporzdemokratie* could reach a point of no return.

The Austrian development seems to be somewhere between these models: we can observe breakaway parties, the decline of corporatism, political abstentionism and a rather hostile attitude towards politics and politicians in general. Austria is exhibiting a kind of 'political secularization', as the old patterns of creating and mobilizing political loyalties no longer work. The pseudoreligious, highly ideological *Lager* subcultures no longer exist, or at least only as ruins, which can be visited like a museum.

The trend which Austria's political culture is following means Westernization, and that means losing its distinct Austrian flavour. It is becoming increasingly western European and, while it is distinguishable from other cultures, it is no longer an extreme, deviant case. In short, Austria's political culture is becoming less and less Austrian and we therefore have to acknowledge the process of de-Austrianization of Austria.

Austria's political culture is increasingly characterized by uncertainties, rather than by the stable certainties of the past; by unpredictabilities, rather than by the significant predictability of consociationalism; by deconcentration, rather than by the peculiar bipolarity of the post-war situation; by individualization, rather than by the paternalistic structures personified by politicians such as Karl Renner, Leopold Figl, Julius Raab and Adolf Schärf.

Does all this mean an increase in the quality of Austrian democracy? The answer must of course be ambivalent: yes and no. Yes, there is an increase in the quality of democracy, because more and more Austrians see themselves as citizens claiming their right to participate directly. They are no longer satisfied by protective mediators and by structures such as political parties and their respective suborganizations which are increasingly perceived as an obstacle to democratic participation. In present-day Austria one can observe numerous preconditions for democracy: citizens' movements, flexible electoral behaviour and a new and positive awareness of conflicts as a social phenomenon. The generation gap and the education gap, in combination with education as a booming industry, are guaranteeing 'Westernization', and indicators of liberal democracy are thus increasingly self-evident in Austria.

But, at the same time, there is also a 'no': new cleavages are becoming more and more significant. A rather new and aggressive feeling of being 'left out' is determining the attitude of 'modernization losers' such as blue collar-workers and farmers, who are increasingly aware that the development of an urbanized, well educated, white-collar middle class indicates a new class struggle. And this new class struggle is articulated by an increasing xenophobic sentiment directed at a new scapegoat fulfilling a very old function – the 'foreigner', a code word which encompasses ethnocentrist and racist attitudes.

The social segment responsible for the new class war attitude is the 'angry young man' with a proletarian outlook, but without a proletarian class consciousness. This attitude is the reason for a typical decline in democratic quality. The number of adult persons legally resident in Austria, but not entitled to participate in the democratic process, is becoming ever larger. This increase of officially disenfranchised persons – 'foreigners' according to the illiberal rules that stem from populist xenophobia – has been growing significantly.

There is a new class society in Austria, which has very little to do with the old one. Its novelty and significance lies in the fact that, politically, the thoughts and actions of the 'underdogs' are increasingly right-wing. The new, well educated middle class is located at the centre and centre left of the political spectrum and increasingly favours the Greens and Liberals. And the two traditional major parties are somewhere in between, like relics from a former age.

Notes

1 See also Bruckmüller's contribution to this volume (Chapter 5).
2 See Nick and Pelinka (1996) and the contributions to this volume by Kramer and Neuhold (Chapters 8 and 11).

Bibliography

Atzmüller, K.F. (1984), *Die Kodifikation des kollektiven Arbeitsrechts*, Vienna: Braumüller.

Bischoff, G. and Pelinka, A. (1995), *Austro-Corporatism: Past – Present – Future*, New Brunswick, NJ: Transaction Publishers.

Bruckmüller, E. (1994), *Österreichbewußtsein im Wandel. Identität und Selbstverständnis in den 90er Jahren*, Vienna: Signum.

Dachs, H., Gerlich, P., Gottweis, H., Horner, F., Kramer, H., Lauber, V., Müller, W.C. and Tálos, E. (eds) (1997), *Handbuch des politischen Systems Österreichs. Die Zweite Republik*, 3rd edn, Vienna: Manz Verlag.

Gerlich, P. and Ucakar, K. (1981), *Staatsbürger und Volksvertretung. Das Alltagsverständnis von Parlament und Demokratie in Österreich*, Vienna: Wolfgang Neugebauer Verlag.

Inglehart, R. (1977), *The Silent Revolution: Changing Values and Political Styles Among Western Publics*, Princeton, NJ: Princeton University Press.

Inglehart, R. (1990), *Culture Shift in Advanced Industrial Society*, Princeton, NJ: Princeton University Press.

Lehmbruch, G. (1967), *Proporzdemokratie: Politisches System und politische Kultur in der Schweiz und in Österreich*, Tübingen: Mohr.

Lijphart, A. (1977), *Democracy in Plural Societies: A Comparative Exploration*, New Haven and London: Yale University Press.

Luther, Kurt Richard (1992), 'Consociationalism, Parties and the Party System' in Kurt Richard Luther and Wolfgang C. Müller (eds) (1992), *Politics in Austria: Still a Case of Consociationalism?*, London: Frank Cass; also appeared in *West European Politics*, **15**, (1), pp.45–98.

Luther, K.R. and Müller. W.C. (eds) (1992), *Politics in Austria: Still a Case of Consociationalism?*, London: Frank Cass; also appeared as special issue of *West European Politics*, **15**, (1).

Luther, Kurt Richard (1997), 'Die Freiheitlichen' in Herbert Dachs *et al.* (eds), *Handbuch des politischen Systems Österreichs. Die Zweite Republik*, 3rd edn, Vienna: Manz Verlag, pp.286–303.

Müller, Wolfgang C. (1997), 'Die Österreichische Volkspartei' in Herbert Dachs *et al.* (eds), *Handbuch des politischen Systems Österreichs. Die Zweite Republik*, 3rd edn, Vienna: Manz Verlag, pp.267–85.

Müller, W.C., Plasser, F. and Ulram, P.A. (eds) (1995), *Wählerverhalten und Parteienwettbewerb. Analysen zur Nationalratswahl 1994*, Vienna: Signum Verlag.

Nick, R. and Pelinka, A. (1996), *Österreichs politische Landschaft*, Innsbruck: Haymon.

Pelinka, A. (ed.) (1994), *EU-Referendum. Zur Praxis direkter Demokratie in Österreich*, Vienna: Signum.

Plasser, Fritz and Ulram, Peter (1995), 'Konstanz und Wandel im österreichischen Wählerverhalten' in Wolfgang C. Müller, Fritz Plasser and Peter A. Ulram (eds), *Wählerverhalten und Parteienwettbewerb. Analysen zur Nationalratswahl 1994*, Vienna: Signum Verlag, pp.341–406.

Plasser, Fritz, Ulram, Peter and Grausgruber, Alfred (1992), 'The Decline of "*Lager* Mentality" and the New Model of Electoral Competition in Austria', in Kurt Richard Luther and Wolfgang C. Müller (eds), *Politics in Austria: Still a Case of Consociationalism?*, London: Frank Cass; also appeared in *West European Politics*, **15**, (1), pp.16–44.

Schneider, H. (1990), *Alleingang nach Brüssel. Österreichs EG-Politik*, Bonn: European Union Verlag.

Steiner, K. (1972), *Politics in Austria*, Boston, MA: Little Brown.

Ucakar, Karl (1997), 'Die Sozialdemokratische Partei Österreichs' in Herbert Dachs *et al.* (eds), *Handbuch des politischen Systems Österreichs. Die Zweite Republik*, 3rd edn, Vienna: Manz Verlag, pp.248–64.

Ulram, P.A. (1990), *Hegemonie und Erosion. Politische Kultur und politischer Wandel in Österreich*, Vienna: Böhlau.

7 From Accommodation to Competition: The 'Normalization' of the Second Republic's Party System?

Kurt Richard Luther

Introduction

The background to the post-war re-establishment of Austria's party system was decidedly inauspicious: for at least three decades the country had experienced profound regime discontinuity; its people had manifestly failed to develop a shared national identity capable of bridging the gap between the mutually hostile identities of its polarized political camps (*Lager*); and Austria's political parties had proved unwilling, or unable, to maintain a functioning multiparty system in the face of economic crises and anti-democratic threats. Yet the Second Republic fairly quickly established a stable, two-party system and, for over 50 years, has been predominantly characterized by domestic peace and levels of economic prosperity that compare very favourably not only with its own inter-war experience, but also with the post-war experience of most Western states.

This was not achieved by a fundamental recasting of governmental institutions; unlike Germany, Austria readopted its ill-fated inter-war constitution.[1] Nor were the key political actors replaced; the establishment of the Second Republic was largely undertaken by the same parties – and indeed by some of the same individuals – that had been involved in setting up the First (see Chapters 1 and 2 in this volume by Weinzierl and Knight respectively). Moreover, although their political ideologies were somewhat attenuated, the post-war *Lager* were fundamentally the same as in the First Republic, as were their party organizations (Wandruszka, 1954; Simon, 1957).

Instead, the successful rebirth of the party system has much to do with the altered circumstances in which the political institutions and party actors found themselves in 1945. Defeated Austria was once again in a dire economic situation but, in marked contrast to the punitive reparations regime imposed after the First World War, the Allies now sought to stimulate reconstruction via the Marshall Plan. Second, for the overwhelming majority of Austrians, the experience of incorporation into Nazi Germany had discredited pan-Germanism and thus, at least by default, helped prepare the ground for the gradual development of an Austrian national identity (Bruckmüller, 1996 and Chapter 5 this volume). Similarly, the Allied occupation of Austria from 1945 to 1955 generated a common desire to get rid of the foreign forces, thereby enhancing aspirations for independent statehood. Third, Nazism and subsequent Allied occupation also facilitated a narrowing of the party system's ideological spectrum. The weak *Kommunistische Partei Österreichs* (KPÖ) was further delegitimized by Soviet occupation of Eastern Austria until 1955 (and subsequently by communist repression in adjacent Hungary and Czechoslovakia), whilst the Allies' anti-fascist consensus militated against a revival of the anti-democratic extreme Right. Indeed, for the crucial first four post-war years the Allies banned Third *Lager* parties. Only three political parties were licensed: the *Österreichische Volkspartei* (Austrian People's Party – ÖVP), the descendent of the pre-war Christian-Socials; the *Sozialistische Partei Österreichs* (Socialist Party of Austria – SPÖ) and the KPÖ.

It was not until 1949 that the Allies permitted the establishment of a Third *Lager* party, the *Verband der Unabhängigen* (League of Independents, or VdU), formed partly to appeal to liberals and those not incorporated into the two main *Lager*, but mainly to attract former Nazis (Riedlsperger, 1978). Yet, by then, the two main *Lager* had been re-establishing their subcultural networks for four years, and it is thus not surprising that their parties succeeded in consolidating a longlasting duopolistic control over Austria's political 'support market'. Accordingly, the VdU enjoyed only a short existence and in 1956 was replaced by the *Freiheitliche Partei Österreichs* (Austrian Freedom Party – FPÖ) (Stäuber, 1974), which, for most of the next 30 years, was rarely able to obtain the support of more than about half of the proportion of the Austrian electorate initially mobilised by the VdU (see Table 7.2 below) (Luther 1987, 1991, 1996a, 1996b and 1997a).

The aim of this chapter is to ascertain the extent to which the party system of the Second Republic has changed from the characteristic contours it had adopted by the 1960s. That enquiry will be structured around the 'working model' for the analysis of party system change advanced by Gordon

Smith (1989).[2] Smith argues that it is first necessary to specify the key 'regulatory' factors – including institutional features and aspects of a country's political culture – that affect the functioning of its party system. He then proposes that one can 'rate' a party system 'in relation to its main defining features', which might include the number and relative size of parties, ideological distance ('polarization') movements in party support ('volatility'), relations between government and opposition and the principal 'sites' or arenas of party interaction (Smith, 1989 pp.350f and 356f). Third, Smith maintains that only after one has identified the 'features or parts of the system which are most immune to change and which provide significant continuity' (1989, p.356) is it possible to proceed to an assessment of the extent of change, which can thus be understood as change in these 'core elements'. He identifies four possible levels of change: 'temporary fluctuations' ('the normal ebb and flows of party fortunes'); 'restricted change' ('permanent, but limited to the extent that most other features of the system remain unaltered'); 'general change', (which 'implies that several of these changes take place at the same time or follow on quickly ... before a new equilibrium is established') and 'transformation', where 'all aspects of the system alter so much that an entirely new party system comes into existence' (1989, pp.353f).

The first focus of this chapter will therefore be upon some of the most significant institutional and 'cultural' variables that together constitute the 'regulatory factors' shaping party competition in the Second Republic. The main empirical section of the chapter will then identify the key features that together constituted the 'core elements' of Austria's post-war party system and will assess the extent to which they have changed. The chapter will conclude with a brief discussion of the possible causes and consequences of that change.

Institutional Variables Shaping the Second Republic's Party System

Aside from the peculiar circumstances of the immediate post-war years, party competition in the Second Republic has been influenced by a number of interrelated contextual variables. Amongst the most important of the institutional factors is Austria's proportional electoral system (Müller, 1996). The system in force until 1970 inflated the electoral 'price' of minor parties' seats. Since the small Third *Lager* party was deemed uncoalitionable and the electoral system reproduced at parliamentary level the sociopolitical stalemate between the two major *Lager*, the electoral system effectively militated in favour of oversized coalitions. The 1970 reforms lowered the electoral hurdle for the minor parties and increased proportionality. The

1992 electoral reform slightly reversed both changes. Elections to the 183-seat national parliament now operate according to a modified party list system. The nine *Länder* are subdivided into 43 regional constituencies, which elect between three and five members, depending upon the size of their resident population. The majority of regional constituencies are entitled to elect between three and five members each. The actual party distribution of regional seats is determined by the Hare quota (total votes cast at *Land* level divided by the number of seats to be allocated within that *Land*). In 1995 some 97 seats were allocated at the regional level, but it is only the largest parties that are successful here (SPÖ 48; ÖVP 32; FPÖ 17). The 'unused' votes of all parties which either win a regional seat or obtain at least 4 per cent of the total national poll proceed to the next stage of seat allocation which takes place at the *Land* level, where in 1995 the Hare formula allocated a further 63 seats (SPÖ 18; ÖVP 16; FPÖ 19; Liberal Forum [LiF] 5; Greens 5). The final distribution is undertaken at the federal level via the d'Hont system, which in 1995 provided the SPÖ, ÖVP and LiF with five further seats each and the FPÖ and Greens with four.

The electoral system is fairly efficient: in 1995, vote wastage was only 2.4 per cent overall, ranging from nil (ÖVP) to 3.2 per cent (LiF). Until 1970 there was an 'effective threshold' of 8.5 per cent, reduced by the 1992 reforms to 2.6 per cent (Lijphart, 1994, pp.25–9 and 39). Despite the 1992 introduction of a formal 4 per cent threshold, the electoral system remains quite 'weak' – that is, proportional. Thus in 1995 the average cost in votes of the parliamentary parties' seats differed by no more than ± 3.3 per cent. That is not to deny that the new threshold constitutes a constant concern for the Greens, who in 1995 obtained merely 4.91 per cent of the national vote and for the Liberal Forum (an'internally created' party formed in February 1993 by five MPs who broke away from the FPÖ), whose vote declined from 5.97 per cent in 1994 to 5.52 per cent in 1995. In 1995 it proved to be an insurmountable hurdle for an anti-EU protest party which obtained over 53 000 votes – that is, twice the average 'price' of the parliamentary parties' seats, but failed to gain representation. Finally, the 1992 reforms sought to strengthen further the system of preference voting first introduced in 1949. Although large numbers of preference votes are cast (966 000 in 1995), only once (in 1983) has a candidate ever been elected by virtue of preference votes, as opposed to his or her position on a party list. Although this could be held to indicate that candidates placed on party lists enjoy popular support, a more credible interpretation is that the parties have retained their control over candidate recruitment, despite superficial attempts to widen it (Nick, 1995; Müller and Scheucher, 1995).

Federalism is a second institutional factor impinging upon the operation of the party system. First, the constitutions of seven *Länder* require *Land* governments to be grand coalitions. Although the role of non-majority parties in *Land* governments is undermined by the *Landeshauptmann*'s power to decide on the allocation and scope of portfolios, the fact remains that parties excluded from national government usually continue to share some of the spoils of office at the *Land* level. Second, notwithstanding their constitutional weakness, the *Länder* do offer considerable scope for the *de facto* exercise of political power (Luther, 1997b). Moreover, given the traditional territorial concentration of SPÖ and ÖVP support, for many years federalism meant that both major parties had *Länder* in which they exercised a virtual political hegemony (Luther, 1989).

A third institutional factor concerns the (paucity of) constitutional and statutory regulation of Austrian political parties. Although the 'electoral party' and 'parliamentary party' are briefly mentioned in the Constitution (Arts 26, 35 and 55), there are remarkably few constitutional or legal norms designed to govern the conduct specifically of political parties (Schaden, 1983). For example, there is no equivalent of Article 21 of the German Basic Law, which requires parties' internal organization to be democratic and permits those which, by their aims or behaviour, 'seek to impair or abolish the free democratic basic order' to be banned. Nazi rule of course left its mark not least in the 1945 *Verbotsgesetz*, promulgated under the auspices of the Allied Military Council, which prescribed life imprisonment for attempts to revive Nazi organizations or ideology. Moreover, in Article 9 of the 1955 State Treaty re-establishing its sovereignty, Austria formally committed itself to continue a policy of denazification and to combat fascist revivals. However, denazification was, from the outset, half-hearted and the state's powers to act against neo-Nazi activities have until recently been used very sparingly. For example, it was not until 1988 (two years after the 'Waldheim affair' had caused Austria's attitude to its Nazi past to be severely criticized), that the militant pan-Germanic National Democratic Party, founded in 1967, was finally deemed by the constitutional court to be a neo-Nazi organization and therefore denied the status of a political party. To encourage the authorities to use their powers more frequently – especially in light of a rash of neo-Nazi attacks since 1990 – the *Verbotsgesetz* was amended in 1992, *inter alia* by the introduction of the possibility of shorter sentences.

Only in 1975 was a specific 'Party Law' introduced, Article I of which has constitutional status. Until then, the Second Republic's 'founding parties' (the SPÖ, ÖVP and KPÖ) had in effect operated extra-constitutionally, whilst newer parties such as the VdU and FPÖ had had to constitute themselves under the terms of the law on associations (*Vereinsgesetz*). To obtain party status under the 1975 law, parties merely have to deposit their statutes with the Ministry of the Interior. Since the law imposes no substantive restrictions on them, but entitles them to benefit from the system of state subsidies, with the introduction of which it was primarily concerned, the parties have naturally all complied. Accurate figures on party finances are notoriously difficult to obtain, but a recent study (Sickinger, 1995) suggests that Austria's parties are among the most generously financed in Europe. The existing system militates against new parties, who, unless and until they overcome the hurdle of parliamentary representation, lack the financial muscle of their established, state-subsidized opponents.

'Cultural' Variables Shaping the Second Republic's Party System

However, the 'format' and 'mechanics' (Sartori, 1976, pp.128f) of post-war party competition have been governed less by formal institutional variables than by the following three interrelated 'cultural' factors. First, until the 1980s Austrian society was dominated by the pillarization of the socialist and Catholic-conservative subcultures in particular. A myriad of *Lager*-specific occupational, educational and cultural associations ensured that the lives of the members of the subculture could be lived 'from womb-to-tomb' within their own milieu (Diamant, 1958; Lorwin, 1974; Powell, 1970; Stiefbold, 1975; Houska, 1985; Luther, 1992; Müller, 1992). They also fostered rival '*Lager* mentalities', characterized by deference, strong partisan attachment and distrust of rival *Lager* (Plasser, Ulram and Grausgruber, 1992). Yet pillarization should not be regarded merely as a sociopolitical given. It was successfully promoted and further refined by the major parties, who consciously used it to structure the electorate, reducing the electoral potential of other parties and thereby consolidating the party system to their advantage (Luther, 1998b; Luther and Deschouwer, 1998).

Pillarization not only facilitated a very high degree of party-political penetration of Austria's socioeconomic system, but also helps explain why Austria has had the highest proportion of party members of any country in the Western world (Beyme, 1985; Katz and Mair, 1992). Table 7.1 contains the membership figures of the major post-war Austrian parties in all general election years since 1949. It also records the size of the electorate and total party membership as a proportion of the electorate (M/E). At least three points are worthy of note. The first is the exceptionally high proportion of the total Austrian electorate mobilized by the parties. Second, the SPÖ and ÖVP are clearly very successful mass membership parties or parties of mass integration (Neumann, 1956). Their organizational density (membership as a proportion of voters) was, for many years, between 25 and 30 per cent. Although it soon ceased to be a mass membership party, the KPÖ's membership density has consistently been even higher than that of the SPÖ and

Table 7.1 Party membership in Austria, 1949–95[1]

Year	ÖVP (Max)[2]	ÖVP (Min)[2]	SPÖ	FPÖ	KPÖ	Electorate	M/E I[3] (ÖVP max)	M/E II[3] (ÖVP min)
1949	485 000	439 000	614 366		150 000	4 391 815	28.45	27.40
1953	505 000	441 000	657 042		*114 000*	4 586 870	27.82	26.42
1956	565 000	498 000	687 972	10 600	*87 000*	4 614 464	29.27	27.82
1959	590 000	509 000	721 737	20 068	*60 000*	4 696 603	29.63	27.91
1962	655 000	532 000	698 705	26 949	*40 556*	4 805 351	29.58	27.02
1966	700 000	543 000	699 432	27 334	*34 778*	4 886 818	29.91	26.70
1970	720 000	561 000	719 389	27 913	29 000	5 045 841	29.65	26.50
1971	715 000	564 000	703 093	28 850	*27 500*	4 984 448	29.58	26.55
1975	715 000	562 000	693 156	31 808	*21 500*	5 019 277	29.12	26.07
1979	720 000	560 000	721 262	37 288	*15 500*	5 186 735	28.81	25.72
1983	720 000	552 000	694 598	37 232	*12 500*	5 316 436	27.59	24.43
1986	695 000	528 000	669 906	36 925	*11 000*	5 461 414	25.93	22.88
1990	670 000	488 000	597 426	42 413	*9 000*	5 628 912	23.43	20.20
1994	579 000	433 000	512 838	43 764	*4 900*	5 774 000	19.81	17.28
1995	*552 000*	*419 250*	490 000	44 153	*4 200*	5 768 099	18.96	16.66

Notes:

1. Italicization denotes estimated figures, based on the assumption of an even trend between years for which figures were available. This has proved necessary mainly in respect of the KPÖ. Since KPÖ membership has since at least the 1960s constituted only a small proportion of total Austrian party membership, the impact of any inaccuracies on the M/E figure will be relatively marginal.
2. Given the indirect nature of ÖVP party membership, the figures are susceptible to double counting (Müller, 1992). We have therefore quoted Müller's maximum and minimum membership figures and have also provided two calculations of M/E.
3. M/E denotes party membership as a percentage of the total electorate (see Katz, Mair *et al.*, 1992).

Sources: Müller (1992, pp.40–49; 1997, p.242); Ucakar (1997, p.259); Luther (1997a, p.293) and Ehmer (1997, p.328).

ÖVP. In 1949 it stood at 70 per cent and in 1970 was still some 65 per cent (albeit of an electorate that had fallen by some 80 per cent). By 1990 the KPÖ had only just under 26 000 voters but, given a membership of circa 9000, its membership density still stood at 35 per cent. By contrast, the membership profile of FPÖ shows this Third *Lager* party to be more akin to the ideal type of a cadre party (Duverger, 1964). A final point worth noting is the decline of between a quarter and a third in the size of the major parties' membership since the peak reached in the 1970s. Conversely, (with the exception of period of the change in leadership from Steger to Haider) the FPÖ's membership has slowly and steadily increased, albeit from a much lower level.

A second 'cultural' factor structuring party competition and arguably the most crucial explanator of the successful reformation of the post-war Austrian party system, is the essentially accommodative role culture of the SPÖ and ÖVP party elite. In 1945 the centrist wings of the two main *Lager* assumed a controlling position in their respective parties and replaced the confrontational orientation which had characterized most of the First Republic with a much greater commitment to accommodation, by means of which they sought to overcome the profound mistrust that still existed between the *Lager*. Confrontational political rhetoric was, of course, not abandoned, especially in the electoral arena where it served to confirm rival '*Lager* mentalities' and ossify pillarized structures (Hölzl, 1974). The *prima facie* paradoxical coexistence of a segmented society on the one hand and elite accommodation on the other is of course the core characteristic of 'consociational democracy' (Lijphart, 1968; 1969; Lehmbruch, 1967; Powell, 1970; Stiefbold, 1975; Luther and Müller, 1992; Luther and Deschouwer, 1998) and the elite's changed orientation has been attributed by some (for example, Lijphart, 1968, p.21) to elite political behaviour deliberately designed to counteract disintegrative tendencies in the system. In the Austrian case, this is typically understood to imply that the post-war elite were persuaded of the merits of democratic cooperation by their experience of regime collapse in 1934 and, in particular, by virtue of their shared political persecution during the Nazi period.[3]

The most frequently cited expression of elite accommodation has been Austria's propensity for oversized, 'grand' coalitions (Engelmann, 1966; Dreijmanis, 1982). Much more pervasive, albeit often less visible and more difficult to quantify, has been *Proporz*, according to which the two parties structured the distribution amongst themselves and their subcultural allies of the majority of public-sector posts and state resources (including access to electronic media) in rough proportion to their subcultures' relative electoral weight. Largely as a consequence of the nationalization of former Nazi enterprises, the state controlled one of the largest nationalized industry sectors of any Western country (Müller, 1985). Accordingly, the parties had enormous scope for economic intervention to protect their client groups' jobs, but also to exercise influence over individual appointment decisions, where party-political criteria were often at least as important as objective performance criteria. In some areas, *Proporz* meant that each *Lager* received an equal share of resources, or employees, whilst elsewhere, the principle of segmental autonomy permitted the *Lager* to run organizations independently (Luther, 1992, pp.72–93). *Proporz* greatly extended the 'reach' of the party system (Luther, 1992), which penetrated the socioeconomic realm to an extent comparable only with 'partocracies' such as Belgium and Italy (Deschouwer, De Winter and Della Porta, 1996). As a system of political patronage, *Proporz* further enhanced the competitive advantage of the two main parties and their associated subcultures, by allowing them to act as gatekeepers in the distribution of spoils.

The pervasive system of *Proporz* meant that, for many Austrians, party membership was regarded as a prerequisite for access to housing, jobs, licences to trade and other benefits for which the political parties and their allied auxiliary associations acted as gatekeepers. This was well documented as late as 1980 (Deiser and Winkler 1982, pp.94–8 and 237) in a survey which examined Austrians' perceptions of why people join political parties. Some 79 per cent said they felt the prospect of career advancement was either a very important, or an important, factor, while 72 per cent similarly evaluated the possibility of obtaining housing more easily. Just under half the sample felt an affinity with a party's values to be important and 23 per cent considered it either insignificant or only slightly relevant. It is interesting to note that when these questions were answered by party members with reference to their own motivation, the results differed sharply. Career prospects and housing were cited as important by only 36 per cent and 26 per cent respectively, whilst 64 per cent said party values had motivated them and 53 per cent mentioned family tradition.

The major parties' accommodative orientation shaped the party system's 'mechanics' (Sartori, 1976) or style as well. The SPÖ and ÖVP came to share in the promotion of various formative 'founding myths' of the Second Republic, including the propositions that Austria had been 'the first victim of Nazi aggression' and that it had in 1955 freely opted for permanent neutrality (Menasse, 1992). The prevalent decision-making style was consensual and reflected in practices such as mutual veto and log-rolling, as well as in the high proportion of laws passed unanimously (Luther, 1992). Over time, cooperation significantly reduced the ideological distance between the major parties, creating bipartisan agreement on major policy areas. Notable examples are permanent neutrality and 'Austrokeynsianism', a policy mix comprising a hard currency policy, the promotion of investment and savings, the depoliticization of incomes and the stabilization of demand by deficit spending (Lauber, 1992).[4]

A final key contextual variable – which has both institutional and behavioural, or cultural dimensions – is 'social partnership', Austria's extra-constitutional system of corporatist decision-making. Established in large measure to help deliver Austrokeynsianism, its core focus has been economic and social policy (Gerlich, Grande and Müller, 1985; Gerlich, 1992). At the centre of the extensive corporatist web was the Joint Commission on Wages and Prices (*Paritätische Kommission für Lohn- und Preisfragen*), set up in 1957. The five corporatist interest groups are inextricably linked to one or other of the two main *Lager*. Most are centralized and very densely organized, not least because membership in three (the Chambers of Labour, Business and Agriculture) is obligatory by law for all relevant population groups, whilst a fourth (the Austrian Trade Union Federation, or ÖGB) in practice enjoys a virtual monopoly of workers' interest representation. The fifth corporatist interest group is the *Vereinigung Österreichischer Industrieller* (Union of Austrian Industrialists, or VÖI). Together, the corporatist actors came to constitute a sort of shadow government and were granted a significant role in policy implementation.

The implications of this system for party competition were profound. Through their organic links to the interest groups, the SPÖ and ÖVP have had privileged access to information and to technical expertise that has in many respects rivalled that of the state bureaucracy. Moreover obligatory Chamber membership, the interest groups' service provision to their members and their quasi-state role in implementing government policy provided the two main *Lager* with additional opportunities to exercise patronage and thus further enhanced membership incentives. Yet, in the long run, the system of social partnership was to have perverse, or unintended, effects for the ÖVP and SPÖ, whose close association with 'their' interest groups had the capacity to make them 'prisoners' of the latter and thus less flexible than parties not entrenched in the corporatist system.

'Core Elements' of the Post-war Party System

Number and Relative Size of Parties

One of the most distinctive features of Austria's post-war party system has been the domination of the national electoral and parliamentary arenas by two very large parties: the ÖVP and SPÖ.[5] As is visible from Table 7.2, from 1945 up to and including 1983, their average combined shares of the national vote and of National Council seats were 90.2 and 94 per cent

Table 7.2 Austrian national election results 1945–95: votes and seats

		1945	1949	1953	1956	1959	1962	1966	1970	1971	1975	1979	1983	1986	1990	1994	1995
SPÖ	(vote)	44.6	38.7	42.1	43.0	44.8	44.0	42.6	48.4	50.0	50.4	51.0	47.6	43.1	42.8	34.9	38.1
	(seats)	76	67	73	74	78	76	74	78	93	93	95	90	80	80	65	71
ÖVP	(vote)	49.8	44.0	41.3	46.0	44.2	45.4	48.3	44.7	43.1	42.9	41.9	43.2	41.3	32.1	27.7	28.3
	(seats)	85	77	74	82	79	81	85	81	80	80	77	81	77	60	52	53[5]
FPÖ (VdU)	(vote)		11.7	10.9	6.5	7.7	7.0	5.4	5.5	5.5	5.4	6.1	5.0	9.7	16.6	22.5	21.9
	(seats)		16	14	6	8	8	6	6	10	10	11	12	18	33[1]	42	40[5]
Greens	(vote)													4.8	4.8	7.3	4.8
	(seats)													8	10	13	9
LiF	(vote)															6.0	5.5
	(seats)														(5)[1]	11	10[5]
Others	(vote)	5.6	5.6	5.7	4.5	3.3	3.5	3.7	1.4	1.4	1.2	1.0	4.1	1.0	3.7	1.6	1.4
	(seats)	4	5	4	3												
Turnout		96.8	96.8	95.8	96.0	94.2	93.8	93.8	91.8	92.4	92.9	92.2	92.6	90.5	86.1	81.9	86.0
SPÖ + ÖVP	vote	94.4	82.8	83.4	89.0	89.0	89.4	90.9	93.1	93.2	93.4	92.9	90.9	84.4	74.9	62.6	66.4
SPÖ + ÖVP	seats	97.6	87.3	89.1	94.5	95.2	95.2	96.4	96.4	94.5	94.5	94.0	93.4	85.8	76.5	93.9	67.8
Fractionalization[2]	F_e	0.55	0.64	0.64	0.60	0.60	0.59	0.58	0.56	0.56	0.56	0.56	0.58	0.63	0.68	0.74	0.72
(Rae index)	F_p	0.52	0.61	0.60	0.55	0.54	0.54	0.53	0.53	0.55	0.55	0.55	0.56	0.62	0.67	0.74	0.72
Effective no. of	N_v	2.22	2.78	2.76	2.48	2.48	2.46	2.39	2.29	2.28	2.26	2.27	2.40	2.72	3.16	3.87	3.59
parties[3]	N_s	2.09	2.54	2.47	2.22	2.20	2.20	2.14	2.15	2.21	2.21	2.22	2.26	2.63	2.99	3.78	3.51
Net volatility[4]			12.17	4.00	5.69	2.97	1.72	6.24	6.65	2.04	0.42	1.31	4.81	9.95	10.09	15.51	3.88

Notes:

1. On 4 February 1993 five of the 33 FPÖ MPs elected in 1990 broke away to form the Liberal Forum.
2. Own calculations of index of electoral (F_e) and parliamentary (F_p) fractionalization (Rae, 1967).
3. Own calculations of Laakso & Taagepera's (1979) index of effective number of parties at the level of votes (N_v) and of seats (N_s).
4. Own calculations of Pedersen (1979, p.4) index (i.e. cumulated gains for *all* winning parties standing at the election).
5. Since December 1995 the FPÖ has gained 2 seats, 1 via a LiF defection and 1 from the ÖVP as a result of a rerun ballot in Burgenland.

Source: Bundesministerium für Inneres (ed.), (1996) *Nationalratswahl vom 17. Dezember 1995*, Vienna: Bundesministerium für Inneres.

respectively. Rae's (1967) well known 'fractionalization index' allows one to generate a single figure which indicates the number and relative size of parties in the electoral, or in the parliamentary arena (F_e and F_p respectively).[6] When one calculates the index for the Second Republic (Table 7.2) one finds that, once the new party system had stabilized in 1956, fractionalization remained remarkably low for some 30 years. In the indirectly elected Bundesrat, concentration was even more pronounced. Between 1945 and 1987, with the minor exception of the years 1949 to 1955, the Bundesrat was the exclusive preserve of the ÖVP and SPÖ.

Since the mid-1980s, however, the electoral arena has witnessed a growth in the number of parties and a significant narrowing in the disparity between their relative strengths, as is well illustrated in Figure 7.1. The logical corollary of Austria's weak electoral system has been an analogous trend in the parliamentary arena. Both changes are captured in the measures of party system factionalization (F_e and F_p), which rose to their highest ever Second Republic values (0.74) in 1994, before dropping back marginally in 1995 (see Table 7.2). Although the procedures governing the appointment of members of the Bundesrat are such that changes in voter behaviour are both underrepresented and delayed, there have nevertheless been tangible alterations here also. Thus by late 1996 the FPÖ's representation had increased to 14, which reduced the SPÖ and ÖVP's combined share of Bundesrat seats from 100 to 78 per cent. The extent of the overall change to Austria's national party system can perhaps be illustrated most clearly by means of the index of the 'effective number of parties' developed by Laakso and Taagepera (1979).[7] Figure 7.2 plots the values of this index for Austria's post-war party system and provides a graphic illustration of the trends from 1945 to 1995. With the exception of the general elections of 1949 and 1953, when the newly licensed Third *Lager* party (the VdU) succeeded in making a considerable electoral impact, until the mid-1980s the degree of fractionalization of the Austrian party system was effectively that of a pure two-party system. By 1994–95 the subsequent sharp rise in fractionalization had left Austria with a degree of fractionalization approaching that of a four-party system. In sum, Austria no longer exhibits the extremely high level of concentration so characteristic of its post-war party system.

Ideological Distance (Polarization)

The failure of the First Republic was largely due to the inability (or unwillingness) of the political elite to find effective strategies to overcome the intense ideological polarization between their respective subcultures. It is thus not surprising that relations between the Second Republic's encapsulated

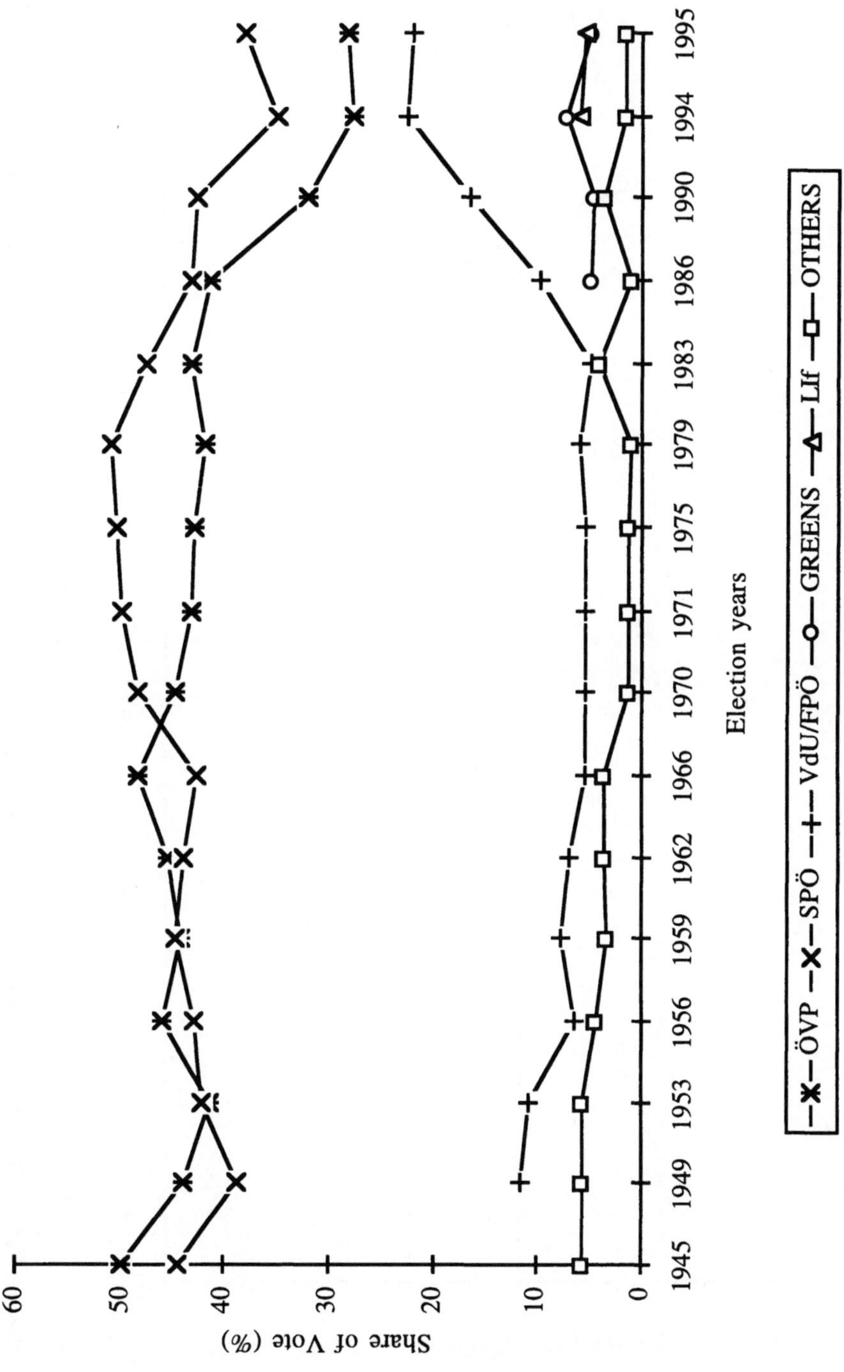

Figure 7.1 Party shares of the vote at elections to the Austrian National Council (1945–95)

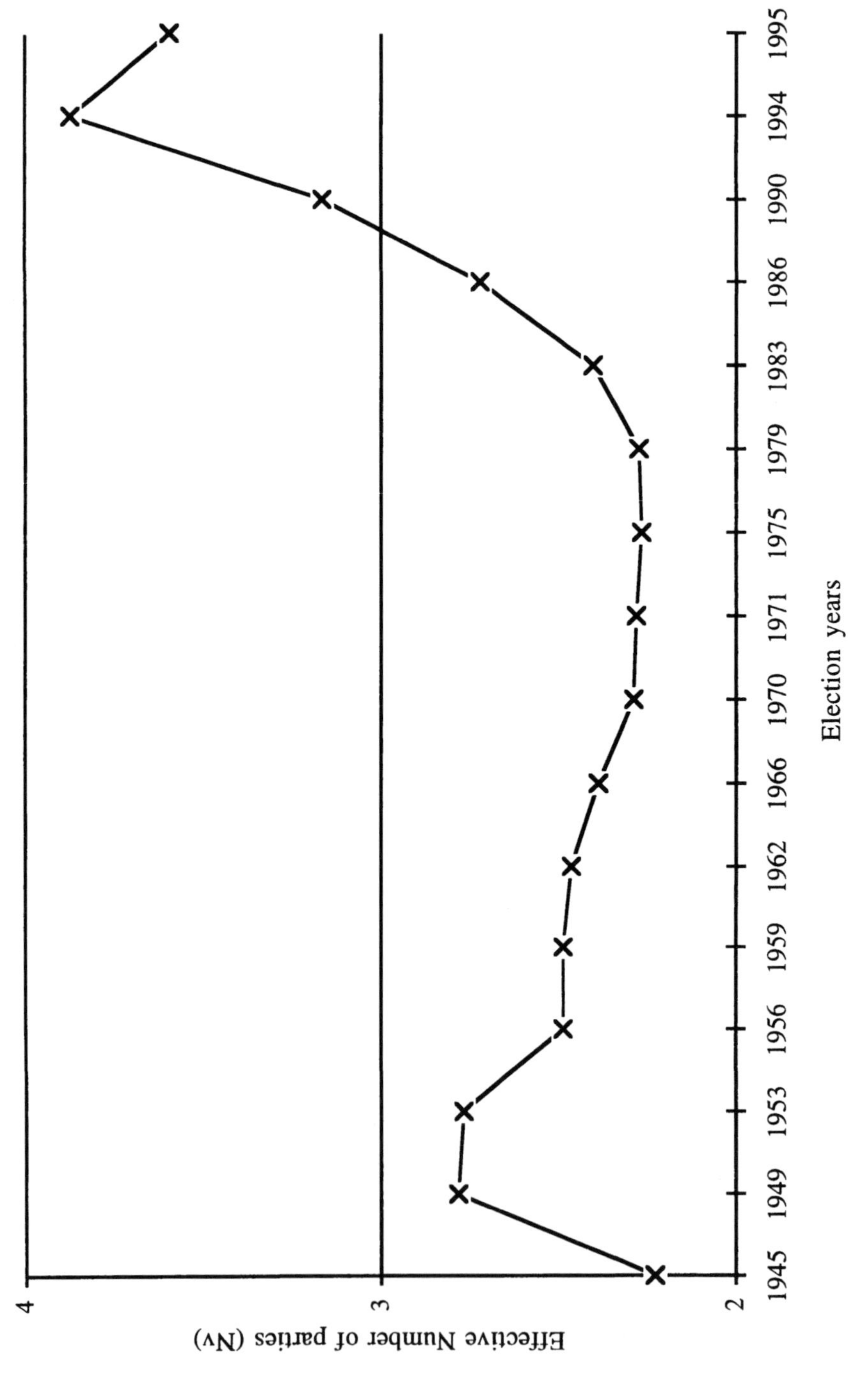

Figure 7.2 Effective number of parties at elections to the Austrian National Council (1945–95)

Lager subcultures was initially also characterized by a considerable degree of suspicion or even outright hostility (for example, Stiefbold, 1975 esp. pp.141–56 and 204–12). The high 'ideological temperature' inherited by the Second Republic's party system was deliberately sustained in the electoral arena by 'propaganda wars' (Hölzl, 1974) in which the parties sought to convince their followers that if they failed to vote for their *Lager* party in sufficient numbers, they ran the risk of their opponents obtaining an absolute majority and putting an end to democracy. The ÖVP claimed that the socialists might erect a 'red dictatorship' akin to the 'people's democracies' already installed in nearby Eastern Europe whilst, for its part, the SPÖ reminded its voters of the role the bourgeois parties had played in the collapse of democracy during the inter-war years and suggested that, without the socialists' moderating influence, an ÖVP government would, for example, scrap workers' welfare benefits and pensions. Both major parties restricted their stated electoral goal to achieving a balance of power, accusing their opponents of secretly harbouring the dangerous and inherently undemocratic ambition of obtaining an absolute parliamentary majority and forming a single-party government. Meanwhile, the Third *Lager* accused both the SPÖ and ÖVP of abusing power for party-political ends and was in turn dismissed by its opponents as little more than a bunch of inveterate old Nazis. Writing about Austrian electoral campaigns from 1945 to 1971, Hölzl (1974, pp.9–14) concluded that, for nearly a quarter of a century, the Second Republic's general elections had constituted 'decisions made in, or partly out of, fear'.

This type of ideological polarization and the profoundly negative campaigning it generated can be regarded as a core element of the first two decades or so of the Second Republic, but it is clear that its credibility was even then being undermined by political practice. In the first place, despite their many deficiencies, the series of grand coalition governments that ruled Austria from 1945 to 1966 gave a lie to the proposition that the rival *Lager* could not be trusted. Notwithstanding their electoral rhetoric, the two major parties had manifestly not only developed a largely bipartisan approach to a range of key foreign and domestic policies, but had established consensual mechanisms such as social partnership for tackling issues over which they did not agree. In other words, ideological polarization in the electoral arena had not prevented the development of both substantive and procedural consensus in government. Moreover, from 1966 onwards, Austria was ruled by a series of single-party governments (ÖVP from 1966–70 and SPÖ from 1970–83), none of which posed the predicted threat to the maintenance of democracy.

Second, the decline of ideological polarization was also reflected in change to the parties' programmatic profiles. Thus Pelinka and Welan (1971, p.285) argued that, in respect of the three historically most emotive and divisive issues (clericalism, attitude to democracy, and the socioeconomic, or property, question), the major parties' programmes were characterized by 'a preponderance of consensus over competition'. That development was later confirmed not only by other qualitative studies, (for example, Kadan and Pelinka, 1979, esp. pp.62–74), but also by more recent quantitative approaches, which *inter alia* subjected all post-war electoral manifestos to frequency and factor analyses (Horner, 1987, 1997; Müller, Philipp and Jenny, 1995). At the risk of oversimplification, three main stages in the development of ideological polarization within the Second Republic's party system can be identified. The first covers the period up to the mid-1960s when, as we have already outlined, the party system was initially characterized by polarized ideological rhetoric which, with few exceptions, was not, however, reflected in political practice. By the end of this first period, the two major parties' programmes had moved much closer in respect of the traditional socioeconomic left–right dimension and thereafter continued to shadow each other, whilst the FPÖ's ideological profile meant that it was largely considered to be beyond the pale. During the second stage (late 1960s to early 1980s), emotionally less charged issues related to modernization and value change gradually became the main conflict dimension of the party system. For their part, the leaders of the Third *Lager* initiated a deliberate change in their ideological profile from that of a backward-looking party, emphasizing protest and German nationalism, towards gradual liberalization, albeit of a distinctly conservative variety (Luther, 1987, 1996a, 1996b). The third stage covers the period since the Greens' entry into parliament in 1983 and Haider's assumption of the leadership of the FPÖ in 1986. It has witnessed the emergence on to the political agenda of new and, in part, very divisive issues, including immigration, internal and external security, European integration, privatization and deregulation and issues connected with the financial viability of the existing welfare state arrangements. Many challenge core elements of the major parties' long-established domestic and foreign policy consensus and thus help explain why governing capacity has become a key conflict dimension (Müller, Philipp and Jenny, 1995, pp.146–61). Second, the Greens' 'post-materialist' agenda has not only enhanced the salience of issues such as the environment, gender and democratization, but also often makes it rather difficult to locate parties on a simple left–right ideological continuum. Third, much of the ideological conflict between the electorally now much weaker 'major' parties and the opposition parties relates to what Dahl (1966, esp. pp.341–4) would term structural as opposed to policy-oriented opposition. Many of the established parameters of party competition (for example, mutual veto, social partnership and *Proporz*) are being subjected to radical attack, especially from

Haider's FPÖ, but also – albeit from a different perspective and in different language – from the Greens. Finally, if one observes the nature of political discourse in the electoral and parliamentary arenas, one cannot fail to notice that it has again become much more polarized.

Movements in Party Support (Volatility)

As a subculturally encapsulated polity with a pronounced '*Lager* mentality' (Stiefbold, 1975; Houska, 1985; Powell, 1970; Plasser, Ulram and Grausgruber, 1992), for many years Austria constituted a classic example of 'frozen' cleavages (Lipset and Rokkan, 1967). We lack survey data from the first two post-war decades, but other evidence (for example, Simon, 1957; Blecha *et al.*, 1964; Engelmann and Schwartz, 1974; Haerpfer, 1985; Haerpfer and Gehmacher, 1984) strongly suggests that, until the early 1980s, the overwhelming majority of Austrian voters were extremely loyal and their voting behaviour was to a very large extent predicated upon the traditional cleavages of class and religion,[8] which in 1969, for example, still accounted for 46 and 36 per cent of variation in voter behaviour (Haerpfer, 1983, p.134).

Since the 1970s, however, Austria has experienced a process of gradual depillarization, caused in part by socioeconomic factors such as Austria's changing occupational structure; urbanization; increasing geographical and social mobility, secularization and rising levels of education. Together, they have significantly reduced subcultural encapsulation; between 1972 and 1990 the proportion of SPÖ and ÖVP adherents living in party-politically consonant social networks declined from 86 to 57 per cent and from 78 to 48 per cent respectively (Plasser, Ulram and Grausgruber, 1992, p.23). Changes to the structure of political communication also fostered depillarization, as the growing salience of electronic media was accompanied by a dramatic fall in the combined share of total Austrian newspaper circulation held by SPÖ and ÖVP party newspapers, which declined from 39 per cent in 1952 to only 9 per cent in 1988 (Müller, 1992, pp.54–7).

The political consequences of depillarization were initially confined chiefly to attitudinal change. For example, between 1954 and 1990 partisanship amongst SPÖ and ÖVP adherents fell from 81 to 43 per cent and 82 to 47 per cent respectively whilst, from 1969 to 1990, uncritical party support in the population as a whole declined from 65 to 34 per cent (Plasser, Ulram and Grausgruber, 1992, pp.25–8). The proportion of party identifiers dropped from 73 per cent in 1954 to 44 per cent in 1994 (Ulram, 1997, p.517). Meanwhile, dissatisfaction with political parties increased and has partly been reflected in the growth in both post-materialist and more chauvinistic, or authoritarian, orientations (Plasser and Ulram, 1982; Deiser and Winkler, 1982; Ulram, 1990; Plasser and Ulram, 1991; Müller, Plasser and Ulram, 1995). In due course, depillarization reduced the efficacy of the major *Lager* parties' two traditional mobilizing techniques. In 1972 59 per cent of respondents had agreed that 'if you have a particular ideology, there is only one party you can vote for and you must stick with it', but after two decades of de-ideologization by the SPÖ and ÖVP, only 37 per cent did so in 1990 (Plasser, Ulram and Grausgruber, 1992, p.24). Material incentives based upon individual and group patronage continued to work for some time but, by the mid-1980s at the latest, they too were considerably weakened. On the one hand, public sector contraction and the state's gradual withdrawal from the socioeconomic sphere reduced patronage opportunities. On the other hand, patronage was increasingly regarded as illegitimate, in part because of a series of corruption cases, but also because of value change and critical reporting in the party-politically more independent print and electronic media. Accordingly, the major parties are often caught in a cleft stick; using patronage to mobilize their traditional supporters frequently results in alienating the electorally increasingly significant proportion of the population which lacks *Lager* partisanship

Although depillarization gradually expanded the previously extremely small pool of floating voters, who no longer held to the dictum 'my party right or wrong', for most of the 1970s there were not only very small changes in parties' electoral fortunes but also the unprecedented sight of a party obtaining a plurality of votes and seats. This apparent contradiction is not as great as it seems, however. The SPÖ's electoral majority was only possible because of the willingness of the predominantly middle-class, non-aligned, personality- and issue-oriented voters to vote for the SPÖ. The unifying elements of the SPÖ's 'electoral coalition' during the 1970s were Kreisky's personality and the appeal of a social–liberal consensus based upon 'economic growth, full employment and its guarantee of stable prices and a tightening of the social welfare net' (Birk and Traar, 1987, p.55). In short, the electoral impact of depillarization was merely postponed by the success of the Kreisky-led SPÖ in more than compensating for the decline in its core vote by attracting and retaining the floating voters. From 1971 to 1979, the SPÖ thus enjoyed three consecutive absolute majorities and there was little or net volatility, since the small individual volatility flows largely tended to cancel each other out.

Accordingly, until the early 1980s, the Second Republic's party system remained characterized by very low levels of net movement in party support. Calculated on the basis of the Pedersen index (the theoretical value of which ranges between 0 and 100),[9] average net electoral volatility between 1953 and 1979 inclusive was merely 3.49 per cent and in 1975 dropped as low as 0.42 per cent (see Table 7.2). Even the relatively high 1966 and 1970 levels (which presaged single-party ÖVP and SPÖ governments respectively) are low by international standards (Pedersen, 1979; Bartolini and Mair, 1990). Significant change at the aggregate level only really started in 1983, with the entry of the Greens on to the political scene, and grew especially from 1986, when, under the leadership of Jörg Haider, the revitalized FPÖ experienced the first of three dramatic electoral victories (see Table 7.2). Although volatility declined again in 1995, it is too early to assume that the period of high volatility is at an end.

Even if it were, depillarization and three consecutive elections with unusually high levels of aggregate volatility have left their mark upon party support. First, even comparing the 1995 election results with 1986, rather than with earlier elections at which the SPÖ and ÖVP still dominated in their respective sociodemographic strongholds, it is clear that there have been fundamental changes in the party-political profile of different social groups (see Table 7.3). Some of the ÖVP's greatest losses have been amongst its traditional core voters: the self-employed (–21 per cent); farmers (–21 per cent); and unemployed women (–18 per cent). The only social group amongst which it still retains majority support is farmers, who account for only approximately 7 per cent of the working population. The SPÖ too has suffered especially badly in its socioeconomic heartland. For many years, it had obtained over two-thirds of the blue-collar vote and, even in 1986, its support amongst skilled workers lay at 56 and amongst the unskilled or semi-skilled it comprised 59 per cent. In 1995, however, the SPÖ was only able to muster the votes of 40 and 43 per cent respectively. For its part, the FPÖ has increased its support the most amongst blue-collar voters of both categories and amongst the youngest age cohort. A very worrying development for both the SPÖ and ÖVP is the ageing of their electorates.

The capacity of sociostructural variables to predict voter choice have been much reduced. To be sure, religiosity is still important, with 59 per cent of all religiously active Austrians voting for the ÖVP. Similarly, union membership predisposes voters to support the SPÖ, as does living in a blue-collar household (Plasser, Ulram, Neuwirth and Sommer, 1995, p.45). Yet between 1969 and 1995, the Alford index of class voting (the proportion of blue-collar minus the proportion of white-collar votes for a social democratic party) declined from 26 to a mere 9 points. Applied to the FPÖ, the index registers 12 (Plasser, Ulram and Seeber, 1996, p.183). Indeed, if one looks not at the political profile of sociodemographic groups but at the sociodemographic profile of party support, one finds a very interesting picture (see Table 7.4). Blue-collar voters now comprise only 24 per cent of the SPÖ's electorate, whilst they make up 35 per cent of the Austrians who cast their vote for the FPÖ. In other words, the SPÖ now shares its

Table 7.3 Voting profile of selected Austrian sociodemographic groups in 1986 and 1995

	1986				1995					Change 1986–96			
	SPÖ	ÖVP	FPÖ	G	SPÖ	ÖVP	FPÖ	G	LiF	SPÖ	ÖVP	FPÖ	G
Men	42	38	12	4	35	26	27	4	5	−7	−12	+15	0
employed	41	38	13	4	34	24	30	4	4	−7	−14	+17	0
unemployed	44	37	11	5	29	25	9	15	19	−15	−12	−2	+10
pensioners					38	33	23	0	3				
Women	43	43	7	5	40	29	16	5	6	−3	−14	+9	0
employed	46	37	7	7	35	26	20	7	8	−11	−11	+13	0
unemployed	34	49	8	7	38	31	14	7	6	+4	−18	+6	0
pensioners	49	44	5	0	50	31	10	1	2	+1	−13	+5	+1
Age													
First-time voters	37	35	14	12									
18–29 years old	39	33	12	11	30	18	29	10	9	−9	−15	+17	−1
30–44 years old	43	37	11	5	36	25	24	5	5	−7	−12	+13	−1
45–59 years old	42	48	6	1	39	33	19	2	5	−3	−15	+13	+1
60–69 years old	44	45	8	1	42	36	14	1	3	−2	−9	+6	0
70 and over	46	43	9	1	46	32	16	0	1	0	−11	+7	−1
Occupation													
self-employed/ professionals	14	60	15	6	18	39	28	7	5	+4	−21	+13	+1
farmers	1	93	5	1	4	72	18	1	1	+3	−21	+13	0
civil servants	49	32	9	6	48	20	17	6	6	−1	−12	+8	0
white-collar	40	36	13	7	32	28	22	7	8	−8	−8	+9	0

blue-collar skilled	56	26	11	4	40	14	35	4	4	−16	−12	+24	0
b–c un/semi-skilled	59	28	8	3	43	11	33	3	3	−16	−17	+25	0
housewives	36	52	8	4	42	34	12	3	4	+6	−18	+4	−1
pensioners	49	41	7	1	45	32	16	1	3	−4	−9	+9	0
in schooling	19	38	9	23	25	22	15	19	18	+6	−16	+6	−4
Education													
obligatory	47	43	6	2									
vocational	45	38	11	3									
pre-university	33	41	10	11									
graduates	19	52	14	10									
vote switchers	10	24	39	22	25	21	34	5	13	+15	−3	−5	−17
non-voters last election	38	25	15	20	27	13	24	12	8	−11	−12	+9	−8
Overall	43	41	17	5	38	28	22	5	6	−5	−13	+5	0

Source: Fessel+GfK, Exit Polls; 1986 (n=2149): Plasser and Ulram (1988, p.84); 1995 (n=2333): Plasser, Ulram, Neuwirth and Sommer (1995, p.31).

Table 7.4 Social structure of Austrian political parties, 1986 and 1995

	1986 SPÖ	1986 ÖVP	1986 FPÖ	1986 G	1995 SPÖ	1995 ÖVP	1995 FPÖ	1995 G	1995 LiF	Change 1986–96 SPÖ	Change 1986–96 ÖVP	Change 1986–96 FPÖ	Change 1986–96 G
Sex													
Men	46	44	61	40	45	46	62	39	41	–1	+2	+1	–1
Women	54	56	39	60	55	54	38	61	59	+1	–2	–1	+1
Age													
18–29 years old	22	20	31	58	18	15	31	52	39	–4	–5	0	–6
20–44 years old	28	25	32	32	27	25	31	34	28	–1	0	–1	+2
45–59 years old	23	27	15	6	23	27	20	11	21	0	0	+5	+5
60–69 years old	12	13	10	2	15	17	9	2	9	+3	+4	–1	0
70 and over	15	15	12	3	16	15	10	1	4	+1	0	–2	–2
Occupation													
self-employed/professionals	2	7	7	6	2	6	6	7	4	0	–1	–1	+1
farmers	0	9	2	1	1	10	3	1	1	+1	+1	+1	0
civil servants	7	5	6	8	9	5	5	9	8	+2	0	–1	+1
white-collar	18	17	27	29	18	21	22	33	34	0	+4	–5	+4
blue-collar	30	14	22	17	24	10	35	17	15	–6	–4	+13	0
housewives	12	18	12	12	12	13	6	6	8	0	–5	–6	–6
pensioners	28	25	19	4	31	30	19	3	13	+3	+5	0	–1
Education													
obligatory	32	30	18	15	29	24	20	12	5	–3	–6	+2	–3
vocational	52	45	56	31	47	41	58	30	33	–5	–4	+2	–1
qualified for university entrance/graduates	16	25	26	54	24	35	22	58	62	+8	+10	–4	+4

Sources: Fessel+GfK, Exit Polls; 1986 (n=2149): Plasser and Ulram (1988, p.85); 1995 (n=2333) Plasser, Ulram, Neuwirth and Sommer, 1995, p.41).

traditional role as the party of the working class with the FPÖ. Although Green voters tend to be slightly younger then LiF voters, there are significant similarities in the profile of the electorate of the Greens and the LiF. Both parties recruit especially well amongst younger age cohorts, women, persons with low levels of religiosity and higher levels of education and white-collar employees, who make up a third of each party's electorate.

To focus exclusively on changes to the sociology and volatility of the Austrian electorate would be to neglect another indicator of de-alignment: the increase in non-voting and in spoilt ballots. Until the late 1980s turnout remained high by international standards and never fell below 90.5 per cent. Since then, however, the incidence of non-voting has increased, reaching over 18 per cent in 1994. If the voters who spoiled their ballots (2.1 per cent of votes cast) are added to these figures, almost exactly 20 per cent of the Austrian electorate failed to cast a valid vote.

To conclude, the significant shifts in party support outlined in this section have had important effects on the structure of party competition. The previously small FPÖ has attained a level of electoral support not much lower than that enjoyed by the SPÖ and ÖVP and party system concentration has thus declined greatly (see above). Second, new parties have emerged and, although they are fishing in the same relatively small (albeit growing) segment of the electoral pool, both appear to have established themselves in the party system. Third, as electoral outcomes have become less predictable, the parties have invested more resources in campaigning which has tended to become increasingly candidate-centred. Fourth, substantial changes have occurred in the sociodemographic composition of the three traditional parties' electorates and is already having a significant knock-on effect on their programmatic profile. For example, in the 1990s the FPÖ has frequently sought to redefine its ideology to reflect its changed electorate. The most recent (1997) – and, for a traditionally anticlerical party, perhaps most surprising change – has been the FPÖ's assertion that it is now a party not only of the workers but also of Christian values. Fifth, even if volatility were to revert to its previously very low level, three successive elections with unusually high levels of volatility (1986–94) mean that Austria is unlikely to resume the pattern of party support typical of the period up to the 1970s. For one, the SPÖ and ÖVP's electoral dominance is unlikely to return. Moreover, the parties' support is likely to remain precarious, since the cumulative effect of a succession of highly volatile elections has been an electorate that is accustomed to changing its vote and is therefore less predictable. Finally, there has clearly been a de-alignment in party support and some factors do seem to have become more important determinants of voting behaviour, such as public versus private sector employment (Plasser, Ulram and Ogris, 1996, pp.190–92). However, it has not yet proved possible to identify a model that adequately explains contemporary voting behaviour (Plasser and Seeber, 1995). Accordingly, it is premature to speak of a re-aligned party system.

Relations Between Government and Opposition

Government office is arguably the prime goal pursued by political parties, so an assessment of the structure of competition for office should offer valuable insights into the nature of a party system. Table 7.5 details the duration and party composition of all post-war Austrian governments. It also contains information on the three aspects of the government formation process which Mair (1996) has argued together offer a useful indication of the extent to which the structure of party competition is open or closed – namely, alternation, innovation and access.[10]

Leaving aside the KPÖ's departure from Figl's first cabinet in 1947, there have been only three cases of partial alternation: 1966, when the ÖVP–SPÖ grand coalition was replaced by a one-party ÖVP government; 1983, when the single-party SPÖ government was extended to include the FPÖ; and, finally, 1987, when in response to Haider's election as leader of the FPÖ, the SPÖ called a snap election, after which it formed the first of a series of SPÖ–ÖVP coalitions that have governed Austria ever since. The only example of wholesale alternation is the replacement of single-party ÖVP rule by a single-party SPÖ government in 1970. Overall, the degree of alternation in the post-war party system has thus been rather low.

The same can be said in respect of innovation. For over 29 of the 50 years since November 1947, when the first ÖVP–SPÖ grand coalition government was sworn in, Austria has been ruled by cabinets comprising this combination of parties. The elections of 1966 and 1970 produced two consecutive innovative governmental formulae: ÖVP and SPÖ single-party governments respectively. In view of the legacy of mutual suspicion inherited from the First Republic, these were important innovations, demonstrating that both parties could be trusted to rule alone. The only other innovation has been the SPÖ–FPÖ coalition of 1983–6 which, although short-lived, may well prove to have (had) a greater long-term influence upon the party system than has hitherto been assumed, in that, as Mair (1966, p.104) has argued, 'a shift in the range of governing options' may act to 'undermine established preferences and promote instability' in the party system.

The range of parties gaining access to government and the length of time they have spent in government presents a very uneven picture. The most impressive record is that of the SPÖ, which has been in government for over 90 per cent of the post-war period and, in terms of office-holding, is thus

Table 7.5 Austrian governments and the structure of government competition since 1945[1]

Cabinet	Date in	Duration (years)	Party composition (chancellor party named first)	Structure of competition[2] Alt	Invtn	Access
Renner	27.04.45	0.6	SPÖ–ÖVP–KPÖ			
Figl (I)	**20.12.45**	**1.9**	**ÖVP–SPÖ–KPÖ**			**0**
Figl (II)	20.11.47	2.0	ÖVP–SPÖ	p	I	3
Figl (III)	**08.11.49**	**3.4**	**ÖVP–SPÖ**	**N**		**3, 4**
Raab (I)	02.04.53	3.2	ÖVP–SPÖ	n		3, 4
Raab (II)	**29.06.56**	**3.0**	**ÖVP–SPÖ**	**N**		**3, 4**
Raab (III)	**16.07.59**	**1.7**	**ÖVP–SPÖ**	**N**		**4**
Gorbach (I)	11.04.61	2.0	ÖVP–SPÖ	n		4
Gorbach (II)	**27.03.63**	**1.0**	**ÖVP–SPÖ**	**N**		**4**
Klaus (I)	02.04.64	2.0	ÖVP–SPÖ	n		4
Klaus (II)	**19.04.66**	**4.0**	**ÖVP**	**P**	**I**	**1, 4**
Kreisky (I)	**21.04.70**	**1.5**	**SPÖ**	**W**	**I**	**2, 4**
Kreisky (II)	**04.11.71**	**4.0**	**SPÖ**	**N**		**2, 4**
Kreisky (III)	**28.10.75**	**3.6**	**SPÖ**	**N**		**2, 4**
Kreisky (IV)	**05.06.79**	**4.0**	**SPÖ**	**N**		**2, 4**
Sinowatz	**24.05.83**	**3.0**	**SPÖ–FPÖ**	**P**	**I**	**2**
Vranitzky (I)	16.06.86	0.6	SPÖ–FPÖ	n		2
Vranitzky (II)	**21.01.87**	**4.0**	**SPÖ–ÖVP**	**P**		**4, 5**
Vranitzky (III)	**17.12.90**	**4.0**	**SPÖ–ÖVP**	**N**		**4, 5[3]**
Vranitzky (IV)	**29.11.94**	**1.3**	**SPÖ–ÖVP**	**N**		**4, 5, 6**
Vranitzky (V)	**12.03.96**	**0.9**	**SPÖ–ÖVP**	**N**		**4, 5, 6**
Klima	28.01.97	?	SPÖ–ÖVP	n		4, 5, 6

Notes:
1. To define a cabinet, the criteria 'same chancellor', 'same party composition' and 'between parliamentary elections' were used. Information for parliamentary election years are in bold.
2. Own application Mair's (1996) criteria to all governments except Renner's provisional government, which preceded the first parliamentary elections of November 1945. Alternation (Alt) relates to change in the party composition of governments. There can be wholesale (w), partial (p), or no (n) alternation. Alternation following parliamentary elections is indicated in upper case. Innovation (Invtn) denotes governments comprising previously unknown party combinations. Access relates to opportunity to participate in government and is indicated here by its obverse: existing parliamentary parties *excluded* from government. (1=SPÖ; 2=ÖVP; 3=KPÖ; 4=VdU/FPÖ; 5=Greens; 6=LiF).
3. From 4 February 1993, when five FPÖ MPs broke away to form the LiF, the excluded parties were 4, 5 and 6.

one of Western Europe's most successful parties. Its only experience in opposition was from 1966 to 1970, since when it has continuously held the chancellorship and from 1970 to 1983 ruled alone. The ÖVP's record is more modest, although still relatively good by Western European standards. The party has been in government for over two-thirds of the post-war period. Between December 1945 and April 1966 it held the chancellorship and was the dominant grand coalition party. From 1966 to 1970, it even succeeded in forming Austria's first single-party government. Since 1970, however, its position has been less exalted. It languished in opposition for 17 years and, from 1987, has had to content itself with the role of junior government party.

The other parties have had little or no government experience. The KPÖ was in parliament from 1945 to 1959, but only held government seats during the rather unusual period up to November 1947. Thereafter, it was a party of opposition. For their part, Third *Lager* parties have been excluded from government for all but 3.6 of the 48 years since the VdU's admission to the party system in 1949. Whether or not the FPÖ has merited (or indeed continues to merit) the label anti-system party, it has for most of its existence certainly been an excluded, or isolated, party. Since 1986 the number of parliamentary parties has increased from three to five, whilst the SPÖ and ÖVP's combined share of parliamentary seats dropped from 91 per cent in 1983 to as low as 63 per cent in 1994. Accordingly, since 1986, the 'grand coalition' has been not nearly as grand as it was up to 1966. Its relationship to the opposition has changed in other significant ways also. It now faces not one, but three, opposition parties: two are new and the parliamentary strength of the third is not far behind that of the junior governing party. Moreover, as mentioned above, the opposition parties devote considerable attention to 'structural' opposition. Finally, the government is faced with 'bilateral opposition' from the Greens on the Left and the FPÖ on the Right. Although this has not involved the 'maximum spread of opinion' typical of 'polarized pluralism' it has resulted in a degree of immobilism and an 'enfeeblement of the centre' (Sartori, 1976, pp.134f).

To summarize, with the exception of the 1983–86 SPÖ–FPÖ coalition, the Second Republic's governmental arena has, since 1947, remained the exclusive preserve of the SPÖ and ÖVP. With one exception, alternation has been at best partial, but usually non-existent, whilst innovation too has been rather limited. In short, a relatively closed structure of competition for office has been and remains a 'core element' of the post-war party system. In view of the fairly profound changes Austria has lately experienced in the number and relative size of parties, in ideological polarization and in its traditionally hyperstable pattern of party support, it is perhaps surprising that the number of parties enjoying access to government has not increased. To be sure, the

Liberal Forum has, from its inception, been regarded as a potential governing party and, since the early 1990s, the Greens have also emphasized their willingness to assume government responsibility. However, to date both have remained in opposition, as has Haider's FPÖ. Although this may be regarded as a measure of the success of the SPÖ and ÖVP in resisting pressure for change, it is unclear how long it will prove possible for them to keep a lid on the head of steam that has been building up since the mid-1980s.

The Site of Decisive Encounters

As Dahl (1966, pp.338–41) has pointed out, parties can compete in a number of different arenas, or 'sites'. In some party systems, there may be sites that are 'decisive', in that 'victory in that encounter entails a rather high probability of victory in the rest' (ibid., p.338). Thus, in Britain, victory in the first-past-the-post elections is usually a 'necessary and sufficient' condition for a party to succeed in changing important government policies (ibid., p.339).

Austria's electoral arena has, of course, always been an important site of encounters between parties, but during the first period of grand coalition government (1945–66), it was not decisive. Neither the SPÖ nor the ÖVP expected to win an absolute majority of parliamentary seats and, on the one occasion when this happened, (November 1945), the parties' shared commitment to accommodation and the exigencies of the occupation prevented the formation of a single-party government. Far more decisive was the government arena, where two parties controlling, between them, 90 per cent or more of parliamentary seats competed to determine government policy. Indeed, Engelmann (1966) concluded of this period that the government arena was not only the site of government policy-making ('the pooling of government'), but also the main location for opposition to government policy ('the pooling of opposition'). Yet many of the key encounters determining government policy were made not in the cabinet itself but in extra-constitutional fora. One was the coalition committee, made up of the ten or so most powerful members of the political elite of both *Lager*, only a few of which held seats in cabinet (Rudzio, 1971). A second was the corporate arena, where the principle of mutual veto had traditionally obtained (Gerlich, Grande and Müller, 1985). It became increasingly important from the late 1950s and, in respect of at least economic and social policy, it indeed constituted the 'site of decisive encounters' of the party system. Through 'their' interest groups, the consent of the two main *Lager* parties thus continued to be indispensable for decision-making, regardless of whether or not they were in government at the time (for example, SPÖ 1966–70 and ÖVP 1970–86). A fifth site in which the two major parties competed for power and influence was the bureaucratic arena. Since 1967 elections have regularly been held for civil servants' representatives and they clearly demonstrate both the extent of party-political activity within the state bureaucracy and the party-political orientation of the different sections of the state apparatus (Luther, 1992, pp.88–91). Through their influence in the bureaucratic arena and their 'osmotic relationship' to the main interest groups, which transferred 'to themselves the regulatory functions of the welfare state' (Secher, 1960, p.961), the SPÖ and ÖVP acted as gatekeepers for a wide range of other state resources. The two major Austrian parties thus exercised influence not only in all areas of public life, but also penetrated deeply into 'civil society'.

The logical corollary of this system was that constitutional structures, such as cabinet and parliament, became 'merely formal instrumentalities of party and group power' (Secher, 1960, p.906). The National Council was largely relegated to the role of a rubber stamp for decisions formally approved in cabinet, but in reality hammered out either in the coalition committee or the structures of social partnership. The role of MPs was to be disciplined lobby fodder, dutifully passing Acts handed down to them. Indeed, until as recently as the 1983–86 parliament, which faced an SPÖ–FPÖ government controlling merely 55 per cent of parliamentary seats, 70–80 per cent of legislation was passed unanimously.

However, since the late 1960s there have been significant changes in the scope of political parties and in the relative salience of the various sites of party competition. At the risk of oversimplification, two phases can be identified. The first lasted until the late 1980s and covers the period of one-party government and the SPÖ–FPÖ coalition. This is a period when the electoral arena became more decisive, since electoral outcomes determined the party composition of government. On the other hand, the influence of the corporate arena also grew, which led to the somewhat paradoxical result that, whilst grand coalition government came to an end, policy-making was still determined by accommodation between the two major *Lager* parties and their associated interest groups. Thus, in many ways, grand coalition government was transferred from the government to the corporate arena.

Since the late 1980s, however, Austria has witnessed a gradual decline in the salience of the corporate arena (Gerlich, 1992). Moreover, although Austria has been ruled by SPÖ–ÖVP grand coalition governments since 1987, the role of the coalition committee is much less influential than it once was. There has been a relative strengthening of the government arena, where the cabinet has 'increasingly become a force in its own right' (Müller, 1992b, p.111). On the other hand, parliament has also reasserted itself. Not only has unanimous voting dramatically declined, but parliament is now much more active than it ever was, with MPs making much more frequent use of procedures such as question time, written questions and committees of investigation. This is partly a consequence of the growing strength of the opposition parties, who until the mid-1980s rarely accounted for more than about 5 per cent of parliamentary seats, but now hold about a third (see Table 7.2). However, even within the governing parties' parliamentary caucuses, there has also been a sharp decline in the hitherto exceptionally high levels of party discipline. In short, there has been a reassertion of formal constitutional structures although, since both the electoral and parliamentary arenas have become less predictable, party government has become more vulnerable.

Conclusion

Writing in the late 1980s (Luther, 1989, p.24), I argued that the Second Republic's party system had experienced change in many of its core features but that, as yet, these amounted only to 'restricted' rather than to 'general' change or 'transformation' (Smith, 1989, pp.353f). This essay has documented significant and relatively speedy change in all the core features of Austria's post-war party system. With the exception of the national governmental arena, the SPÖ and ÖVP have lost their longstanding position of predominance. Instead, there are three nearly equal-sized parties and two minor parties. Moreover, the FPÖ's rapid growth continues to pose a significant threat to the ÖVP's position as the second-largest party, whilst Haider's structural opposition challenges Austria's traditionally consensual style of party interaction. It therefore now seems appropriate to conclude that the Second Republic's party system has undergone 'general change', even if a 'new equilibrium' (Smith, 1989, p.354) has still not been established.

When considering the factors that cause (or prevent) party system change, it is important to consider not only variables exogenous to the party system (for example, institutional factors, sociocultural and economic change and changes in the international environment), but also endogenous factors such as the role of the parties and political actors themselves. For they can and do (at least in part) shape their own environment and effect their own futures through their behaviour and the strategic choices they make. Thus the decline of the major parties can, to some extent, be regarded as a consequence of the behaviour of their own elites. There has been a fundamental change in the degree of popular acceptance of the traditional methods used by parties to structure and mobilize their support, as well as of the traditional style of political decision-making. Some of the parties' strategies and behaviours have thus had a perverse, or unintended, effect and are in part responsible for the predicament in which the traditional parties now find themselves. Conversely, the success of the FPÖ in particular has much to do with Haider's not inconsiderable political skills.

The Second Republic has witnessed significant change in the character of the party-political elites, amongst whom traditional ideological orientations have largely given way to a more technocratic approach. In part, this is a consequence of generational change, as politicians with personal experience of Austro-fascism and Nazi occupation were gradually replaced. In the case of the ÖVP, and in particular the SPÖ, it is also related to the fact that these parties have been in government so long. The resulting 'governmentness' of the two major parties has contributed to the alienation of the party elite from their grassroots, which has further undermined already weakening *Lager* loyalties. It is amongst the political elites of the opposition parties that the greatest changes are apparent, however. The Greens (at least initially) brought an unconventional approach to the political process; they emphasized matters such as the environment and gender equality rather than *Lager* politics; engaged in direct action; and included within their ranks a relatively large proportion of women. The political elite of the LiF is certainly much more conventional in its background and style. However, the LiF's location on the political spectrum opens up a hitherto inconceivable range of coalition permutations that offer the opportunity for Haider's political isolation to be extended (Luther, 1995).

The greatest change in Austria's party-political elite has, of course, been in the FPÖ. Since the period of Steger's leadership (1980–86), when technocracy and careerist ambitions greatly shaped the behaviour of the party elite (Luther, 1996a, 1996b), Haider has eschewed consensual conventions and has pursued an aggressive and populist style that challenges most of the fundamental features of the post-war party system. Moreover, the loyalty of the FPÖ party elite is oriented less to the party, as such, than to Haider himself, to whom most directly owe their positions. Electorally, the FPÖ has been by far the most successful of Europe's new breed of right-wing protest parties. It has also exercised a considerable indirect influence upon the policy of the governing parties, which have sought to steal its thunder on issues such as immigration. However, electoral success does not necessarily translate into government participation – at least not unless a party wins an absolute majority. Since the FPÖ is highly unlikely to be able to do so, its prospects of entering government depend on it finding other parties willing and able to enter into coalition with it.

The SPÖ's and ÖVP's deliberate strategy of isolating the FPÖ from the national governmental arena illustrates well the extent to which political actors can influence the nature of the party system. Although the two parties have become more vulnerable in the electoral and parliamentary arenas, where competition has taken on a new significance and a new edge, they have so far succeeded in excluding Haider from national government. This may be regarded as refusing to accommodate the electorate's expressed preference for change and thus as merely increasing public resentment at the traditional elite's unresponsiveness. However, if we accept Mair's (1996) proposition that change in the structure of competition for government may well serve to further destabilize a party system, then the strategy of exclusion may well prove to be the SPÖ's and ÖVP's best hope of avoiding even more radical change to the party system.

Whichever interpretation proves to be correct, it is important to stress that the changes which the Second Republic's party system has undergone since the 1980s (and in particular since the rise of Haider's populist FPÖ) should not necessarily be regarded as pathological. For nearly 40 years, the Second Republic's party system was characterized by unusually high levels of both stability and accommodation. Since then, Austria has witnessed a gradual process of depillarization and a concomitant depoliticization of its civil society. New party actors have emerged in the electoral and parliamentary arenas, and there has been a significant strengthening of opposition parties not based upon segmented subcultures. The 'site of decisive encounters' has started to shift from extraconstitutional structures such as Austria's corporate system of Social Partnership towards formal institutions such as government and parliament, where party interaction is now both much more competitive and less predictable. These developments have certainly made life more difficult for the SPÖ and ÖVP in particular; they have lost their former predominance and are now much more vulnerable to changes in electoral support. However, there is nothing fundamentally unhealthy in a shift from a system of party competition characterized by hyperstability and accommodation to one in which uncertainty and competition are the order of the day. Indeed, inasmuch as it denotes a move away from the exceptionalism of Austrian post-war politics, this development can, in some respects, be regarded as a 'normalization' of the Second Republic's party system.

Notes

1 For an evaluation of the formal powers and actual working of governmental institutions, see Müller (1992b) and Dachs *et al.* (1997).

2 For an earlier and rather different utilization of some of Smith's ideas, see Luther (1989), which *inter alia* places rather more emphasis on regional features of the Second Republic's party system. For a fuller version of this chapter, see Luther (1998a).

3 This accuracy of proposition has been widely challenged, however (for example, Menasse, 1992, pp.83f).

4 Surveys of Austrian national identity have regularly shown neutrality and consensual economic policy-making to be the object of considerable public pride (see Chapter 5 in this volume by Bruckmüller).

5 For reasons of space, this chapter can only deal with the national level. On the party systems at the *Land* level, where one of the two major parties have often exercised an hegemonic role and where recent changes to the number and relative size of parties have in many cases been even more pronounced than at the national level, see Dachs (1992) and Luther (1989).

6 Rae's model of party system fractionalization is based on the probability that any two randomly selected voters will have chosen different parties in any given election. The index of electoral fractionalization (F_e) is one minus the sum of the squares of each party's decimal share of the vote. Parliamentary fractionalization (or F_p) is calculated in an analogous way. The higher the value, the more fragmented the party system is, with the theoretical range being from 0 (total concentration in one party) to 1, where there are as many parties as voters.

7 See Table 7.1. The effective number of parties in the electoral and parliamentary arenas (N_v and N_s respectively) denotes 'the number of hypothetical *equal*-size parties that would have the same total *effect* on fractionalization of the system as have the actual parties of *unequal* size' (1979, pp.4f; italics in the original). Technically, it carries the same information as the Rae index, from and into which it can thus be readily converted. However, it has the advantage of generating figures that are intuitively more meaningful.

8 For a discussion of research into Austrian political parties which highlights *inter alia* the problems caused by the absence of longitudinal data stretching back to the 1950s and 1960s, see Müller (1993, esp. pp.441–5). For a theoretical justification of the proposition that low levels of aggregate volatility such as those exhibited by Austria between 1953 and the 1980s can be taken to indicate low individual volatility also, see Bartolini and Mair (1990).

9 The Pedersen (1979, p.4) index is calculated by adding up the percentage gains for all winning parties, or the percentage losses of all losing parties.

10 'Alternation' refers to discontinuity in the party composition of consecutive governments. There can be wholesale alternation (that is, no continuity), partial alternation, or no alternation. An innovative government is one whose party composition introduces a previously unknown formula. Access denotes the extent to which all or most parties have the opportunity to participate in government. Table 7.5 provides information on the obverse phenomenon: the parliamentary parties *excluded* from government.

Bibliography

Bartolini, S. and Mair, P. (1990), *Identity, Competition and Electoral Availability. The Stabilisation of European Electorates 1885–1985*, Cambridge: Cambridge University Press.

Beyme, Klaus von (1985), *Political Parties in Western Democracies*, Aldershot: Gower.

Birk, F. and Traar, K. (1987), 'Der durchleuchtete Wähler in den achtziger Jahren', *Journal für Sozialforschung*, **27**, (1), pp.3–74.

Blecha, Karl, Gmoser, Rupert and Kienzl, Heinz (1964), *Der durchleuchtete Wähler. Beiträge zur politischen Soziologie in Österreich*, Vienna: Europa Verlag.

Bruckmüller, Ernst (1996), *Nation Österreich. Kulturelles Bewußtsein und gesellschaftlich-politische Prozesse*, 2nd edn, Vienna: Böhlau.

Dachs, Herbert (ed.) (1992), *Parteien und Wahlen in Österreichs Bundesländern 1945–1991*, Sonderband 3 of *Österreichisches Jahrbuch für Politik*, Vienna: Verlag für Geschichte und Politik.

Dachs, Herbert *et al.* (eds) (1997), *Handbuch des politischen Systems Österreichs. Die zweite Republik*, 3rd edn, Vienna: Manz.

Dahl, R.A. (ed.) (1966), *Political Opposition in Western Democracies*, New Haven: Yale University Press.

Deiser, R. and Winkler, N. (1982), *Das politische Handeln der Österreicher*, Vienna: Verlag für Gesellschaftskritik.

Deschouwer, K., De Winter, L. and Delle Porta, D. (eds) (1996), *Partocracies Between Crisis and Reforms: The Cases of Italy and Belgium*, Special Issue of *Res Publica*, **38**, (2), Leuven: Politologisch Institut.

Diamant, Alfred (1958), 'The Group Basis of Austrian Politics', *Journal of Central European Affairs*, **18**, pp.134–55.

Dreijmanis, J. (1982), 'Austria – the "Black" – "Red" Coalitions', in E.C. Browne and J. Dreijmanis (eds), *Government Coalitions in Western Democracies*, New York: Longmann, pp.791–809.

Duverger, M. (1964), *Political Parties. Their Organisation and Activity in the Modern State*, 3rd edn, London: Methuen.

Ehmer, Josef (1997), 'Die Kommunistische Partei Österreichs' in Herbert Dachs *et al.* (eds), *Handbuch des politischen Systems Österreichs. Die zweite Republik*, 3rd edn, Vienna: Manz, pp.323–32.

Engelmann, F.C. (1966), 'Austria: The Pooling of Opposition' in R.A. Dahl (ed.), *Political Opposition in Western Democracies*, New Haven: Yale University Press, pp.260–83.

Engelmann, Frederick and Schwartz, Mildred (1974), 'Partisan Stability and the Continuity of a Segmented Society: The Austrian Case', *American Journal of Sociology*, **79**, (4), pp.948–66.

Gerlich, Peter (1992), 'A Farewell to Corporatism' in K.R. Luther and W.C. Müller (eds) (1992), *Politics in Austria. Still a Case of Consociationalism?*, London: Frank Cass, pp.132–46.

Gerlich, Peter, Grande, Erich and Müller, Wolfgang C. (1985), *Sozialpartnerschaft in der Krise. Leistungen und Grenzen des Neokorporatismus in Österreich*, Vienna: Böhlau.

Haerpfer, C. (1983), 'Nationalratswahlen und Wahlverhalten seit 1945' in Peter Gerlich and Wolfgang Müller, (eds), *Zwischen Koalition und Konkurrenz. Österreichs Parteien seit 1945*, Vienna: Braumüller, pp.111–49.

Haerpfer, C. (1985), 'Austria' in Ivor Crewe and David Denver (eds), *Electoral Change in Western Democracies. Patterns and Sources of Electoral Volatility*, New York: St Martin's Press, pp.264–86.

Haerpfer, C. and Gehmacher, E. (1984), 'Social Structure and Voting in the Austrian Party System', *Electoral Studies*, **3**, pp.25–46.

Hölzl, Norbert (1974), *Propagandaschlachten. Die österreichischen Wahlkämpfe 1945 bis 1971*, Vienna: Verlag für Geschichte und Politik.

Horner, Franz (1987), 'Austria 1945–1979', in Ian Budge, David Robertson and Derek Hearl (eds), *Ideology, Strategy and Party Change: Spatial Analyses of Post-War Election Programmes in 19 Democracies*, Cambridge: Cambridge University Press, pp. 270–93 .

Horner, Franz (1997), 'Programme- Ideologien: Dissens oder Konsens' in Herbert Dachs *et al.* (eds), *Handbuch des politischen Systems Österreichs. Die zweite Republik*, 3rd edn, Vienna: Manz, pp.235–47.

Houska, J.J. (1985), *Influencing Mass Political Behaviour. Elites and Political Subcultures in the Netherlands and Austria*, University of California: Institute of International Studies.

Kadan, Albert and Pelinka, Anton (1979), *Die Grundsatzprogramme der österreichischen Parteien. Dokumentation und Analyse*, St Pölten: Niederösterreichisches Pressehaus.

Katz, Richard and Mair, Peter (eds) (1992), *Party Organizations in Western Democracies. A Data Handbook*, London: Sage.

Katz, Richard, Mair, Peter *et al.* (1992), 'The Membership of Political Parties in European Democracies, 1960–1990', *European Journal of Political Research*, **22**, pp.329–45 .

Laakso, M. and Taagepera, R. (1979), '"Effective" Number of Parties: A Measure with Application to West Europe', *Comparative Political Studies* **12**, (1), pp.3–27.

Lauber, Volkmar (1992), 'Changing Priorities in Austrian Economic Policy' in K.R. Luther and W.C. Müller (eds), *Politics in Austria. Still a Case of Consociationalism?*, London: Frank Cass, pp.147–72.

Lehmbruch, Gerhard (1967), *Proporzdemokratie: Politisches System und politische Kultur in der Schweiz und in Österreich*, Tübingen: Mohr.

Lijphart, Arend (1968), 'Typologies of Democratic Systems', *Comparative Political Studies*, **1**, (1), pp.3–44.

Lijphart, Arend (1969), 'Consociational Democracy', *World Politics*, **21**, (2), pp.207–25.

Lijphart, Arend, (1994), *Electoral Systems and Party Systems. A Study of Twenty-Seven Democracies, 1945–1990*, Oxford: Oxford University Press.

Lipset, Seymour Martin and Rokkan, Stein (eds) (1967), *Party Systems and Voter Alignments: Cross-National Perspectives*, New York: The Free Press.

Lorwin, Val (1974), 'Segmented Pluralism. Ideological Cleavages and Political Cohesion in the Smaller European Democracies', *Comparative Politics*, **3**, pp.141–75.

Luther, Kurt Richard (1987), 'The Freiheitliche Partei Österreichs: Protest Party or Governing Party?' in Emil Kirchner (ed.), *Liberal Parties in Western Europe*, Cambridge: Cambridge University Press) pp.213–51.

Luther, Kurt Richard (1989), 'Dimensions of Party System Change: the Case of Austria', *West European Politics*, **12**, (4), pp.3–27.

Luther, Kurt Richard (1991), 'Die Freiheitliche Partei Österreichs', in Herbert Dachs *et al.* (eds), *Handbuch des politischen Systems Österreichs*, Vienna: Manz, pp.247–62.

Luther, Kurt Richard (1992), 'Consociationalism, Parties and the Party System' in Kurt Richard Luther and Wolfgang C. Müller (eds), *Politics in Austria. Still a Case of Consociationalism?*, London: Frank Cass, pp.45–98.

Luther, Kurt Richard (1995), 'An End to the Politics of Isolation? Austria in Light of the 1994 Elections', *German Politics*, **4**, (1), April, pp.122–39.

Luther, Kurt Richard (1996a), 'Friedrich Peter' in Herbert Dachs, Peter Gerlich and Wolfgang C. Müller (eds), *Die Politiker. Karrieren und Wirken bedeutender Repräsentanten der zweiten Republik*, Vienna: Manz, pp.435–45.

Luther, Kurt Richard (1996b), 'Norbert Steger' in Herbert Dachs, Peter Gerlich and Wolfgang C. Müller (eds), *Die Politiker. Karrieren und Wirken bedeutender Repräsentanten der zweiten Republik*, Vienna: Manz, pp.548–57.

Luther, Kurt Richard (1997a), 'Die Freiheitlichen', in Herbert Dachs *et al.* (eds) *Handbuch des politischen Systems Österreichs. Die zweite Republik*, 3rd edn, Vienna: Manz, pp.286–303.

Luther, Kurt Richard (1997b), 'Bund-Länder Beziehungen: Formal- und Realverfassung', in Herbert Dachs *et al.* (eds), *Handbuch des politischen Systems Österreichs. Die zweite Republik*, 3rd edn, Vienna: Manz, pp.907–19.

Luther, Kurt Richard (1998a), 'From Moderate to Polarized Pluralism? The Austrian Party System in Transition' in David Broughton and Mark Donovan (eds), *Changing Party Systems in Western Europe*, London: Pinter.

Luther, Kurt Richard (1998b), 'Must what goes up always come down? Of pillars and arches in Austria's political architecture', in Kurt Richard Luther and Kris Deschouwer (eds), *Political Parties and Party Systems in Consociational Democracy*, London: Routledge, forthcoming.

Luther, Kurt Richard and Deschouwer, Kris (eds) (1998), *Political Parties and Party Systems in Consociational Democracy*, London: Routledge, forthcoming.

Luther, Kurt Richard and Müller, Wolfgang C. (1992a), 'Consociationalism and the Austrian Political System' in Kurt Richard Luther and Wolfgang C. Müller (eds), *Politics in Austria. Still a Case of Consociationalism?*, London: Frank Cass, pp.1–15.

Luther, Kurt Richard and Müller, Wolfgang C. (eds) (1992b), *Politics in Austria. Still a Case of Consociationalism?*, London: Frank Cass; also a special issue of *West European Politics*, **15**, (1).

Mair, Peter (1996), 'Party Systems and Structures of Competition' in Lawrence LeDuc, Richard G. Niemi and Pippa Norris (eds), *Comparing Democracies. Elections and Voting in Global Perspective*, London: Sage, pp.83–106.

Menasse, Robert (1992), *Das Land ohne Eigenschaften. Essay zur österreichischen Identität*, Vienna: Sonderzahl.

Müller, Wolfgang C. (1985), 'Die Rolle der Parteien bei Entstehung und Entwicklung der Sozialpartnerschaft. Eine handlungslogische und empirische Analyse', in Peter Gerlich, Erich Grande and Wolfgang C. Müller, *Sozialpartnerschaft in der Krise. Leistungen und Grenzen des Neokorporatismus in Österreich*, Vienna: Böhlau, pp.135–224.

Müller, Wolfgang C. (1991), 'Das Parteiensystem' in Herbert Dachs *et al.* (eds), *Handbuch des politischen Systems Österreichs*, Vienna: Manz, pp.181–96.

Müller, Wolfgang C. (1992), 'Austria (1945–1990)', in Richard Katz and Peter

Mair (eds) (1992), *Party Organization. A Date Handbook on Party Organizations in Western Democracies, 1960–90*, London: Sage, pp.21–120.

Müller, Wolfgang C. (1992a), 'Austrian Governmental Institutions: Do They Matter?' in Kurt Richard Luther and Wolfgang C. Müller (eds), *Politics in Austria. Still a Case of Consociationalism?*, London: Frank Cass, pp.99–131.

Müller, Wolfgang C. (1993), 'After the "Golden Age": Research into Austrian Political Parties Since the 1980s', *European Journal of Political Research*, **23** pp.439–63.

Müller, Wolfgang C. (1996), 'Wahlsystem und Parteiensystem in Österreich 1945–1995' in Fritz Plasser, Peter Ulram and Günther Ogris (eds), *Wahlkampf und Wahlentscheidung. Analysen zur Nationalratswahl 1995*, Vienna: Signum, pp.235–52.

Müller, Wolfgang C. (1997), 'Die Österreichische Volkspartei' in Herbert Dachs *et al.* (eds), *Handbuch des politischen Systems Österreichs. Die zweite Republik*, 3rd edn, Vienna: Manz, pp.265–85.

Müller, Wolfgang C., Philipp, Wilfried, Jenny, Marcelo (1995), 'Ideologie und Strategie der österreichischen Parteien: Eine Analyse der Wahlprogramme 1949–1994' in Wolfgang C. Müller, Fritz Plasser and Peter Ulram (eds), *Wählerverhalten und Parteienwettbewerb. Analysen zur Nationalratswahl 1994*, Vienna: Signum, pp.119–66.

Müller, Wolfgang C. and Scheucher, C. (1995), 'Das verstärkte Vorzugsstimmensystem: Durchbruch zur Persönlichkeitswahl? Bilanz der Nationalratswahl 1994' in Wolfgang C. Müller, Fritz Plasser and Peter Ulram (eds) *Wählerverhalten und Parteienwettbewerb. Analysen zur Nationalratswahl 1994*, Vienna: Signum, pp.323–40.

Müller, Wolfgang C., Plasser, Fritz and Ulram, Peter (eds) (1995), *Wählerverhalten und Parteienwettbewerb. Analysen zur Nationalratswahl 1994*, Vienna: Signum.

Neumann, Friedrich (ed.) (1956), *Modern Political Parties. Approaches to Comparative Analysis*, Chicago: University of Chicago Press.

Nick, Rainer (1995), 'Die Wahl vor der Wahl: Kandidatennominierung und Vorwahlen', in Wolfgang C. Müller, Fritz Plasser and Peter Ulram (eds), *Wählerverhalten und Parteienwettbewerb. Analysen zur Nationalratswahl 1994*, Vienna: Signum, pp.67–117.

Pedersen, M. (1979), 'The Dynamics of European Party Systems: Changing Patterns of Electoral Volatility', *European Journal of Political Research*, **7**, pp.1–26.

Pelinka, Anton and Welan, Manfred (1971), *Demokratie und Verfassung in Österreich*, Vienna: Europa Verlag.

Plasser, Fritz and Seeber, Gilg (1995), 'In Search of a Model: Multivariate Analysen der Exit Polls 1986–1994' in Wolfgang C. Müller, Fritz Plasser and Peter Ulram (eds), *Wählerverhalten und Parteienwettbewerb. Analysen zur Nationalratswahl 1994*, Vienna: Signum.

Plasser, Fritz and Ulram, Peter (1982), *Unbehagen im Parteienstaat. Jugend und Politik im Parteienstaat*, Vienna: Böhlau.

Plasser, Fritz and Ulram, Peter (1988), 'Großparteien in der Defensive. Die österreichische Parteien- und Wählerlandschaft nach der Nationalratswahl 1986' in Anton Pelinka and Fritz Plasser (eds), *Das österreichische Parteiensystem*, Vienna: Böhlau, pp.79–102.

Plasser, Fritz and Ulram Peter (eds) (1991), *Staatsbürger oder Untertanen? Politische Kultur Deutschlands, Österreichs und der Schweiz im Vergleich*, (Frankfurt-am-main: Peter Lang).

Plasser, Fritz, Ulram, Peter and Grausgruber, Alfred (1992), 'The Decline of *Lager* Mentality and the New Model of Electoral Competition in Austria' in Kurt Richard Luther and Wolfgang C. Müller (eds) (1992), *Politics in Austria. Still a Case of Consociationalism?*, London: Frank Cass, pp.16–44.

Plasser, F., Ulram, P., Neuwirth, E. and Sommer, F. (1995), *Analyse der Nationalratswahl vom 17. Dezember 1995*, Vienna: Zentrum für Angewandte Politikforschung.

Plasser, F., Ulram, P. and Ogris, G. (eds) (1996), *Wahlkampf und Wahlentscheidung. Analysen zur Nationalratswahl 1995*, Vienna: Signum.

Plasser, F. Ulram, P. and Seeber, G. (1996), '(Dis-)Kontinuitäten und neue Spannungslinien im Wahlverhalten: Trendanalysen 1986–1995' in Fritz Plasser, Peter Ulram and Günther Ogris, (eds), *Wahlkampf und Wahlentscheidung. Analysen zur Nationalratswahl 1995*, Vienna: Signum, pp.155–209.

Powell, G.B. (1970), *Social Fragmentation and Political Hostility: An Austrian Case Study*, Stanford: Stanford University Press.

Rae, D. (1967), *The Political Consequences of Electoral Laws*, New Haven: Yale University Press.

Riedlsperger, Max (1978), *The Lingering Shadow of Nazism: The Austrian Independent Party Movement Since 1945*, Boulder, Col.: East European Quarterly.

Rudzio, W. (1971), 'Entscheidungszentrum Koalitionsausschuß – Zur Realverfassung Österreichs unter der großen Koalition', *Politische Vierteljahresschrift*, **12**, pp.87–118.

Sartori, G. (1976), *Parties and Party Systems. A Framework for Analysis*, Vol. I, Cambridge: Cambridge University Press.

Schaden, Michael (1983), 'Parteien und Rechtsordnung' in Peter Gerlich and Wolfgang C. Müller (eds), *Zwischen Koalition und Konkurrenz. Österreichs Parteien seit 1945*, Vienna: Braumüller, pp.225–47.

Secher, Herbert (1960), 'Representative Democracy or Chamber State?: The Ambiguous Role of Interest Groups in Austrian Politics', *Western Political Quarterly*, **13**, pp.890–909.

Sickinger, Hubert (1995), *Politikfinanzierung in Österreich – ein Handbuch*, Vienna: Thaur.

Simon, Walter B. (1957), *The Political Parties of Austria*, Columbia University PhD thesis.

Smith, Gordon B. (1989), 'A System Perspective on Party System Change', *Journal of Theoretical Politics*, **1**, (3), pp.349–63.

Stäuber, R. (1974), *Der Verband der Unabhängigen (VdU) und die Freiheitliche Partei Österreichs (FPOe) Eine Untersuchung über die Probleme des Deutschnationalismus als Einigungsfaktor einer politischen Partei in Österreich seit 1945*, St Gallen: Kolb.

Stiefbold, R. (1975), 'Elites and Elections in a Fragmented Political System' in Rudolf Wildenmann (ed.), *Sozialwissenschaftliches Jahrbuch für Politik*, Munich and Vienna: Günther Olzog Verlag, pp.119–227.

Ucakar, Karl (1997), 'Die Sozialdemokratische Partei Österreichs' in Herbert Dachs *et al.* (eds), *Handbuch des politischen Systems Österreichs. Die zweite Republik*, 3rd edn, Vienna: Manz, pp.248–64.

Ulram, P. (1990), *Hegemonie und Erosion: Politische Kultur und politischer Wandel in Österreich*, Vienna: Böhlau.

Ulram, P. (1997), 'Politische kultur der Bevölkerung' in Herbert Dachs *et al.*, *Handbuch des politischen Systems Österreichs. Die zweite Republik*, 3rd edn, Vienna: Manz, pp.514–25.

Wandruszka, Adam (1954), 'Österreichs politische Struktur: Die Entwicklung der Parteien und politischen Bewegungen' in H. Benedikt (ed.), *Geschichte der Republik Österreich*, Vienna: Verlag für Gesellschaft und Politik, pp.289–485.

PART III
EXTERNAL RELATIONS

8 Austrian Foreign Policy from the State Treaty to European Union Membership (1955–95)

Helmut Kramer

Introduction

The period I have been asked to cover in this analysis of the major characteristics of and challenges to Austria's post-war foreign policy embraces over four decades. It starts with the *annus mirabilis* of 1955, when Austria regained its full independence and extends to include January 1995, the month in which, along with Sweden and Finland, Austria joined the European Union.[1] During these 40 years, Austria worked its way up from a country grappling with the aftermath of war, with economic scarcity, social unrest and deep political cleavages, to a well accepted position in the club of the economically most advanced and politically most stable countries in Europe. Indeed, economic and financial surveys of per capita income, economic competitiveness and quality of life nowadays rank Austria in the top ten or 15 countries in the world.

It could be argued with some justification that the Austrian government's foreign policy contributed significantly to this 'success story'. With its active outlook, its flexibility and its initiatives in many fields of international politics, it can be regarded as one of the main showpieces of Austria's rise in the international system. This positive evaluation of the Second Republic's foreign policy is widely shared by the Austrian people. Opinion polls consistently show the 1955 State Treaty and the policy of active neutrality to be important factors underpinning the strong popular allegiance to the principles of an Austrian identity and to Austria as an independent small state (see Chapter 5 by Bruckmüller in this volume). However, such assessments require qualification. The 1980s witnessed significant changes in the international environment for Europe's neutral small states. The ensuing 'identity crisis' in Austria's foreign policy and especially in its security policy was reflected in a rather emotive domestic debate on their future direction. Moreover, this debate has continued into the 1990s, as has the absence of a domestic foreign policy consensus and a clear policy direction.

In order to achieve a clearer understanding of Austria's foreign policy record from 1955 to 1995, this chapter will adopt the main hypothesis of a recent essay by Gerhard Botz and Alfred Müller on Austria's development after 1945. The essence of their argument is that the growth and reinforcement of national political identity is closely related to the extent to which the population of a given nation perceives the existence of some sort of distinctiveness, or 'difference', by means of which the contemporary situation of their nation is distinguished from its historical profile. In short, their argument is predicated on the notion of the political importance of 'historical memory' (Holzer, 1995, p.120). The first passage of the essay by Botz and Müller reads as follows:

> The Austria of the years since 1945 – and this holds true without qualification until around 1990 – is characterised much more than in any other historical period by two persistent traits: first, by a form of identity which succeeded in establishing itself independently and second, by an explicit wish for a distinctive difference. (Botz/Müller, 1995, p.7).

According to this perspective, the international and foreign policy status of the Second Austrian Republic stands in marked contrast to the experiences of the Austrian population in the period between the First and Second World Wars. The Austrian First Republic of the 1920s was, to quote a widely used phrase, 'a state nobody wanted', in which political and economic sovereignty was restricted to a minimum by massive pressure and intervention on the part of foreign powers (Kramer, 1996a). Thus Bruno Kreisky writes in his memoirs that, in his youth, Austria and Vienna had been reduced to the status of a 'passive object of world history' (Kreisky, 1986, p.20). This was a period in which the only foreign policy which the government in Vienna actively pursued was the *Anschluß* with Germany. After the destruction of democracy in 1933–34 by its authoritarian corporatist regime, in 1938 Austria was finally wiped out as an independent state by German occupation.

Austria's powerless and essentially reactive foreign policy of the 1920s and the 1930s was, to a significant extent, the consequence of a very difficult international environment, referred to in the words of a contemporary foreign policy notable as 'a situation in which the world worked against Austria' (Hornbostel, cited in Kramer, 1996a, p.15). In sharp contrast, post-1945 Austria managed to develop and maintain a very different and much more successful foreign policy strategy and style. Based on a very *active foreign policy* interpretation of neutrality and using, with great skill, the full range of available *small state strategies*, Austria's foreign policy-makers succeeded in actively probing the international environment and utilizing it for the successful realization of national foreign policy goals. For post-Second World War Austria, this meant attaining and safeguarding national independence, satisfying basic social and economic needs and strengthening political cohesion and national identity. Such an active foreign policy required political flexibility, being open to changes and new constellations in the international system, as well as 'competence based on solid homework on international issues' (Andrén, 1984, p.53). It represented a clear break (or *difference*) vis-à-vis Austria's tragic foreign policy experiences in the past and, as was mentioned above, it worked very successfully in the period from after the war until the beginning of the 1980s. From the end of the 1970s, however, as the international constellation changed and closed some of the former windows of opportunity for neutral small states in Europe and in global politics, Austria's politics of neutrality and its small state foreign policy perspective faced growing difficulties.

I will argue in this chapter that the concept of 'difference' can also be fruitfully applied to an analysis of Austrian foreign policy since 1955, and particularly since the mid-1980s. Put simply, the success story of Austrian foreign policy in the period from 1955 (or 1945) until the 1980s can be regarded as being to a significant extent both causally and contextually related to the growing 'identity crisis' in Austria's foreign policy since the mid-1980s. From 1955 until the late 1970s Austria had been successful in its main foreign policy goals. It had achieved a relatively high level of international acceptance, had become a member of the club of the economically most prosperous states of the world and had witnessed a strengthening of political cohesion between its political subcultures, *inter alia* through the development of an overarching Austrian national identity. As a consequence, Austria's foreign policy lost much of its purposiveness and its mission-mindedness, as well as the self-confidence and qualities of 'transforming leadership' (as per James McGregor Burns) characteristic of this period of active neutrality foreign policy. The sense of 'difference' which this period had generated was, as we have outlined above, one which contrasted Austria's post-war success favourably with its inter-war failure. From the mid-1980s, however, a new form of 'difference' can be hypothesized – namely, one linked to a distinct break in foreign policy orientation and philosophy. It could be considered to constitute a process – and a crisis – of 'normalization' or 'Westeuropeanization'.[2]

From the State Treaty to the 'Kreisky Era'

There are many examples of an active foreign policy and of skilful negotiating tactics on the part of the Austrian government in the difficult political constellation after the end of the Second World War. By reacting flexibly to the negotiating positions (and the disagreement amongst) the Allied powers in Austria, the government in Vienna managed gradually to restrict the extensive control which the Western powers and the Soviet Union exerted as occupying authorities. For example, Austria succeeded in its efforts to become a beneficiary of the US Marshall Plan, making it the only country under partial Soviet occupation that received European Recovery Programme funds. Indeed, Austria received the highest per capita allocation of all the countries benefiting from the Marshall Plan. But the most telling, and politically most important, examples of an active foreign policy – for which a broad domestic political consensus on the basic goals and the general orientation of domestic and foreign policy was a necessary prerequisite – can be found in the period starting with the attainment of full sovereignty by the Austrian State Treaty in May 1955.

The Moscow Memorandum of April 1955 – the main political breakthrough leading to the final political *rapprochement* between the Soviet Union and the Western powers on the question of Austria's independence – specified that, after signing the State Treaty, Austria would have to make a declaration that would commit it 'to permanent neutrality as practised by Switzerland' (Stourzh, 1975, p.164). Austria's history and its geopolitical position between NATO and the Warsaw Pact differed, of course, from those of its western neighbour. Austrian foreign policy-makers decided from the very beginning that they would follow a policy of neutrality that 'would take more risks and be more dynamic than Swiss policy' (Bonjour, 1980, p.80). The goal of the Austrian government was 'to do everything possible to make its contribution to international understanding through active co-operation in organisations encompassing the whole world' (Declaration of Foreign Minister Figl at the signing of the State Treaty, quoted by Csaky, 1980, p.409). A profile of 'active neutrality' began to develop. In contrast to Switzerland, Austria became a member of the United Nations in December 1955. In March 1956 it was also admitted to the Council of Europe and became a signatory of its European Convention on Human Rights.

According to the Finnish political scientist Harto Hakovirta in his study on the European neutrals in the East–West conflict, 'Though East–West crises are tests of neutrality, their consequences for neutral states are not always negative; crises also provide the opportunity to demonstrate what neutrality means in practice' (Hakovirta, 1988, p.144). The uprising in late autumn 1956 of the Hungarian population against the communist regime and its bloody repression by the Soviet army were to become the first major test of Austrian neutrality in which a very active foreign policy orientation can be attributed to the government in Vienna and to the Austrian people. As pointed out in a case study on Austria's foreign policy stance in 1956, Austria's behaviour during the Hungarian uprising was 'courageous' and even 'provocative' towards the Soviet Union, especially when compared to the restraint of the West, which was at the time tied up with the Suez Crisis (Eger, 1981, p.34). The firm and clear position adopted by the Austrian government and the decisive measures taken to secure its borders and to safeguard neutrality were fully supported by the Austrian population. It should be stressed that Austria's very positive international image in the West and in the international community at large, on account of what the United Nations called Austria's 'exemplary achievement' in absorbing and caring for the Hungarian refugees (Eger, 1981, pp.68f), was above all due to the spontaneous outpouring of help on the part of the Austrian people. This 'foreign policy from below' clearly shaped and reinforced the government's decision to speak out without reservation against any form of ideological neutrality and 'neutralism' in this conflict.

One could enumerate many other examples of Austria's active foreign policy strategy, carefully examining and probing the international constellation for 'windows of opportunity', especially in its relations with the Soviet Union and its Eastern European satellites. The foreign policy of Chancellor Julius Raab (1953–61) and Bruno Kreisky (foreign minister 1959–66, chancellor 1970–83) towards Austria's eastern neighbours was based on 'attaining maximum confidence in the West – i.e. America – and a minimum of distrust in the East – i.e. in Russia' (Kreisky in *Basta*, October 1984, p.40). Once the chill in Austro-Soviet relations caused by Austria's reaction to the Hungarian uprising in late 1956 had faded away, a new degree of acceptance of Austria's neutrality policy developed in Moscow. As in the case of Soviet policy towards Finland after 1956–57, Soviet relations with neutral Austria were shaped to fit Khrushchev's pursuit of a new foreign policy strategy of easing tensions in Europe and the world by means of a stated commitment to 'peaceful coexistence' between different social systems, as well as between Superpowers and small states. Austria's neutrality came to be seen by the Soviet Union as an important factor enhancing stability and a positive element of peaceful development in Central Europe. Of particular importance for Austria's role as a 'window to the Eastern world' (Josef Klaus, Austrian chancellor 1964–70) was its *Besuchsdiplomatie* ('diplomacy of state visits') in Eastern Europe during the 1960s. Kreisky was only the second Western foreign minister to visit Poland (March 1960), and the first in Romania (July 1963), Hungary (October 1964) and Bulgaria (July 1965). Given Austria's long historical association with this region, it was easier for Austrian foreign policy actors than for most of their Western colleagues to understand the specific and differing positions of their eastern and south-eastern European neighbours. Moreover, they were acutely aware that, in its reconstruction and the process of its transformation into a developed Western economy, Austria had benefited greatly from many positive external and internal factors which were tragically lacking in the post-war development of neighbouring countries such as Czechoslovakia and Hungary.

Another important example of how Austrian policy sought to help transform relations to its Eastern European neighbours in the direction of strengthening détente in Europe is Austria's role in the CSCE process. Together with other European neutrals (notably Finland), Austria contributed decisively to the preparation and passage of the Final Act of the Conference for Security and Cooperation in Europe in Helsinki in August 1975. The government in Vienna concentrated its efforts on persuading the United States and other Western countries, which at first displayed little interest in the political project of a CSCE process initially proposed by the Soviet Union, to take an active part in it. 'By actively using their independence from existing blocs and groups in setting up communication between opposing interests and in supporting the search for solutions' (Zemanek, 1984, p.20) the European neutrals and non-aligned states (N+N Group) made themselves available for technical and political 'good offices' to ensure the successful continuation of the CSCE process through, for example, the CSCE follow-up conferences in Belgrade (1977–78), Madrid (1980–83) and Vienna (1986–89) (Birnbaum, 1987; Lehne, 1991).

The CSCE process and Austria's role in it is a very vivid and significant example of the second general characteristic of Austria's foreign policy in the period from 1955 to 1980, namely a *small state* foreign policy perspective and style. One can distinguish two main levels at which small state foreign policy strategies operate and where small states are inclined to utilize particular forms of behaviour.[3] The first level is in the field of bilateral relations. Here, small states try to counter their relative weakness in power and foreign policy resources by diversifying the focus and the direction of their foreign policy to as many dimensions and sectors as considered necessary and feasible. Besides the need to have as broad and extensive a diplomatic profile as possible (and a diversified trade relations regime to parcel out its economic dependence), small states invest in international domains and foreign policy questions which are important to them and less important to both the bigger and the very big actors in the international system. In his seminal work on 'small state strategies against dependence', Daniel Frei defined this as recognizing the 'difference in the distribution of attention' in the international system and gambling with it (Frei, 1977, p.213). Opportunities for selective optimization of the small state's international functions and capabilities are sought and niches for 'free-rider' strategies exploited. This strategy of 'free-riding' brings us to a very difficult borderline between, on the one hand, positive strategies through which small states try to outwit bigger or less legitimate foreign policy players – what the Swiss political scientist, Alois Riklin, defines as 'the legitimate clever trick (*Schlaumeierei*) of the small state vis-à-vis great powers' (Riklin, 1991–92, p.2) – and, on the other hand, to rather problematic and 'negative' foreign policy behaviour, such as attempts to circumvent and violate existing rules and norms of international behaviour as in the case of international sanctions or illegal arms deliveries to countries in war.[4]

But the level at which the inventory of small states' foreign policy strategies is most visible and important relates to pursuit of multilateral foreign policy, as manifested above all in active involvement in international organizations such as the United Nations (UN) and other multilateral and supranational forms of political and economic association. The focus on multilateral foreign policy activities can be seen as a form of rational choice behaviour and wise foreign policy investment, since participation in the UN or in other international associations (for example, transnational associations such as the Socialist International or the International Democratic Union) is largely based on the equality of all actors, regardless of size. These multilateral activities of small states and their 'good services' in conference diplomacy and conflict mediation can also be seen as sometimes innovative contributions directed at strengthening and transforming the international system into a more democratic and a more stable order – one more suitable for the realization of the small states' foreign policy needs and interests. Of special importance for small neutral states are multilateral policies aimed at strengthening détente, as well as international confidence-building measures. The active participation of the small European neutral countries in the CSCE and their good record in helping to bring about and maintain the CSCE process in the 1970s and 1980s led to a positive evaluation of the political utility of their neutral status and to its wider international acceptance. Thus the 'right of being neutral' was incorporated into the first principle of the 1975 Final Act of the CSCE.

Successful 'specialisation in *cooperation* on the European scene' (Agh, 1988, p.233) and the active role Vienna played as an international meeting place[5] made the status of the neutral small state internationally more attractive. Moreover, Austria played an active and quite prominent role in the UN, especially in the 1970s: Kurt Waldheim was elected Secretary-General in

1971 and reappointed for another term in 1976; Austrian representatives served as chairpersons of important UN commissions; and Vienna was developed into the third seat of UN headquarters. This elevated Austria's international reputation and helped mobilize international support for Austria's own foreign policy interests. Austria's activity in, and support for, the UN could even be regarded as an investment designed to safeguard and strengthen national security. This is certainly the line Bruno Kreisky took in a 1979 interview when he argued that 'International Organisations based in Austria are important from a security and political point of view. They are as valuable as big stores of arms which might never be used' (*Financial Times*, 21 August 1979).

In an essay on the 'constants' and the 'variables' in Austria's neutrality policy, Karl Zemanek, the current doyen of Austria's international law, writes:

> Austria's intensive and special involvement in the multilateral processes in the contemporary international system is the nearest example of a self-chosen neutral 'role' that one can find.

And he traces the multilateral emphasis of Austrian neutrality policy and the differences between Austria and Switzerland in this domain back to the historical trauma of the loss of Austrian independence in 1938:

> When Austria regained her independence and adopted neutrality in 1955, she faced a twofold task: re-establishing herself on the international scene from which she had been absent for 17 years; and seeking recognition for her newly-acquired status. Not recognition in a formal legal sense, but recognition in a political sense, as a useful and indispensable member of the international community in her new existence. (Zemanek, 1984, p.20).

From this perspective, Austria's foreign policy record in the period from 1955 to the beginning of the 1980s, when the favourable international context for an active neutrality policy began to deteriorate and the 'windows of opportunity' started to close, can be seen as a process whereby a state originally in a situation of high external dependence and characterized by an uncertain international status transformed its position into that of an actor increasingly active in, and accepted by, the international community.

This might be an appropriate point at which to introduce the impact of personality and of leadership upon the development and implementation of Austrian foreign policy. The contributions of Austria's leading foreign policy personalities (especially Raab and Kreisky) seem to be a suitable example for James McGregor Burns' concept of 'transforming leadership', in which political activity, political influence and political aspiration is oriented towards changing and transforming politics and society to a higher level and thus 'producing social change that will satisfy followers' authentic needs' (Burns, 1978, p.4; see also Zemanek, 1984, p.23). Emphasizing the role of leadership and political personalities does not imply ignoring the importance of 'constants' such as political context and political structures, nor analysing political processes in elitist terms by exaggerating the role of 'great men' as 'creators of history' (Carlyle). Transforming leadership, as defined by Burns, is enhanced and made possible by 'democratic politics' – that is, by a creative and active two-way relationship between leaders and 'followers'.

> The transforming leader recognises and exploits an existing need or demand of a potential follower. But, beyond that, the transforming leader looks for potential motives in followers, seeks to satisfy higher needs, and engages the full person of the follower. The result of transforming leadership is a relationship of mutual stimulation and elevation that converts followers into leaders and may convert leaders into moral agents. (Burns, 1978, p.4).

An examination of Austria's active foreign policy reveals a number of examples of this complex relationship of mutual support between the Austrian government and the Austrian population. In the difficult days of the Hungarian crisis in 1956, for example, the 'followers' acted as a 'critical mass' influencing, activating and controlling the 'leaders' and a similar case can be made for the events of August 1968, when Warsaw Pact troops invaded Czechoslovakia. Moreover, political personalities like Raab and Kreisky 'gave Austria a political profile far beyond her potential' (Zemanek, 1984, p.23) and, in the process, opened up the Austrian people to a world in which their country's political role and status gained a very positive acceptance that contrasted very favourably with its position in the first half of this century.[6] Henry Kissinger's opinion of Bruno Kreisky, the main architect of this transformation, is that he was 'a shrewd and perceptive chancellor, who had parlayed his country's formal neutrality into a position of influence beyond its strength' (Kissinger, 1979, p.1204).

Austrian Foreign Policy and the 'Crisis of Normalization' in the 1980s

The 'Kreisky era' of Austrian foreign policy formally came to an end as a consequence of the parliamentary election of 1983, at which Kreisky's SPÖ (*Sozialistische Partei Österreichs)* lost its absolute majority. However, changes had already become visible during the later years of Kreisky's chancellorship. Austrian foreign policy-makers were confronted with a much more difficult international environment. Kreisky's distinctive and active foreign policy approach to matters such as the Arab–Israeli conflict and North–South relations had, in large measure, been responsible for a significant deterioration in Austria's relations with the United States, and Austria had also adopted a more defensive and rigid policy towards developments in Eastern Europe, as manifested in Kreisky's handling of the Polish crisis in 1980. The new crisis in the relationship between the Soviet Union and the United States under President Reagan had reduced the European neutrals' room for manoeuvre, as well as their opportunities to offer political 'good offices' (as in the CSCE process) and to support new initiatives in multilateral foreign policy and in the UN. In addition to the shrinking importance of the Third World, which had been a main foreign policy focus in the Kreisky years, Austria's 'integration environment' (Väyrynen, 1987, p.37) had been considerably rearranged. The increased economic and political momentum of the European Community, particularly the Single Market project scheduled for completion in the early 1990s, caused Austria and the other European neutrals to reconsider their relationship to the EC (Luif, 1988; Schultz, 1992).

The new foreign minister of the coalition government formed at the end of 1986 between the SPÖ and the ÖVP (*Österreichische Volkspartei*) was Alois Mock, party leader of the ÖVP since 1979. He made a clear conceptual and programmatic break with Kreisky's globally-oriented foreign policy and provided a new definition of Austria's foreign policy guidelines. They included a 'realistic neutrality policy' based on 'Austria's real interests' and 'natural self-restraint'. The central aim was now 'to assert a regional rather than a global line of vision' (Luchak, 1987, p.229), with the emphasis on Europe (the European Community) and on Austria's neighbours. Mock's foreign policy direction had already been partly initiated and prepared by Kreisky's successors in the SPÖ – namely, by Chancellor Sinowatz (replaced in mid-1986 by Vranitzky) and by SPÖ foreign ministers Gratz and Jankowitsch. Increasing restraint was shown in statements and initiatives on international issues. Thus it was asserted that Austria should be careful not to expose itself 'to the charge of being a small state that wants to be, so to speak, the schoolmaster of the world and give out grades in morality' (Gratz, 1984, p.34). This led to a noticeable weakening of Austria's political profile in the Middle East and in multilateral foreign policy, the only exception being the CSCE, where Austria hosted the CSCE follow-up conference in Vienna (1986–89) and continued to be active in the context of the N+N group.[7]

This new conception of Austrian foreign policy, with its focus on a 'realistic' foreign and neutrality policy and an emphasis on a narrower European sphere, constituted a distinctive change. The optimistic and activistic approach to international affairs and to Austria's foreign policy opportunities which had characterized the period from 1955 to the beginning of the 1980s had been replaced by a more pessimistic perspective vis-à-vis the international system and Austria's role within it. In one of his first interviews as foreign minister, Alois Mock declared, echoing the basic tenets of the 'realists' in international relations theory, that 'international relations are basically a jungle, a sort of wilderness' (Mock, 1987, p.5).[8]

Alterations in the structure of Austria's international environment constitute a significant explanation of this break in Austria's foreign policy attitude and philosophy. Relevant changes include strategic changes and changes in the balance of power, but also the trend towards a 'multicentric' world with many new foreign policy actors and new levels of policy-making in the international system (Rosenau, 1990; Kramer and Quendler, 1995). Together, such developments exacerbated a growing 'identity crisis' in Austria's foreign policy, especially since the significant foreign policy reorientation they demanded became the subject of continuous haggling and infighting between the two government parties and of a growing organizational and conceptual crisis in the Austrian foreign ministry.[9]

The change in Austrian foreign policy from the mid-1980s is in part also attributable to problems within the country's domestic arena. A crucial area concerned economic developments. By international standards, the Austrian economy had been very successful during the 1960s and 1970s. From 1983, however, Austria was faced with recession, rising unemployment and a structural crisis in the nationalized industries. 'Becoming a member of the European Community as soon as possible is seen (by Vienna) as a kind of panacea for all the economic and political misfortunes of the country' was the commentary of the *Neue Zürcher Zeitung* on the hopes of the SPÖ–ÖVP government and the Austrian business community that closer contacts would bring about the structural reform and economic modernization that could not be accomplished without that kind of *deus ex machina* (*Neue Zürcher Zeitung*, 31 August 1988; Schneider, 1990, p.104).

In addition to these economic factors, Austria was suffering a serious image and identity crisis. Throughout the Second Republic, Austria had been able to count on the advantage of a very good international image. Now, however, a series of scandals resulted in Austria acquiring 'the worst image abroad that any European state has been confronted with in recent times' (*Die Presse*, 11 February 1988). Examples of such scandals include revelations concerning illegal arms exports;[10] the 1985 'wine scandal', which related to the widespread illegal artificial sweetening of Austrian wine and threatened both the image and profitability of the country's wine producers; and the 1985 'Reder affair', when an international outcry arose over the handshake with which the Freedom Party's federal defence minister,

Friedhelm Frischenschlager, welcomed back to Austria a former SS officer who had been released from imprisonment in Italy for crimes committed during the Second World War.

In terms of its negative impact on Austria's international image (and arguably also its significance for Austria's national identity), the most important scandal was, however, the 'Waldheim affair'. Although Waldheim was elected Austrian president in June 1986 probably despite, rather than because, of the heated international debate over his wartime record (Luther, 1987), that did not mark an end to the controversy regarding his past activities and his flawed recollection thereof. Indeed, the 'Waldheim affair' became a serious burden for Austria's foreign policy and international prestige. After Waldheim took office, the number of official state visits to Vienna dropped dramatically, and meetings with Western foreign ministers had to be moved to provincial capitals 'because that way the foreign guests could avoid paying the obligatory visit to the president' (*Die Presse*, 6 July 1988). Austria also had to endure the ultimate ignominy of its president being placed on the United States' 'watch list' and thus being refused entry to the United States.

Although the 'Waldheim affair' was clearly based upon exceptional circumstances, in general, the emotional atmosphere and the mid-1980s 'identity crisis' of Austria's foreign policy can be interpreted as a 'crisis of normalization'. First, the new structural conditions in Austria's international environment had reduced the usefulness of the previously successful small state strategy 'mix' of pursuing national foreign policy interests whilst contributing (in cooperation with other European neutrals and non-aligned countries) 'good offices' in multilateral foreign policy. Second, the very success of Austria's foreign policy meant that the country was in the process of losing its former foreign policy 'drive'. The latter had assumed the status of a specific trademark of the post-war political system and, as such, helped underscore the difference between the Second Republic and Austria's past. The crisis of Austria's international image and aspects of the troubled political–psychological identity of Austrians and of their political and economic class became mixed with the issue of EC membership. A rather agitated and emotional public debate ensued regarding European union membership. At the level of Austria's foreign policy actors involved in the negotiations for European Union membership, Austria's changed foreign policy outlook became particularly apparent in very deferential attitudes and statements that reflected their lack of self-confidence and direction.[11]

Austrian Foreign Policy after 1989

The dramatic European developments which started in 1989 (the collapse of the communist regimes in Eastern Europe, the reunification of Germany and the disintegration of the Soviet Union into 15 successor states in late 1991) brought a further fundamental change in Austria's international environment. The *de facto* end of the East–West-conflict, in the context of which Austrian neutrality had been developed, led to the adoption of a looser and more flexible interpretation of Austria's neutrality status. Austria, which was a non-permanent member of the UN Security Council in 1991 and 1992, took part not only in the economic sanctions against Iraq but also allowed the US-led alliance against Saddam Hussein to transport war materials across the country. Giving precedence to UN law over the law of neutrality signified a substantial change in Austria's neutrality policy from an 'integral' to an 'differential' concept of neutrality (Rotter, 1991; Zemanek, 1991). For Austria which, because of its geographic position, had until 1989 'been pressed to the edge of the West, the reform process in the East offered an historic opportunity to move into the centre of Europe' (Thomas Klestil in 1989, who succeeded Waldheim as Austrian president in July 1992).

In Europe's post-1989 'new political architecture' the EC (from November 1993 the European Union or EU) had become the most important economic and political centre of gravity between the Atlantic and the Urals. At the beginning of the 1990s the most promising candidates for the EC's strategy to enlarge the Community were without doubt Norway and the prosperous neutral countries of Austria, Finland, Sweden and Switzerland. In view of their close economic interaction with EC countries and their expected net contributions to the EC budget, no insurmountable problems were envisaged in the membership negotiation. But before the dramatic changes in the political landscape of Europe during the autumn and winter of 1989, Finland, Sweden and Switzerland perceived neutrality and EC membership as incompatible and favoured a strategy of deepening the multilateral links between the European Free Trade Area (EFTA) and the EC. The reactions of the governments in Stockholm, Helsinki and Bern were therefore rather reserved when the Austrian government dashed ahead on the issue of EC membership in the summer of 1989. Yet once the fundamental changes to the European international environment had commenced and, in addition, Finland and Sweden had begun to face serious economic problems, the two Scandinavian countries and Switzerland reconsidered their position and applied for EC membership in the summer of 1991 and spring of 1992.[12]

The membership negotiations between Brussels and Austria, Finland and Sweden started in February 1993, with Norway joining the negotiations in

April that year. By the end of 1993 agreement was reached between Austria and the EU on most of the important questions, and a compromise formula was devised regarding the issue of neutrality. A three-day marathon negotiation in Brussels in early March 1994 led to agreement between the negotiating parties concerning the regulation of issues of special sensitivity for Austria, such as agriculture, the question of transit traffic and of second homes. Since membership of the EU affects fundamental principles of the Austrian Constitution, the law on accession passed by parliament in May 1994 had to be submitted to a national referendum, which was held on 12 June 1994. Contrary to the fears expressed in some quarters, the 'masses' followed their 'leaders'; some 82.4 per cent of the Austrian electorate participated and, of these, a majority of 66.6 per cent voted in favour of joining the EU. Similar referenda in Finland and Sweden in the autumn of 1994 resulted in majorities of 56.9 per cent and 52.3 per cent respectively, while in Norway a majority of 52.5 per cent rejected EU membership. After ratification of their treaty of accession by the national parliaments of the 12 EU member states, Austria, together with Finland and Sweden, became a member of the EU on 1 January 1995.

These developments might have been expected to cause the government's foreign policy record during 1994 and 1995 to be evaluated by the Austrian media and public as quite successful and positive. The coalition government could argue that its EC policy, which placed Austria at the forefront of the group of EFTA countries racing towards Brussels, had been based on a correct and quite sensible reading of the far-reaching changes in the international environment initiated by the historic events of 1989. Furthermore, it could point to the fact that the EU referendum of 12 June 1994 showed very strong support on the part of the Austrian population for the outcome of the negotiations with the EU, as well as for the general economic and political aspirations of the enlarged EU's goals. In addition, Austria's position vis-à-vis the reforming countries of Eastern Europe – which expect substantial Austrian support for their efforts to join the EU – could and should enable Austria to play an important role with the EU. The trade relations with, and direct investment of, Austrian businesses in Eastern Europe, especially in Hungary, the Czech and Slovak Republics and Slovenia increased considerably in the early 1990s. In comparison with other OECD countries, Austria's financial aid and technical assistance to the reforming countries was substantial. Austria's share of overall OECD wealth is about 1 per cent, but from 1990–92, its share of OECD bilateral credits to transition countries amounted to 4.7 per cent and in 1993 constituted the highest aid-to-GDP ratio of any OECD country – namely, 0.21 per cent.

An examination of the political atmosphere and foreign policy debate after June 1994 produces a very different picture, however. The positive attitude of the Austrian public towards the EU and EU membership has been dwindling and support in opinion polls declined to an historic low.[13] There is continuous infighting between the SPÖ and ÖVP over foreign policy positions, especially in security policy and on the role of neutrality in the evolving European security system. Fierce disputes persist also between the social democratic chancellor, the ÖVP foreign minister and the Austrian president (an ÖVP nominee) concerning their respective political and constitutional responsibilities in the field of foreign policy-making and the representation of Austria in the EU. Austria's lack of a clear and coherent strategy within the EU – where Austrian nominations for important posts are dealt with in the traditional clientelist fashion – is widely criticized. There is much concern that Austria is not making the most of the political and economic opportunities offered by the transformation process in Eastern Europe.[14] The lack of a consensus on a dynamic interpretation of Austrian foreign policy interests – as apparent in the ambivalent attitude of government representatives towards Austria being a 'small state'[15] – corresponds with a pessimistic and – in many sectors of the Austrian population – distinctively xenophobic view of the Austrian public on large-scale immigration, organized crime and other types of non-military threat in the Europe of the 1990s.

Conclusion

To sum up, a 'crisis of normalization' in Austrian foreign policy has been developing since the mid-1980s and is still underway. Austria's government and the Austrian public face a situation in which they have to cope with an international constellation characterized by a high degree of complexity and instability, as well as with a 'new European political architecture' which has, to a significant extent, failed to find a definite and clearly ordered structure.

The foreign policy which Austria conducted in the period from 1955 to the end of the 1970s was characterized *inter alia* by three key elements of 'difference' vis-à-vis that of the 1920s and 1930s: it was based on a small state strategy, an active interpretation of Austrian neutrality, and was also very successful. In view of the altered national and international circumstances in which it now finds itself, that policy requires at least adaptation, if not fundamental change. This process of change and the ensuing 'identity crisis' of Austrian foreign policy should not, however, lead an economically developed and politically stable European country, such as Austria, to a deterministic and passive interpretation of foreign policy-making and its foreign policy interests.

Austria has the potential to build upon the economic and political advances it achieved in the course of its increasing 'normalization' and 'Europeanization' to develop a new foreign policy perspective that would constitute a 'difference' in terms of not only its own rather muddled and reactive foreign policy strategy in the 1980s and the first half of the 1990s, but also the foreign policies of other countries. This could involve a revival of Austria's active foreign policy and a strategy predicated on a vision of Austria in Europe, in which the pursuit of Austria's legitimate national interests could be combined with a contribution towards developing Europe into a region of economic and political stability and of social justice. As a new member of the EU, Austria's greatest challenge and most promising foreign policy opportunities undoubtedly lie in a revitalized and assertive international strategy which seeks not only to make a significant contribution to the successful transformation of the former communist countries in Eastern and South-eastern Europe, but also to assist them in the realization of their EU accession strategies.

Another foreign policy domain in which transforming leadership and historical hindsight will be much needed, and where Austria's foreign policy could and should renew, reinforce and restructure its former global foreign policy outlook, concerns Austria's support for the strengthening of a democratic and just international order. This will require the pursuit of an active and politically innovative policy both within the UN and in other fora of international cooperation. But such a reactivated foreign policy would have to come to terms with the changes to the structure and processes of the international system brought about by the end of the East–West bloc structure.

Seen from this perspective, Austria's crisis of foreign policy-making has parallels in most of the other Western countries and has mainly been driven and moulded by structural tendencies and constraints caused by the increasing pace of globalization and the concurrent crisis of the 'nation state'. Accordingly, one of the most urgent and important tasks and prerequisites for reform for foreign policy-makers is to try to obtain a systematic understanding of the changed realities of the national and international systems and of possible foreign policy options. This is a task and a challenge for which a better and more fruitful dialogue between practitioners and academic experts could and should be useful.[16]

Notes

1 For a more detailed and systematic analysis of Austria's foreign policy in the Second Republic see Kramer (1996b).

2 The latter term is used by Anton Pelinka and other analysts of Austrian domestic politics (see Chapter 6 by Pelinka in this volume).

3 The term 'small state' is used here to refer to the group of economically advanced Western type European states with less than 15 million inhabitants (see Höll, 1983).

4 Austria was one of the few Western countries in which Krugerrands could still be freely traded until 1985, despite UN sanctions towards South Africa's apartheid regime (see the documentation on Austrian firms circumventing the UN sanctions in Sauer and Zeschin, 1984). Austria's below average development aid payments and other manifestations of the economic reserve which Austria displayed towards the demands of the Third World for a New Economic Order are discussed in the literature as a 'free-riding-strategy' (see Supper, 1983). Another dark area of Austria's Third World policy during the 1970s was the sale of arms to dictatorial regimes. For example, Austria continued to sell arms to Latin American dictatorships such as Argentina, Bolivia and Chile even after US President Carter had banned US arms exports to them because of their violation of human rights. State-owned Austrian companies also sold arms in the crisis region of the Middle East, including to both Iraq and Iran during the first Gulf War (Pilz, 1982).

5 Vienna was, for example, the venue for meetings in 1961 and 1979 of the leaders of the two superpowers and from 1973 to 1989 was hosting the Mutual Balanced Forces Reduction talks.

6 Asked a few months before his death in August 1990 what he regarded as the most important achievements of his political career, Bruno Kreisky answered: '1) the systematic fight for a role for Austria in the world; and 2) that upward social mobility was possible for all classes in Austria' (*Basta*, December 1989, p.50).

7 But we can observe in the CSCE process since the mid-1980s a distinct weakening of the former political cohesion of the N+N group, that is to say, a growing polarization between Switzerland's more conservative stance in matters of military policy and the Scandinavian neutrals (Zielinski, 1990, p.265; Lehne, 1991, p.181).

8 Although both in his years as opposition leader and when taking charge of the foreign ministry in 1986–87, Mock had sharply criticized Kreisky's foreign policy as 'unrealistic', 'moralistic' and 'missionary', the conflict in the former Yugoslavia changed Mock's foreign policy views in a more active, interventionist direction with an explicitly 'idealistic' touch (see Mock in *Oberösterreichische Nachrichten*, 7 July 1993 and the comment by Gerfried Sperl in *Der Standard*, 11 September 1992).

9 Funding for the foreign ministry has been parsimonious since 1959, when it was established as an independent administrative entity. In the days of active neutrality policy, the organizational and financial limitations of the *Ballhausplatz* had at least partly been compensated for by an active and self-confident diplomatic service. See Neuhold (1993) and Kramer and Quendler (1995).

10 See note 4 supra.

11 One could cite numerous statements in which Foreign Minister Mock claimed that, if Austria were to remain outside the European Union, it would without doubt become a 'second class country' (*Kurier*, 31 May 1994) or a 'country with a colonial status' (*Profil*, 2 February 1992).

12 After the negative outcome of a referendum in the autumn of 1992 on Swiss membership of the European Economic Area, Switzerland opted out of the EC accession process.

13 In an opinion poll conducted in July 1995 only slightly more than one third of Austrian respondents expressed the view that the 1994 referendum decision in favour of EU entry had been wise (*Kurier*, 24 July 1995).

14 It has, for example, been expressed by Erhard Busek, who was, until April 1995, vice-chancellor and ÖVP party leader (see *Wiener Journal*, February 1996).
15 Until the 1980s the term 'small state' was widely applied as an official self-definition of Austria by its political and diplomatic representatives. It has of late been increasingly substituted by the terms 'smaller state', or (as on page two of the Austrian government's 1994 official report on the negotiations with Brussels) 'middle-sized' European country. The term 'small state' is still used by Austrian politicians claiming preferential treatment for Austria because it is a 'small country'. Thus when asserting Austria's neutrality was compatible with EU membership Foreign Minister Mock stated: 'You know, we are a small state. I'm sure there will be concessions for us' (*Der Standard*, 1 February 1993).
16 A mutually beneficial discourse between practitioners of foreign policy and universities and research institutes has been not a easy one and rather the exception in Austria (Quendler 1994).

Bibliography

Agh, A. (1988), 'The Foreign Policy of Small States in Western Europe', *Development and Peace*, **9**, Autumn.

Andrén, Nils (1984), 'Sweden: Neutrality, Defense and Disarmament' in Hanspeter Neuhold and Hans Thalberg (eds), *The European Neutrals in International Affairs*, Boulder Col. and Vienna: Westview and Braumüller.

Birnbaum, Karl (1987), 'The Neutral and Non-Aligned States in the CSCE Process' in Bengt Sundelius (ed.), *The Neutral Democracies and the New Cold War*, Boulder Col.: Westview.

Bonjour, Edgar (1980), 'Österreichische und schweizerische Neutralität. Zwei Leitbilder konvergieren', *Schweizer Monatshefte*, **10**.

Botz, Gerhard and Müller, Alfred (1995), 'Identität und Differenz in Österreich. Zu Gesellschaftsgeschichte, Politik- und Kulturgeschichte vor und nach 1945', *Österreichische Zeitschrift für Geschichtswissenschaften*, **1**, (6).

Burns, J.M. (1978), *Leadership*, New York: Harper & Row.

Csaky, E.M. (1980), *Der Weg zur Freiheit und Neutralität. Dokumentation zur österreichischen Außenpolitik 1945–1955*, Vienna: Böhlau.

Eger, R. (1981), *Krisen an Österreichs Grenzen*, Vienna: Böhlau.

Frei, Daniel (1977), 'Kleinstaatliche Außenpolitik als Umgang mit Abhängigkeit' in Daniel Frei, (ed.), *Die Schweiz in einer sich wandelnden Welt*, Zürich: Schulthess.

Gratz, Leopold (1984), 'Europa muß seine politischen Interessen stärker betonen – auch gegenüber den Supermächten, International-Gespräch mit Außenminister Leopold Gratz', *International*, **5**.

Hakovirta, H. (1988), *East–West Conflict and European Neutrality*, Oxford: Oxford University Press.

Höll, O. (ed.) (1983), *Small States and Dependence in Europe*, Boulder Col.: Westview.

Holzer, Gabriele (1995), 'Plädoyer für eine zeitgemäße außenpolitische Doktrin' in Hochschülerschaft der Technischen Universität Wien (ed.), *VorSätze–NachSätze. Diskurs über die Republik*, Vienna and Klagenfurt: Wieser.

Kissinger, H. (1979), *The White House Years*, Boston: Little, Brown.
Klestil, Thomas (1989), 'Die Entwicklung aus österreichischer Sicht', *Österreichisches Jahrbuch für Internationale Politik*, **6**.
Kramer, Helmut (1996a), 'History and International Context', in Volkmar Lauber (ed.), *Contemporary Austrian Politics*, Boulder Col. and London: Westview.
Kramer, Helmut (1996b), 'Foreign Policy' in Volkmar Lauber (ed.), *Contemporary Austrian Politics*, Boulder Col. and London: Westview.
Kramer, Helmut and Quendler, Franz (1995), 'The Role of Diplomacy and Foreign Ministries in the "New Political Architecture" of Europe after 1989 – The Case of Austria', Paper presented to the Second Pan-European Conference on International Relations, Paris, 13–16 September 1995.
Kreisky, B. (1986), *Zwischen den Zeiten. Erinnerungen aus fünf Jahrzehnten*, Berlin: Siegler.
Lehne, S. (1991), *The Vienna Meeting of the Conference on Security and Cooperation in Europe*, Boulder Col.: Westview.
Luchak, John M. (1987), 'Amerikanisch–österreichische Beziehugen von 1955–1985. Neutralität und der Ost-West-Konflikt', Vienna: PhD thesis.
Luif, P. (1988), *Neutrale in die EG? Die westeuropäische Integration und die neutralen Staaten*, Vienna: Braumüller.
Luther, Kurt Richard (1987), 'Austria's Future and Waldheim's Past: The Significance of the 1986 Elections', *West European Politics*, **10**, (3), July.
Mock, Alois (1987), 'Kontinuitätund neue Akzente, Interview mit Außenminister Alois Mock', *International*, **1**.
Neuhold, H. (1993), *Internationaler Strukturwandel und staatliche Außenpolitik. Das österreichische Außenministerium vor neuen Herausforderungen*, Vienna: Braumüller.
Pilz, P. (1982), *Die Panzermacher. Die österreichische Rüstungsindustrie und ihre Exporte*, Vienna: Verlag für Gesellschaftskritik.
Quendler, Franz (1994), 'Bridging the Gap: The Austrian Case' in Michel Girard *et al.* (eds), *Theory and Practice in Foreign Policy-Making. National Perspectives on Academics and Professionals in International Relations*, London and New York: Sage.
Riklin, Alois (1991–92), 'Die dauernde Neutralität der Schweiz', *Jahrbuch des Öffentlichen Rechts der Gegenwart*, Neue Folge **40**.
Rosenau, J.N. (1990), *Turbulence in World Politics. A Theory of Change and Continuity*, Princeton: Princeton University Press.
Rotter, Manfred (1991), 'Von der integralen zur differentiellen Neutralität', *Europäische Rundschau*, **2**, (19).
Sauer, W. and Zeschin, T. (eds) (1984), *Die Apartheid-Connection. Österreichs Bedeutung für Südafrika*, Vienna: Verlag für Gesellschaftskritik.
Schneider, H. (1990), *Alleingang nach Brüssel*, Bonn: Europa Union Verlag.
Schultz, Mark D. (1992), 'Austria in the International Arena: Neutrality, European Integration and Consociationalism' in Kurt Richard Luther and Wolfgang C. Müller (eds), *Politics in Austria: Still a Case of Consociationalism?*, London: Frank Cass.

Supper, Meinhard (1983), 'Die Rolle der Sozialpartner in der Außenpolitik' in Renate Kicker *et al.* (eds), *Außenpolitik und Demokratie in Österreich. Strukturen-Strategien-Stellungnahmen*, Salzburg: Neugebauer.

Stourzh, G. (1975), *Kleine Geschichte des Staatsvertrages*, Graz: Böhlau.

Väyrynen, Raimo (1987), 'Adaptation of a Small Power to International Tensions' in Bengt Sundelius (ed.), *The European Neutrals in International Affairs*, Boulder Col.: Westview.

Zemanek, Karl (1984), 'Austria's Policy of Neutrality: Constants and Variables' in Hanspeter Neuhold and Hans Thalberg (eds), *The European Neutrals in International Affairs*, Boulder Col. and Vienna: Westview and Braumüller.

Zemanek, Karl (1991), 'The Changing International System: A New Look at Collective Security and Permanent Neutrality', *Austrian Journal of Public and International Law*, **42**.

Zielinski, M. (1990), *Die neutralen und blockfreien Staaten und ihre Rolle im KSZE-Prozess*, Baden-Baden: Nomos.

9 Austria and its Immediate Neighbours: Hungary

László J. Kiss

Neighbourhood and History

The coordinates of Hungarian–Austrian relations since 1989 were set by unprecedented changes in European, regional and global history: the collapse of the Soviet empire inside and outside the USSR, the unification of Germany and Austria's admission to the European Union. But even in a chapter as short as this, some historical recapitulation is required.

A glance down the centuries of Austro-Hungarian relations reveals examples of everything possible in the ties between two countries: confrontation and productive coexistence, cultural division and fruitful symbiosis. As Hungarian national awareness developed in the late seventeenth and early eighteenth centuries, the underlying framework of Hungarian–Austrian relations was laid by the Hungarian movement for independence from the Habsburgs and its aftermath. This produced a specific dichotomy in Hungarian political attitudes and behaviour between cooperation with Austria and its dynasty, and confrontation with them. The *kuruc* party, who took the latter course, accused the *labanc*, the compromisers with the Habsburgs, of being treacherous hirelings. The *labanc* branded the resisters provincial escapists. The revolution of 1848–49, as an episode of resistance and warfare in Austro-Hungarian relations, is still interpreted differently in the two countries. The Austro-Hungarian *Ausgleich* or Compromise of 1867, on the other hand, laid the foundations within a supranational, multicultural empire for Hungary's most successful drive for modernization so far. Also part of the two countries' common past is recognition of many intellectual, scientific and artistic achievements in the Danubian monarchy as the products of a cultural and social interpenetration that makes them equally Hungarian and Austrian. The composer Franz Lehár and the playwright Ferenc Molnár will serve as examples (Fodor, 1995, pp.13–17).

One common experience of history is that the conflicts in the relations of the two countries almost always caused damage to both sides, while cooperation between them was mutually advantageous. This experience was exceptionally well confirmed on the one hand by the mutually advantageous *Ausgleich* of 1867, and on the other by the consequences of the break-up of the Austro-Hungarian monarchy in 1918, which for both countries marked the start of a traumatic decline in status from middle-ranking powers to small states. Despite the differences in national outlook, the collapse of the monarchy was a loss both to Hungary and to Austria, and a victory and a gain to the other successor states (Mlynar, 1985). It can hardly be overlooked that the Hungarian leadership in 1938 was inclined to interpret the *Anschluß* as a case of 'one of our friends becoming a neighbour instead of the other'. Nor can it be forgotten that the Iron Curtain of the Cold War descended along the Hungarian–Austrian border and, while Hungary was under Soviet occupation, Austria counted as an 'advance guard' of the hostile West.

Three Geopolitical Patterns of Neighbour Relations

After the conclusion of the Austrian State Treaty in 1955, the main features of bilateral relations between the two neighbours were subject to three main geopolitical patterns, depending on the changes in East–West relations and conditions at home.

Between 1955 and 1962, neutral, independent Austria and Soviet-dominated, Warsaw Pact member, Hungary, had the specific role of peripheral states between two worlds. They were two abutments, two mutually opposed perimeters, even though the division and ideological crusading of the Cold War did not obliterate the underlying cohesive awareness of their common past and culture. It was Vienna, not Budapest, which managed to profit from this perimeter position in a divided Europe, as the West's 'observation point' – a 'bridgehead' of Western culture and freedom. Austrian neutrality was perceived in Hungary as an important step towards desatellization in Central Europe, especially in 1956. According to a typical pattern of perception, Hungary had lost its function as 'connecting link' between the Soviet Union and Austria in military–strategic terms, which seemed to open up a prospect to Hungary for a neutral option. After the defeat of the Hungarian Revolution of 1956, Austria became, in the eyes of Hungarians, not just the escape route – the gateway to the desired freedom of the West – but a decisive geopolitical gauge of comparison, and this it remains to the present day.

As a consequence of the Easternization of Stalinism, Hungary was wrested out of the organic context of a Central European development closely related with the rest of Europe. Actually, the COMECON, as a poor man's club, was an effective means to isolate the Soviet-dominated East European countries both from the world economy and from one another. The defeat of the Hungarian Revolution in 1956 could be described as a reaffirmation of Easternization.

Traditional neighbourly relations revived in the early 1960s, as the post-1956 repression in Hungary came to an end. For Budapest, Austro-Hungarian bilateralism was a means of breaking out of its international isolation – a testing ground for a policy of coexistence – which began quite early on to acquire a subregional significance of its own. It was Austria that displayed most active exchanges with Hungary. The two countries' relations began to improve from 1961, and in November 1962 Hungary concluded a long-term trade agreement with Austria – the first such agreement with a non-Soviet bloc country. Visits of high-ranking officials also became frequent. Bruno Kreisky's visit to Budapest in January 1964 was the first undertaken by an Austrian foreign minister for about 30 years. During his visit, several agreements were concluded, including the establishment of a common committee for the inspection of border incidents. In July 1964, when Hungarian Deputy Premier Jenö Fock visited Austria, his Austrian counterpart, Bruno Pittermann, expressed the intimacy with Hungary as follows: 'When we visit Hungary, we feel as if we were in our neighbour's garden, not in a foreign country.'[1] The improvement in relations was apparent in the conclusion of a new long-term commercial agreement in 1962, in the elevation of diplomatic relations between them to ambassador level in 1965, and not least in the fact that 'Austro-Hungarian friendship' gained a mention. Vienna now again became Hungary's gateway to the West.

The pragmatic features of Kádár's reform-communist policy, the use of consumption in actively depoliticizing Hungarian society ('goulash communism') and the social 'policy of alliances' via partial liberalization would have been impossible without an opening to the West. Austria was never fully 'in between' the two blocs, despite its neutrality. Its Western orientation at the ideological, political and economic levels did not prevent it from pursuing an active neutrality policy for which the term 'bridge-building' was often used. What was more astonishing was that these 'services' were also accepted by the Soviet Union, which played an important additional role in developing a 'special Austro-Hungarian relationship' (see Chapter 11 in this volume by Neuhold). From Austria's point of view, the active policy of neutrality deriving from the State Treaty, the pursuit of a good-neighbourly policy and the role of mediator played as a member of the neutral and non-aligned group in the CSCE process all strengthened Vienna's position and pointed beyond the structures of the Cold War. In the 1980s, the bilateral relations and the subregional forms of cooperation that emerged – the non-governmental Alps–Adriatic Partnership and the intergovernmental Quadrangolare unveiled in Budapest in 1988 (today's Central European Initiative) – all contributed to a latent, 'creeping' realignment in Hungarian foreign policy – that is, to a loosening of one-sided bloc relations and expansion of 'trans-bloc' East–West cooperation.

In 1985 the Austrian Institute for International Affairs in Laxenburg issued an analysis of Hungarian–Austrian relations in its 'Neighbourhood Studies' series (Mlynar *et al.*, 1985). There the authors remarked, on the one hand, on the high degree of institutionalization in the bilateral relations, which extended from agreements, reciprocal recognition of university studies and academic degrees through cooperation between border areas to the abolition of visa requirements. The authors of the book reached the conclusion that these bilateral relations were not a general model for the East–West relationship, but *special* relations inapplicable to other countries, and as such attributable far more to political goodwill than to economic ties. The press, not without irony, celebrated as a return to *k. und k.*, the period of 'Kreisky and Kádár', in which pragmatism and kinship of mentality found expression.

The multiple *Mitteleuropa* debate which broke out in the 1980s raised the question of historical awareness and identity and of a political reorientation in both Vienna–Brussels and Budapest–Moscow relations, along with the rediscovery of the former transnational Central European cultural sphere. For Hungary, the debate denoted, on the one hand, a reassessment of the common past, dovetailing into the process of intellectual preparation for the democratic changes. On the other, the *Mitteleuropa* debate emphasized the 'otherness' of a Hungary, deeply rooted in the profound layers of regional development as opposed to the Soviet type of development, the protest against the division brought about by the Yalta system, and ultimately the demand that the artificial geographical, political, military and cultural incongruence of what Kundera called 'kidnapped Central Europe' should cease. Thus the *Mitteleuropa* debate was one of the important intellectual fermenters of the 'de-East-Europeanization' process.

The dismantling of the Iron Curtain and opening of the Hungarian–Austrian frontier to East Germans in September 1989 was not simply a milestone in bilateral relations or a *par excellence* Hungarian foreign-policy recommencement, but a watershed in global, European and regional history. The disintegration of the Soviet bloc and the Soviet Union created a radically different geopolitical environment for both countries. Austria and Hungary would no longer be on the periphery of two realms of European politics, and the collapse of the Soviet bloc brought an end both to the 'trans-bloc' experiments and to the traditional, bridge-building, mediating role Austria played through its active policy of neutrality.

The perimeters reverted to being parts of an internal historical region and registered the reappearance of this. The waves of arriving Hungarian shoppers showed Vienna and the Eastern province of Burgenland, treated so adversely during the Cold War, that Hungarian purchasing power could act as an economic stimulant. The collapse of the multinational states which had arisen out of the ruins of the Habsburg Empire (bloody in Yugoslavia's case, peaceful in Czechoslovakia's), along with the ethnoterritorial practices in former Yugoslavia, showed how fragile the security situation was for both Austria and Hungary, and led to the recognition that nationalism had not only defeated the dynasties, but in its post-communist form, proletarian internationalism, as well. One aspect of the new situation was that, for the first time in twentieth-century history, the countries of Eastern Central Europe, as 'security orphans' after the Cold War, were without the direct control and influence of an *Ordnungsmacht* of the kind France and, later, Germany had had after the disintegration of the Austro-Hungarian monarchy, or the Soviet Union had had since the Second World War. The new situation also showed that the idea of any kind of Central European federation (perhaps Austrian-led) had become an anachronism. The idea of Central Europe was manifest in operational terms in the subregional forms of cooperation (the Alps–Adriatic Partnership, the Central European Initiative, cooperation among the Visegrád countries and so on), not as alternatives to the EU, but as means of 'informal integration' directed towards the EU and the acquisition of Euro-compatibility. Austria's ceaseless preparations for EU membership and the new democratic Hungarian government's proclamation in 1990 of Euro-Atlantic integration as a foreign policy priority demonstrated both the identity of the two countries' foreign policy objectives and the difference between them in terms of readiness and capability for integration. In contrast with Hungary, Austria displayed a high level of preparedness for EU membership and moved to the Western core by joining the EU in 1995, but still has not gone all the way with regard to security policy, its permanent neutrality having lost its geographical function but remaining deeply ingrained in Austrian mentality. Hungary has no success story, or tradition of sitting on the fence – only the frustrating experience of seeking a neutral status in 1956.

Therefore the question is: when and how (in terms of time as well as of the political and economic costs), will Hungary be able to reach the 'integration threshold' necessary for participation in the EU and in NATO, and how will the willingness and ability of an integrated West to admit Hungary evolve in conjunction with the country's internal development? (Kiss, 1995, pp.249f)

A New Stage in Bilateral Relations: Strategic Neighbourhood

Austria's strategic foreign-policy objective was attained on 1 January 1995, when it obtained EU membership. This gave Hungary a common border with the European Union, which meant the Hungarian–Austrian relationship had outgrown the customary framework of bilateralism: the relations between them gained extra value, and their neighbourhood assumed strategic significance in terms of Budapest's prospects of Euro-Atlantic integration. Austria brought to the EU as a historical and geopolitical dowry, so to speak, the first appearance there of a 'Central European dimension', foreshadowing the next possible surge of expansion of the integration process.

Hungary is not simply in an area of contact between the Germanic, Slav and Latin cultures, but at the post-Cold War conjunction of a pre-modern sphere of the Bosnian type, a modern sphere of post-communist nation-states and, as a neighbour of the new EU member Austria, a post-modern sphere. This post-modernism differs from the anarchic conditions of the pre-modern sphere and the territorial sovereignty and ethnic exclusiveness of the modern sphere by denoting greater security and prosperity gained through greater openness, the adoption of multiculturalism, an end to the significance of frontiers, and a process of integration and transnational development based on intensive and mutual interference in each other's internal affairs. Hungary is not interested in changing the territorial status quo, but in promoting changes within the territorial status quo in Central and Eastern Europe. These changes should lead to a new humanitarian order based on international minority protection, democratization and modernization.

Austria as an EU member is a partner country affected by all three of Hungary's foreign policy priorities: Euro-Atlantic integration, neighbourhood policy and Hungarian minorities. East–Central Europe and the neighbouring countries with EU association agreements have gained enhanced importance for Austria's security interests. Vienna has a short-term interest in easing, and a medium-term interest in ending, its peripheral position in the EU. This means it has to redefine the historical bridging and mediating functions which it has performed in the region. Austria's basic interest lies in furthering the integration of its neighbouring East–Central European states and acting as a kind of network-maker. Austria's political, economic and cultural role can only reach fruition if it becomes an inner region of the EU, instead of being a kind of screening station on the group's outside border.

Austria, as an EU member, is also working to maintain the positions it has gained in East–Central Europe as one of the foremost foreign investors and economic partners. Here Hungary retains its position as the leading partner.

Austria is Hungary's second or third largest trading partner after Germany and the CIS region, and Hungary is Austria's top economic partner in the region. Austria took 10.9 per cent of Hungary's exports in 1994, and supplied 12 per cent of its imports. Hungarian import liberalization coupled with a highly restrictive system of Austrian agricultural imports led to a rapid rise in Hungary's trade deficit with Austria, from US$450 million in 1992 to US$566 million in 1993 and, despite a surge in exports in 1994, to US$584 million in 1994.

Austria is estimated to have invested US$1 billion so far in Hungary, where there is an Austrian stake in about 4700 firms. There is a major Austrian presence in Hungarian sugar refining, distilling and confectionery, building materials, road construction, civil engineering, paper, steel-making and retail trading. Hungary accounts for about two-thirds of the Austrian joint ventures formed in East–Central Europe, which constitute one-third of all Austria's capital exports. Austria has become Hungary's third largest investor country after the United States and Germany, although the proportion is now falling, due to stronger attraction of capital by the likewise neighbouring Czech Republic and Slovakia.

Consequences of the 'Switch' to Europe: Reassessing Bilateral Relations

Austria's admission to the EU created a new situation in bilateral relations, with the earlier cooperation, freed by removal of the Iron Curtain, giving way to regulation by the European Union. The effects can be felt in several areas: tighter border defences and controls, grading of goods consignments, curbs on the migration of labour, and so on. It is no concidence that assessments of the consequences of Austria's admission to the EU for bilateral relations and ways of saving previous bilateral concessions by incorporating them in the Europe Agreement have become central topics at high-level and expert meetings. Budapest wants the arrangements favouring Hungarian agricultural products, as well as the export conditions for manufactures, to be unchanged by Austria's entry, arguing that the EU Commission promised to transfer such valid bilateral agricultural agreement quotas with EFTA countries to the Europe Agreement. There is a strong desire on the Hungarian side that the conversion of the Hungarian–Austrian border into a Hungarian–EU border should not make crossing procedures more difficult, particularly as the citizens of the two countries make 6 million visits a year in each direction. Budapest's aim is to make border crossings by citizens of EU countries and of Hungary easier, because Austria's accession to the Schengen Agreement, which significantly tightens controls on the borders round the EU, could bring radical changes. Another Hungarian goal is to allow more Hungarians to take employment in Austria, making it possible for commuting employees, seasonal workers and skilled trainees to be employed there.

The differences between the areas of 'high policy' and 'low policy' are conspicuous. While high-level Austrian political leaders show great constructiveness, the representatives of particular ministries concentrate on the requirements of adapting to Europe and fulfilment of the tasks set by Brussels. There is no doubt that Austria, as a new member of the EU, is going to be preoccupied with its own affairs until it has managed to build up the influence due to it within the organization. So Hungarian diplomats must show activity and initiative in pursuing the benefits to be gained from Austria's EU membership, by getting to know what experiences Austria had in its preparations, entry negotiations, technical adaptation, legal harmonization and so on.

It is not yet possible to gauge accurately what effect EU admission will have on both Austrian public opinion and the trend of opinion concerning Hungary's membership of the EU. So Hungarian foreign politics must apply the tools of cultured foreign policy and avail itself increasingly of the means of public diplomacy in order to keep the Austrian public and opinion-makers informed about the historical contacts between the two peoples and the need to make this stretch of the EU's external border internal.

Apart from high-level meetings, help in this can be obtained from direct working relations between the local authorities of Austrian provinces and Hungarian counties and between towns and villages, through the so-called Regional Forum or through the Regional Council. A steady 'socialization' of Hungarian–Austrian relations is apparent in the activity, since 1993, of the Hungarian–Austrian Forum for Dialogue, where the two countries' leading politicians and intellectual figures have a chance to meet annually, as they do at the Pannonia Club founded in the same year in Vienna. The lobbying effect of these meetings is also increasing.

One perceptible area of bilateral relations is formed by the Hungarian community in Austria, who number 60 000–70 000 people. The preservation of their cultural identity and instruction in their native language have been assisted by the establishment, in the autumn of 1992 in Oberwart, of grammar-school teaching in German, Croatian and Hungarian. At the beginning of 1993, in line with an Austrian government decision, the status of 'ethnic group' (*Volksgruppe*) was extended to cover not only the Hungarians of Burgenland, but those of Vienna and the Vienna district. These relations are augmented by the cultural institutions operating in the two capital cities – for instance, the famous Collegium Hungaricum in Vienna, the Austro-Hungarian Action Foundation, with its emphasis on teaching the German language, and so on. The previously high level of cultural, educational, scientific and scholarly cooperation between the two countries has become somewhat overshadowed by work in other fields, but this is due, above all, to the expanded Austrian and Hungarian cultural diversification resulting from the change of system in Eastern Europe.

The New Dimensions of Subregional Cooperation

The qualitative change in the geopolitical situation, particularly Austria's membership of the EU, has added a new dimension to the forms of subregional cooperation. The 'bloc-blurring' and 'bloc-overarching' policies of encouraging Westernization through the subregional forms of cooperation (the Alps–Adriatic Partnership and the Central European Initiative) have lost their earlier significance, but the political effects of the policy of anticipated adaptation to the EU ('informal integration' and 'integration or Europeanization from below') can hardly be ignored. This is especially the case in respect of the opportunities which Austria's EU membership offers for the development of border regions. Of course, the activity of the Austro-Hungarian border areas is by no means fortuitous. The building of such relations began almost 20 years ago between various public administrative bodies and between firms. There are also places for the district and local government bodies of the border counties and provinces on the widest variety of the specialized committees of the Austrian–Hungarian Territorial Development Commission, which operates under the Chancellor's Office and the Hungarian Ministry of Environmental Protection and Territorial Development – in other words, at government level.

The cooperative activity of firms has exceeded all expectations. Although Austria takes third place as an investor in Hungary, its role in the sphere of small and medium-sized businesses in the border zone (Györ-Sopron-Moson and Vas counties) is decisive. Also increasing in frequency are cross-border activities by private, grassroots associations. As a further side-effect of Austria's EU membership, the regional disparities within Hungary will increase further, in favour of the parts of the country bordering on Austria.

With Austria's entry into the EU, it has become possible for Hungary to link directly into the trans-European transport, energy, information and environmental protection systems. Cross-border cooperation may be assisted by the infrastructural projects to be implemented under the EU's INTERREG 2 and PHARE programmes.

Austria, on the perimeter of the EU, has an interest in developing cross-border cooperation to benefit its eastern provinces and promote a Central European subregional system that also embraces interregional relations.

Analysts expect Europe's growth areas to shift from north-west Europe towards the south German, north Italian, Swiss and Austrian regions. In this connection, an Austrian plan to develop a Euro-region in the Vienna-Bratislava-Györ triangle (*Euregio Danubiensis*) is seen by both Hungarian and Austrian analysts as likely to yield one of the most promising areas for growth in Europe. The Austrian side in such a prospective Euro-region is recommending policy coordination among the three cities and districts, extending to the fields of environmental protection, public transport and urban development, with coordination of transport fares, joint establishment of a national park on the Danube wetlands, foundation of a 'European secondary school' for Hungarian, Slovak and Czech boarders and so on. It can hardly be denied that there would be obstacles to such a plan, particularly in Hungarian–Slovak and Slovak–Austrian relationships. Yet it has to be recognized that, apart from the common integration objectives it would serve, such a cooperation scheme would offer additional development prospects to Western Slovakia and Bratislava, not to mention the prospect of extending the region to cover Prague and Budapest as well.

Conclusion

Austria's membership of the EU does not replicate the peripheral situations of the Cold War. What we are witnessing is the emergence of a new pan-European architecture, in which the Austrian–Hungarian relationship also has a contribution to make to a strategic objective: anchoring Hungary and the region to the European centre of modernization – to the European Union (Mangott and Neuhold, 1995).

Note

1 *Magyar Külpolitika Dokumentumai 1963*, 1964 East Europe May 1965, p.17.

Bibliography

Fodor, Gábor (1995), 'Anknüpfungspunkte der Nachbarschaft', *Europäische Rundschau*, **23** (2).

Kiss, László J. (1995), 'Hungary' in Hanspeter Neuhold, Peter Havlik and Arnold Suppan (eds), *Political and Economic Transformation in East–Central Europe*, Boulder Col., San Franciso and Oxford: Westview Press.

Mangott, Gerhard and Neuhold, Hanspeter (1995), 'Six Reformist Countries on the

Road to Transformation', in Hanspeter Neuhold, Peter Havlik and Arnold Suppan (eds), *Political and Economic Transformation in East–Central Europe*, Boulder Col., San Fransciso and Oxford: Westview Press.

Mlynar, Zdenek (1985), 'Die Österreich-ungarischen Beziehungen als Sonderfall der Ost-West-Beziehungen' in Zdenek Mlynar, Hans-Georg Heinrich, Toni Kofler and Jan Stanovsky (eds), *Die Beziehungen zwischen Österreich und Ungarn: Sonderfall oder Modell?*, Vienna: Wilhelm Braumüller.

Mlynar Z., Heinrich, H.-G., Kofler, T. and Stanovsky, J. (eds) (1985), *Die Beziehungen zwischen Österreich und Ungarn: Sonderfall oder Modell?*, Vienna: Wilhelm Braumüller.

Neuhold, H., Havlik, P. and Suppan, A. (eds), *Political and Economic Transformation in East–Central Europe*, Boulder Col., San Fransciso and Oxford: Westview Press.

10 Austria's new neighbours: the Slovenian perspective

Walter Lukan

I am neither a prophet nor a political scientist. I am a historian and my contribution will therefore be less of a prospective than a retrospective account. It will illustrate the main line of development of relations between Austria and Slovenia and will consider the possible impact of recent trends upon future developments. The prospective element is thus based on, but not aimed at, the past.

The retrospective must start from the time when Slovenians and German Austrians were still living in a common state, the Austro-Hungarian monarchy, which committed involuntary suicide as a consequence of its inability to solve the problem of multinationality. The Slovenians also contributed to this, in calling for a Slovenia which did not exist as an independent administrative unity and in demanding a federalization of the state. From 1897 onwards, in search of support for their aims, they turned their eyes increasingly towards the South, with the result that towards the end of the First World War they succumbed to a fairly uncritical Yugoslavism. This was partly due to the lack of alternatives. The Slovenians would have preferred to stay with Austria, but the heads of state were not prepared to negotiate their nationalist political programme – the creation of a South Slav state in the framework of the Habsburg monarchy – until the bitter end. At the end of October 1918 Slovenia emerged for a short period as an administrative unit. It initially formed part of the 'State of Slovenians, Croats and Serbs', but on 1 December 1918 hastily became part of the 'Kingdom of Serbs, Croats and Slovenians'. 'Slovenija', was abolished in 1921 by the centralist St Vitus Day Constitution. It was not until 1945 that the 'Socialist Republic of Slovenia' was founded within the framework of communist Yugoslavia's emergence from the Second World War. In 1990 the 'Socialist Republic of Slovenia' discarded the word 'socialist' and on 25 June 1991 declared itself independent.

During the period from 1918–91, Austro-Slovenian relations therefore have to be carefully distinguished from the interstate relations between Austria and Yugoslavia. In other words, relations were carried out on a lower, regional level: on the one side were the Austrian *Länder* of Carinthia and Styria and on the other the *Dravska Banovina* in the inter-war period, or, from 1945, the (S) R[epublic] Slovenia. Moreover, it is worth noting that the positions of the two states were not always identical with those of their respective regional units. On the whole, the stance adopted at state level were more moderate. Indeed, Austria maintained a Consulate General in Ljubljana from the end of the 1920s until 1938 and again after the Second World War until 1992, when it was transformed into an embassy on recognition of Slovenia's in international law by Austria.

The demise of the Danubian monarchy undoubtedly establishes the first deep incision in the relations between Slovenians and German Austrians. The university cities of Vienna, until 1918 the 'second home of the Slovenians', as the Slovenian writer and politician Matjaz Kmecl once said, and of Graz were very important cultural centres for Slovenians. All but a few Slovenian students and professors now left Austrian universities and followed the call of the University of Ljubljana, which had been newly founded in 1919. This was followed by the foundation of other Slovenian cultural institutions, including the Slovenian Academy of Sciences in late 1938. It was a kind of cultural revolution which, as in the political sphere, manifested itself in a completely new geocultural orientation. Slovenian and Serbo-Croat found their way into schoolbooks, literature, theatre and the fine arts and, when Slovenians looked to Europe, they rarely sought out Graz or Vienna, but Paris. French was in fashion as a foreign language, whilst everything German-speaking was suppressed, especially in the school system. The heyday of the *Reclam Hefte* (a series of very cheap paperback editions of the most important texts in German literature, published to enable everyone to establish their own private library) as upholders of culture was over. The German theatre in Ljubljana was closed down, and it was even concluded that one could do without a lecturer in German at the new university.

Slovenian reservations about neighbours to the north, and Carinthian and Styrian reservations about their southern neighbours, were reinforced by border fighting which ended, in the case of Southern Carinthia, with a referendum in favour of Austria and, for Lower Styria, without a referendum in favour of the Southern Slav state, Slovenia. The sentimental days of commemoration of the referendum on both sides of the border merely increased mutual resentments. But even before that, in the propaganda preceding the referendum, longlasting stereotypes had been created. In Carinthia, Slovenians were 'balkanized' – that is thrown into one pot with the 'uncivilized Serb' whilst, on the Slovenian side, the people of Carinthia were stylized as aggressive German nationalists. These long-lived images still have an effect today.

Both sides had their own minorities, and reciprocity in policy towards minorities was much talked about, although the mutual reciprocity was actually expressed not in the promotion but in the suppression of those minorities. In addition, there was supposed or real irredentism, the latter also being articulated in schoolbooks. In a word, political relations between Austria (Carinthia/Styria) and the South Slav state had become predominantly conflictual. Even a tour to Slovenia by a choir of Slovenian Carinthians could result in political problems. Only economic relations developed normally.

Austrian interest in cultural exchange with its southern neighbour was probably motivated by a latent conviction of cultural superiority. One spoke – mainly in newspapers, but also diplomatic and academic circles, which reflected a broad spectrum of opinion – of a cultural gradient. The view that Austria's cultural contacts with South Slav peoples, including Slovenians, were on the whole a one-way-street, since cultural impulses were generated by Austria, was still supported during the Second Republic, albeit by fewer people. Nowadays, this prejudice, in so far as it exists, is limited to the lower classes of the population. In view of the attitudes described, it is hardly surprising that Austro-Slovenian cultural relations have remained marginal. A few translations of Austrian writers (Rilke, Zweig, Werfel, Gagern) on the one side, and one Cankar translation, as well as performances of the Vienna Boys' Choir and of the Burgtheater on the other, are all there is to report.

One might have expected that the reserved, almost hostile attitude towards Austria of the Slovenian population and especially of the Slovenian intelligentsia would have changed from the second half of the 1920s. Newspaper reports and minutes of the Austrian Consulate General in Ljubljana point in that direction. Renewed efforts at teaching German in secondary schools were also to be noted. One of the main reasons for Slovenians' altered views towards Austria is certainly to be sought in their disillusion and dissatisfaction with Yugoslavian conditions. This dissatisfaction, however, did not extend to questioning the Yugoslavian state.

The events of the Second World War had significantly increased old fears and their traumatic potential. Slovenians' existence had been seriously threatened by National Socialism and the resentments they felt to Austria, which had been perceived as German nationalist, not only remained but became even more pronounced with the establishment of the Second Republic. New territorial claims by Yugoslavia and the earlier expulsion of the German-speaking minority from Yugoslavian territory, as well as their almost total annihilation by Tito's partisan army took their toll. Thus the German-speaking minority in Slovenia became practically non-existent, apart from small fragments, about which more will be said below. The Slovenian minority in Carinthia, however, remained as – one is tempted to say – an object of conflict.

In view of these preconditions and the different social systems that prevailed in the two countries, it is perhaps surprising that, as early as the 1950s, there developed a mutually positive relationship between the Austrian and Yugoslav states and in particular between Austria and the constituent Yugoslav republic of Slovenia. The State Treaty of 1955 played a special role in this context. One indicator of this promising development concerned economic relations, in which Slovenia became the strongest of Austria's economic partners among Yugoslavia's six republics. Another pertains to cultural relations, which were of an incomparably more intense and more diverse nature than in the inter-war period. One exception has to be made, however: there was not so much progress in the state–institutional sector, which did not have an Austro-Yugoslavian framework cultural programme until 1972, on top of which there were somewhat absurd problems in negotiating implementation treaties. A moot point, for example, was the spelling of place-names in the text of the Treaty.

In taking the initiative to launch the first post-war cultural contacts, the Slovenians played the role of a catalyst and the government of Carinthia utilized its Slovenian links in this area. Cultural contacts started even before the Yugoslavian declaration of early 1951 that the state of war with Austria had come to an end, and during the period when the 1945 model school regulations for minorities were still in force in Carinthia. As mentioned above, it was precisely that minority or ethnic group which was later to become the bone of contention in intrastate relations, where it was of course primarily Slovenia on the Yugoslavian side which exerted the pressure. But it has to be emphasized that this issue had relatively little effect on the otherwise positive development of bilateral good neighbourly relations. Nevertheless, the high point of this conflict, which essentially revolved around (non-)compliance with Article 7 of the Austrian State Treaty, will be discussed here. Matters escalated as a result of the 1958 Carinthian school strike, which a year later led to the abolition of the 1945 school regulation mentioned above. This was followed by the so-called *Ortstafelsturm*, the 1972 'sign-post offensive', in which bilingual signposts were defaced, but which led to an Austria-wide campaign of solidarity on behalf of the Carinthian Slovenians – a development which obviously did not remain unnoticed in Ljubljana. The last major conflict on this issue resulted in an exchange of notes between Austria and Yugoslavia, concerning the Law on Ethnic Groups (*Volksgruppengesetz*) and the subsequent secret census of the native language in 1976. Finally, Ljubljana responded negatively to an amendment of the Law for the Protection of Minorities in Schools (*Minderheitenschulgesetz*) in Carinthia, which had been designed as a compromise and inititated by the German nationalist *Kärntner Heimatdienst* and the *Freiheitliche Partei Österreichs* (FPÖ) following a popular initiative. The amendment produced a partial segregation of German- and Slovenian-speaking pupils who had previously been taught together. Since then, there have been no reports of further conflicts in the question of minorities in Carinthia that might have led to disagreements between Slovenia and Austria.

The year 1989 witnessed the start of the final phase in the demise of Yugoslavia, the related process of democratization and in Slovenian strivings for independence. The first free elections took place in April 1990 and in December 1990 the overwhelming majority voted for the independence of Slovenia. These developments were met with much sympathy by the Austrian people and the Austrian media. From 1989 to 1991, Austria officially still supported the process of reforming the whole state of Yugoslavia; for example it supported the EFTA–Yugoslavia solidarity fund. It cannot therefore be claimed that Austria had distanced itself from Yugoslavia early on, even though the frequent visits of Slovenian and Croatian politicians to Vienna in the first half of 1991 may have led some people to reach that conclusion. The situation did not become confrontational until the Yugoslav army intervened in Slovenia after the latter's declaration of independence, whereupon Austria sent about 6000 troops to the Slovenian border on 28 June 1991. It was then that the Yugoslav government made the accusation in its statement of 7 July that Austria had already been supporting tendencies towards the disintegration of Yugoslavia for quite some time. In its reply of 16 July, Austria rejected this accusation and, after pointing out that the tendencies towards disintegration were caused by domestic factors, emphasized the principles of sovereignty of nations. In the following months, Austria took steps in unison with the EU member states, but also played an active role regarding the question of the diplomatic recognition of Slovenia and Croatia. Examples are the 28-state initiative of 6 November 1991 and the Austrian federal government resolution of 10 December 1991 regarding recognition in international law of Slovenia and Croatia, which was accomplished on 15 January 1992.

In general, it may be said that Austria supported the new state of Slovenia from its very inception. Even Austria's armed presence at the border during the short war at the end of June and the beginning of July 1991 had greatly helped Slovenia, since the Yugoslav People's Army was not able to act as it might have wished. In those critical days the Slovenian civilian airline was able to relocate to Klagenfurt, and Austria helped Slovenia a great deal in other aspects of her international passenger traffic. After Slovenia's recognition, Austria successfully supported Slovenia's membership of international organizations such as the CSCE (24 March 1992), the UN (22 May 1992) and the Council of Europe (14 May 1993). She currently supports Slovenia's wish for a treaty of association with the European Union. However, there was a minor irritation concerning Slovenia's relationship to the EU when Austria's foreign minister, Alois Mock, who in other respects had gained undisputed merit in his efforts on behalf of Slovenia, took Italy's side on the question of Italian property in Istria. This led to the Slovenian application for association with the EU being blockaded by the Berlusconi government. Examined more closely, it is clear that Mock's actions were in support of the Slovenian foreign minister, Lojze Peterle, who had negotiated the preliminary treaty of Aquileia with the Italians and had consequently been forced to resign. Mock's actions concerning Istria were therefore designed more as a gesture of support to his fellow Christian Democrat, Peterle, than as a frustration of the interests of the Slovenian state.

There were also disagreements over the Slovenian wish automatically to enter treaties which Austria had previously signed with the former Yugoslavia, especially the Austrian State Treaty. In this case, Austria refused, but again reasserted that any diminution in minority rights was out of the question. Moreover, as Thomas Klestil pointed out in an interview prior to his election to the Austrian presidency, Slovenia retained the option of championing the interests of the Slovenian national group in Austria vis-á-vis the Austrian government through the relevant provisions of the CSCE (*Slovenski vestnik* [Klagenfurt], 11 March 1992). Whilst on a state visit to Ljubljana in November 1992, Chancellor Franz Vranitzky, for his part, agreed with the Slovenian head of government, Janez Drnovsek, during a joint press conference that 'relations had never been better' with regard to the Slovenian minority in Austria. In general, this may well be true. Those problems which presently exist are created by the leadership of the Slovenian minority in Carinthia itself in their assessment of its future political strategy. While the socialist group broadly pursues a kind of intercultural plan akin to that of the Green Party, the Slovenians who are Christian-oriented show some sympathy for the idea of a so-called 'Chamber of the Peoples' (*Volksgruppenkammer*) – an old concept rediscovered by Jörg Haider when he was governor of Carinthia and opposed to such a chamber. In any case, the disagreement within the national group over these two models has absorbed unnecessary energies.

Slovenia protects its Hungarian and Italian minorities (1991: 8503 and 3074 persons respectively) in an exemplary manner and, although the Gypsies (2293) are treated less well, they are at least recognized by the Constitution as an indigenous ethnic group. A new minority or, more precisely, one which had been believed no longer to exist, is now being added – namely the 'German-speaking ethnic group'. In its memorandum of 12 June 1992 Austria claimed the right to represent this minority vis-à-vis the Slovenian government and, at the same time, called for equality with Hungarians, Italians and Gypsies. As already stated above, the German-speaking minority, which had probably comprised significantly over 20 000 persons in the inter-war period had, as a result of the Nazis' resettlement policies and annihilation by Tito's army, almost ceased to exist. According to the 1948 census, only 1824 people remained, most of them detained in camps and deprived of citizenship rights. After the dissolution of the camps they were given back these rights *de facto*, but not *de jure*. The census of 1991 recorded 1543 German-speaking people, of whom about 500 are supposed to be descendants of those settled previously. The 'Bridge of Freedom' society, which aims to organize the 'Old Austrians', cites a figure of between 2–3000. Until now, Slovenia has taken the view that experts should examine the problem since this issue entails delicate questions of property. By means of its decree of 21 November 1944, the wartime government of the Yugoslavian Peoples' Liberation Front had declared all ethnic Germans to be enemies of the state and their property to be confiscated. Unlike Italy, Austria did not associate the resulting problems of compensation with the EU negotiations for Slovenia.

By comparison with the question of the *Juznjaki* – that is, the migrants from former Yugoslavia (in total, about 140 000 people), who have in some cases been living in Slovenia for several generations and more or less enjoy only the status of foreign workers, the question of the German-speaking minority is a relatively small problem which will hardly effect Austro-Slovenian relations.

In general, it may be concluded that since 1991 Austro-Slovenian relations have been very positive and stand on a very high level both economically and culturally. As far as the economic sector is concerned, one may just mention the bilateral agreement of November 1993, which provides both parties with maximum benefit in respect of customs duties and other taxes. However, it is difficult to say how quickly the problem of the Krsko nuclear power station can be resolved. As it would take too long to list all the many initiatives in the cultural and academic field I will only mention the Austrian East- and South-East European Institute, of which I am a member. It is funded by the Austrian Federal Ministry for Science, Research and the Arts and supports a branch at Ljubljana, whose task it is to promote academic cooperation between Austria and Slovenia.

When discussing the events of the Second World War, I mentioned the deep-rooted fears and traumata, which nowadays seem to have been largely overcome. This is to some extent a question of generational change, but pragmatic reasons also play a part: no one in Austria seriously fears territorial claims by the small state of Slovenia and, in Slovenia, the image of a German bridge to the Adriatic will soon also disappear. Yet one should not underestimate irrationality in this matter and, above all, the part played by historical myths (although one should equally not overestimate them either). I mention in this context only the *karantanischer Fürstenstein* on the provisional Slovenian banknotes (coupons), which gave rise to heated emotions on both sides of the Karawanken mountains. Representatives of national historiography – those people whose task it is to furnish the appropriate historical basis for a modern nation – could undoubtedly claim a partial success for their efforts from the reactions of the Slovenian and Austrian public (in Carinthia even the *Land* parliament protested). I was recently told by the head of the Ljubljana division of the Austrian East- and South-East European Institute that, in Slovenia, the Habsburg ghost, although frail, still wanders about. My colleague was asked in all seriousness by a high-ranking and worried Slovenian politician how strong the forces in Austria were for the restoration of the Habsburg monarchy!

At the beginning of this chapter, I mentioned the year 1918 and how, whilst not losing sight of Europe, Slovenians underwent a geopolitical and geocultural reorientation towards the South. Today, Slovenia prefers to have very little to do with the Balkans, but very much to do with Europe, and Austria is an important part of that policy for Slovenia. In respect to progress in the areas of democratization and the rule of law, I would rank contemporary Slovenia alongside the Czech Republic and Hungary. The practice of reform, however, does not always match up with the theory. Bureaucracy as an unwanted 'upholder of tradition' is a not inconsiderable hindrance. In the economic sector too, there are many obstacles to be overcome in the adjustment to a market economy. In past years Austria has shown that it is willing to cooperate in this, and not, as in the past, with a raised index finger.

Bibliography

Bister, F.J. and Vodopivec, P. (eds) (1995), *Kulturelle Wechselseitigkeit in Mitteleuropa. Deutsche und slowenische Kultur im slowenischen Raum vom Anfang des 19. Jahrhunderts bis zum Zweiten Weltkrieg*, Ljubljana: Oddelek za zgodovino Filozofske fakultete Univerze v Ljublijani.

Höll, O. (ed.) (1988), *Österreich–Jugoslawien: Determinanten und Perspektiven ihrer Beziehungen*, Vienna: Braumüller.

Holzner, J. and Wiesmüller W. (eds) (1986), *Jugoslawien–Österreich. Literarische Nachbarschaft*, Innsbruck: Institut für Germanistik der Universität Innsbruck.

Karner, S. and Schöpfer, G. (eds) (1990), *Als Mitteleuropa zerbrach. Zu den Folgen des Umbruchs in Österreich und Jugoslawien nach dem Ersten Weltkrieg*, Graz: Leykam.

Lukan, Walter (1991), 'Graz und die Slowenen – kulturelle Wechselbeziehungen', *Wirtschafts- und Kulturbeziehungen zwischen dem Donau- und dem Balkanraum seit dem Wiener Kongreß*, Graz: Abteilung Sudosteuropäische Geschichte des Institutes für Geschichte der Universität Graz, pp.193–210.

Mencinger, Joze and Suppan, Arnold (1995), 'Slowenien' in Werner Weidenfels (ed.), *Mittel- und Osteuropa auf dem Weg in die Europäische Union. Bericht zum Stand der Integrationsfähigkeit*, Gütersloh: Verlag Bertelsmann Stiftung, pp. 195–222.

Mihelic, D. (ed.) (1994), *Dunaj in Slovenci*, Ljubljana: Zveva zgodovinskih društev Slovenije.

Necak, Dusan (1993–94), 'Einige grundlegende Angaben über das Schicksal der deutschen Volksgemeinschaft in Slowenien nach 1945', *Südostdeutsches Archiv*, **36/37**, pp.163–71.

Rumpler, H. and Suppan, A. (eds) (1988), *Geschichte der Deutschen im Bereich des heutigen Sloweniens 1848–1941*, Vienna: Verlag für Geschichte und Politik.

Siegl, Walter (1993), 'Die österreichische Jugoslawienpolitik', *Österreichisches Jahrbuch für internationale Politik 1992*, Vienna: Böhlau Verlag, pp.14–31.

Suppan, A. (1996), *Jugoslawien und Österreich 1918–1938. Bilaterale Außenpolitik in europäischen Umfeld*, Vienna: Verlag für Geschichte und Politik.

Weilguni, W. (1990), *Österreichisch–jugoslawische Kulturbeziehungen 1945–1989*, Vienna: Verlag für Geschichte und Politik.

11 Austria in Search of its Place in a Changing World: From Between the Blocs to Full Western Integration?

Hanspeter Neuhold

Austria's International Status During the East–West Conflict

The political sea change of 1989–91 – the collapse of the communist regimes in the crumbling Soviet bloc and the resulting end of the East–West conflict – entailed far-reaching consequences for all European states. For Austria and Europe's other neutrals – countries sometimes referred to, during the Cold War, as being situated between East and West – these effects were more fundamental than for the members of the Western bloc, if less sweeping than for the previously communist states. In the case of the latter countries, both their internal regimes and their foreign policies have undergone a radical transformation (Neuhold, Havlik and Suppan, 1995). By contrast, the former maintained their domestic political and economic systems as well as their international orientation, albeit in a different, less hostile environment. The neutrals also saw no reason to modify their internal structures. However, the foundations of their international status were called into question.

These challenges are better understood if the international positions held by these countries before and after the watershed years of 1989–91 are compared. As regards post-1955 Austria, it was a permanently neutral state located in the centre of Europe, but firmly Western with regard to its political and economic system. With closer scrutiny, Austria's international status during the East–West conflict was characterized by components that are somewhat contradictory but, then again, Austrians are obviously good at living with contradictions. As the Austrian writer Robert Menasse put it, Austrians have developed a unique 'either-and-or' approach (Menasse, 1993, pp.16ff). Austria's success in squaring several political circles during the Cold War can be demonstrated by taking a closer look at five aspects of its international status prior to the changes at the beginning of the 1990s (Neuhold, 1994a, pp.465–94).

Ideological Orientation

Permanent neutrality did not constitute an obstacle to Austria's Western ideological orientation. The European neutrals have in fact always emphasized that their status does not require equidistance or abstention with regard to political values (Verdross, 1978, p.45). They have also never made a secret of their preference for the Western camp of pluralistic, market-oriented democracies that guarantee liberal, individualistic human rights. In Austria's case, this position was reflected, *inter alia*, in the country's early admission to the Council of Europe - in 1956, only a year after the re-establishment of Austria's full sovereignty through the State Treaty. Moreover, Austria has pursued an active human rights policy, not only within the Council of Europe but also in other international fora.

Economic Relations with Western Europe

Neutrality also did not prevent the countries concerned from developing rather intensive economic relations with their main partners in Western Europe. Until recently, a two-tier approach evidently provided a solution that was satisfactory in economic terms and at the same time compatible with the obligations resulting from the international law of neutrality. On the one hand, Austria, Sweden and Switzerland were founding members of the European Free Trade Association (EFTA) which, as its name implies merely provides for the establishment of a free trade area and imposes no obligations which would conflict with those entailed by neutrality. On the other hand, membership in the supranational European Community (EC) was at the time considered incompatible with the status of permanent neutrality (Verdross, 1978, pp.60ff). The principal impediment was said to be the possibility of a unilateral embargo being imposed on the (private) export of war material against only one belligerent; such a measure could be decided by a majority vote and would also be binding on neutral members who would find themselves in a minority position. At the same time, Austria in particular had, because of the bulk of its trade and other economic relations with countries that belonged to the Community, to avoid discrimination by the EC as much as possible. A way out of this dilemma was agreed upon by the conclusion, in 1972–73, of bilateral free trade arrangements between the European Economic Community (EEC) and the European Coal and Steel Community (ECSC), on the one hand, and Austria as well as the other European neutrals, on the other (Straßer, 1972). These agreements contained provisions designed to safeguard neutrality. Thus, each side had the right to terminate the treaties provided it gave twelve months' notice. Each contracting party was also entitled to take measures that it deemed necessary in the event of war or grave international tensions.

Active Neutrality Policy

Austria's Western orientation at the ideological, political and economic levels did not prevent it from pursuing an active neutrality policy for which the term 'bridge-building' was often used. That offers of good offices and mediation by the European neutrals in Cold War disputes were appreciated by the West hardly came as a surprise. What was more astonishing was that these services were also accepted by the East. One explanation for this seems to lie in the neutrals' reputation as impartial 'honest brokers' in the exercise of those third-party functions. Another reason may have been the fact that the European neutrals were the only acceptable candidates for these services, because at least the West would have objected to 'bridge-building' by non-European members of the Non-aligned Movement. In any event, Austria's policy of neutrality was quite successful. For example, Vienna hosted two US–Soviet summit meetings in 1961 and 1979, as well as the Mutual and Balanced Force Reduction (MBFR) negotiations on conventional disarmament between the North Atlantic Treaty Organization (NATO) and the Warsaw Treaty Organization (WTO) from 1973 to 1989. In addition, Austria joined forces with eight other neutral and non-aligned participants in the Conference on Security and Cooperation in Europe (CSCE) process. This 'N+N' group played a third-party role which undoubtedly exceeded its material power potential (Neuhold, 1987).

Security Policy

In the field of security policy, neutrality meant that Austria could not count on pledges of military assistance by powerful allies. Instead, the country had to rely primarily on its own defensive efforts. Like the other neutrals, Austria practised the only reasonable security strategy, one based on the 'disproportionate entrance and occupation price'. The objective of this doctrine was not the ability effectively to repel a major attack by either of the Cold War's military blocs over an extended period of time – an unattainable goal for a small neutral country with relatively modest means – but rather to convince potential aggressors that the costs of an actual attack in terms of human casualties and the loss of war material, time and political prestige outweighed the limited benefits to be gained by attaining direct control over the neutral's territory and other resources. Although Austria took its national defence less seriously than Sweden, Switzerland and Finland[1] – a strange attitude in light of the country's particularly exposed and vulnerable geostrategic location – its 'dissuasion strategy' seems to have worked. Like the other neutrals, Austria was not drawn into any armed conflict throughout the Cold War. A pertinent question, however, is whether this positive result was really achieved through Austria's military preparedness or whether Austria and the other neutrals benefited, first and foremost, from the strategic balance between the Atlantic Alliance and the WTO. This second reason is increasingly acknowledged in neutral states, which NATO spokespersons have occasionally criticized as 'free-riders'. Such criticisms were not unfounded, especially in Austria's case. Moreover, a security policy which relies too much on 'bridge-building' efforts runs the risk of proving inadequate if and when it cannot prevent the resort to armed force.

Geopolitical and Geostrategic Position

Although Austria is situated in the geographic centre of the European continent, it found itself in a peripheral geopolitical and geostrategic position during the East–West confrontation. Although, in ideological terms, Austria was the easternmost bastion of the Western camp, Austrians learned to live quite comfortably in the shadow of the Iron Curtain. Austria also tried to develop good relations with the 'socialist' countries and was particularly successful in its 'special relationship' with Hungary; the new 'K+K' (Kreisky and Kádár) system even survived the new Cold War of the early 1980s (Mlynar *et al.*, 1985). The negative exception was the failure to achieve a durable thaw vis-à-vis Czechoslovakia, for which the main blame lay with the hardliners in Prague. They did not want their country to open up for more than two decades after the crushing of the 'Prague Spring' in 1968 (Bielka, 1983, pp.195ff and 224ff).

In its general Ostpolitik, the Austrian government tried to drill small holes into the Iron Curtain by working for the resolution of individual humanitarian hardship cases and by fostering economic and cultural cooperation. Austria did not, however, challenge the bipolar bloc system on the European continent. The *Quadrangolare*, which was launched in November 1989 and has in the meantime grown into the Central European Initiative (with 16 instead of four participating states), was initially still based on this approach (Neuhold, 1991).

After 1955 many Austrians came to feel that they lived in the best of all possible worlds: between East and West geographically and with respect to the military bloc structures; in the West ideologically, politically and economically, but at the same time 'building bridges' from the Western to the Eastern bank; somehow outside Europe in the field of security, according to a widespread (albeit unrealistic) assumption, shielded by permanent neutrality from being engulfed in a military showdown between the two blocs and from being affected by the consequences of such a confrontation.

Austria's Position in the 'New Europe'

A look at Austria's international status today leads to a *prima facie* puzzling conclusion. The recent political upheavals have apparently had no impact on Austria. It continues to be a permanently neutral state and a pluralistic, market-oriented democracy in the heart of Europe. However, on closer analysis, all these characteristics now appear in a different light and have acquired a new meaning. While the above-mentioned contradictions have disappeared, new problems and challenges have arisen in their place.

Geopolitical/Geostrategic Position

Today, Austria's geographic, geopolitical and geostrategic positions coincide. The country's Western political and economic orientations no longer distinguish and separate it from some of its neighbours. All of the latter have opted for the Western models in these fields. As a result, Austria now entertains normal relations with the post-communist states as well – that is, its relations are not restricted primarily to the official, intergovernmental level, but cover all areas of international interaction. In turn, this normalization requires a new attitude towards the peoples in the reform countries. They can no longer be regarded as pitiable caged victims with whom only scarce contacts and ties exist. Instead, they have become partners, but also competitors, who must be taken seriously and treated on an equal footing. The transformation processes in the former communist bloc have also produced winners and losers in Austria. Although the overall economic balance of the transformation processes in neighbouring countries is decidedly favourable for the Austrian side, the loss of jobs in non-competitive sectors has further fuelled xenophobia, whose growth can be observed not only in Austria but throughout Western Europe. Indeed, it is not a foregone conclusion that open borders lead to better understanding between neighbours; the result may instead be increasing apprehension and hostility.

At the beginning of the changes brought about by the collapse of communism in the Soviet bloc, Austria was faced with the danger of sliding once again towards the periphery, this time bordering on a zone of economic stagnation and political instability. However, today its neighbours to the north and east are (with the exception of Slovakia at the political level) amongst those former communist countries that stand the best chances of permanent success in their transition to Western democracies and market economies.

Permanent Neutrality

Austria's permanent neutrality has become increasingly problematic. There are a number of reasons for this (Krejci, Reiter and Schneider, 1993). First, with the end of the East–West conflict, during which it was established in 1955, Austria's neutrality has lost its principal 'conflict of reference' and the crucial geostrategic functions on which its vital acceptability depended. It goes without saying that (permanent) neutrality cannot be declared in a political vacuum, but requires a conflict in which it is practised. Moreover, the eventual success of neutrality hinges not only on the neutral's good intentions, it must also be appreciated by other countries, particularly by the conflicting parties and the great powers. They will view a neutral stance favourably if they also expect to benefit from it.

In the past, Austria served as a buffer between NATO and the WTO. At the same time, it constituted, together with Switzerland, a neutral thorn in the Atlantic Alliance's flesh by separating NATO's central front (the Federal Republic of Germany) from the southern tier (Italy). This fact may help to explain the Soviet Union's readiness to agree to the withdrawal of its troops from Northern and Eastern Austria in the State Treaty – a move which caught quite a few observers by surprise in 1955 (Stourzh, 1985).

A second question facing Austria's permanent neutrality, and one more and more frequently posed, concerns the identity of the parties between which Austria intends to remain neutral. In answering this question, it could be argued that we have, since 1989, not witnessed the 'end of history', let alone of international conflicts. In Europe the number of conflicts has not decreased, but dramatically increased. Consequently, the need for third-party 'bridge-building' has also grown. For the neutrals, however, this mounting demand has gone hand-in-hand with the loss of their privileged position in this area. Nowadays, good offices, mediation and similar services are performed more frequently by countries that belong to military alliances. For instance, the historic breakthrough between Israel and the Palestine Liberation Organization in November 1993 was accomplished near Oslo. Vancouver hosted the first summit meeting between Presidents Clinton and

Yeltsin in April 1993. The Hague was chosen for the headquarters of the agency charged with monitoring compliance with the 1993 Chemical Weapons Ban. The fact that these three cities are situated in NATO countries proved to be no political handicap. By contrast, according to Austrian diplomats, Vienna was ruled out at an early stage as the venue of the 1993 US–Russian summit conference because it evoked negative Cold War associations. The 'N+N' group has ceased to exist within the Organization for Security and Cooperation in Europe (OSCE, as the former CSCE is called since 1 January 1995).[2]

Third, permanent neutrality seems less and less capable of serving its main purpose as a security strategy for the country that has opted for this status. As a matter of fact, the end of the East–West conflict has fundamentally transformed the security constellation in Europe in two important respects (Neuhold, 1994b, pp.21ff; Ghebali and Sauerwein, 1995). On the military level, the spectre of nuclear annihilation has receded, although both the United States and Russia will still possess 'overkill capabilities' even after the full implementation of the START I and II Treaties. Moreover, the danger of the proliferation of nuclear weapons and other weapons of mass destruction worries decision-makers and security experts more than ever, but is inadequately understood by public opinion. The man (and woman) on the street, however, are well aware of the renewed resort to conventional military force. During the era of bipolar deterrence, such force was blocked by the threat of escalation across the nuclear threshold by the party facing defeat on the conventional level. Today, 'Clausewitz is back', as Willem van Eekelen, the former Secretary-General of the Western European Union (WEU), put it (Eekelen, 1993, p.23). Now that the use of armed force can again be limited, both geographically and with regard to the weapons employed, war reappears to be an 'acceptable' option for the continuation of policy by other means.

To make matters worse, the return of conventional warfare is not just a theoretical option. The potential for conflict abounds in Eastern Europe, where an explosive mix of old and new sources of disputes exists. On the one hand, the Cold War did not eliminate, but merely 'froze' ethnic–nationalistic, religious and territorial issues whose roots often date back to past centuries. On the other hand, such traditional controversies are frequently exacerbated by 'modern' causes of conflict, particularly socioeconomic tensions and political instability during the transition by the reformist countries to robust democracies and successful market economies. The tragedies in the former Yugoslavia provide only the most dramatic and depressing illustrations of force being resorted to in order to 'settle' such issues (Neuhold, 1994c, pp.109ff).

For Austria, however, the main military problem is not the threat of a direct attack, but rather the possibility of a spillover of military hostilities from its neighbouring countries on to its own territory. This is a challenge which Austria should really be able to cope with, provided it takes its defence seriously enough. During the East–West conflict, it was tacitly assumed that, if the country was attacked by one bloc (in all likelihood, the WTO), the other would come to its rescue to prevent the aggressor from upsetting the precarious overall balance. By contrast, foreign military assistance seems less certain today, unless Austria abandons its neutrality and joins an alliance.

In any event, like NATO as a whole and other European countries individually, Austria adapted its military doctrine according to the formula 'leaner but meaner' (Danzmayr, 1991; Fasslabend, 1993, pp.585ff). Emphasis is placed on the principles of flexibility, mobility and modernization. Instead of the previous static area defence based on large militia forces, Austria has switched to the concept of border protection and accords priority to a relatively small, but well trained and well equipped rapid reaction force. At the same time, the country's mobilization strength is to be reduced considerably.

The real problem looms in a short- or mid-term perspective; the increasing costs of sophisticated, up-to-date weapon systems means that smaller states will become less and less able to afford them on an individual basis. In addition, European states are faced with non-military threats and risks that are more serious than those they have encountered hitherto. This is particularly true of Austria, whose location exposes it to the most likely source of these challenges – namely, East–Central and Eastern Europe. Today's non-military threats and dangers include transboundary ecological hazards *à la* Chernobyl, mass migration, political and religious terrorism and organized, internationalized and professionalized, non-political crime ranging from car theft to drug and plutonium trafficking. These challenges cannot be met by individual states acting by themselves, but require collective responses. International cooperation in these areas, however, does not run counter to neutrality.

A fourth problem for permanent neutrality seemed to be that it might constitute a possible stumbling block on the road to Austria's admission to EC membership. Unlike Sweden, Finland and Switzerland, Austria expressly stated in its 1989 application to the EC that it assumed it would be able to maintain its neutral status as a member of the Communities.[3] Austria's 'long march to Brussels' lasted longer than the admission of the other EFTA members, which applied two or three years later than Austria but acceded to the EU at the same time, on 1 January 1995. Thus, Austrians received particularly instructive first-hand insights into the complexities of EC/EU procedures and decision-making (Neuhold, 1995, pp.15ff). However, among the four candidate countries where referenda on membership were held, Austrian voters expressed the strongest support for joining the Union.[4]

Eventually, the interest in the 'EFTA enlargement' also grew on the EU's side. After the rejection of the Maastricht Treaty in the first Danish referendum, the close vote in France and because of widespread opposition in other member countries, it had become clear that a further deepening of integration within the Union was out of the question for the time being. In any event, contrary to accusations by opponents of EU membership in the applicant countries, the results of the negotiations on admission were not a sell-out of their national interests. They were more favourable to the EFTA states than a reflection of the power relationship between them and the Union.

This is particularly true of the solution found for the neutrality issue. Initially, 'EC fundamentalists' had insisted that neutrality be abandoned prior to accession to the Communities/Union or that the neutral applicants must agree to join NATO and the WEU in the future.[5] Eventually, however, the pragmatists within the EU prevailed. As a result, the Union contented itself with a Joint Declaration which was annexed to the Final Act of the Treaty of Accession. In this declaration, the new member states agree that they will be ready and able to participate fully and actively in the Common Foreign and Security Policy (CFSP) as defined in the Treaty on European Union (Regelsberger, 1993; Jürgens, 1994).

As a matter of fact, the Treaty of Maastricht (in particular its relevant Article J), is compatible with the obligations of neutrality.[6] Article J.4, paragraph 1, merely envisages a common defence policy and a common defence as possibilities for the future.[7] Under Article J.4, paragraph 2, decisions and actions of the Union that have defence implications are entrusted to the WEU; however, EU members are not obligated to also join this West European alliance. Moreover, the CFSP 'shall not prejudice the specific character of the security and defence policy of certain Member States' – a formulation which also leaves room for neutrality (Art. J.4, paragraph 4). Furthermore, decisions within the framework of the 'second pillar' have to be taken unanimously, thus giving each member state a veto. This principle also applied to possible revisions of the CFSP provisions at the 1996–97 Intergovernmental Conference (IGC), so that the neutrals could prevent new provisions contrary to their status if they so wished.

European Union Membership

Membership of the EU marks the third major change in Austria's international status.[8] In addition to economic advantages – first and foremost, lower prices and lower inflation rates, additional foreign investment, increased exports, the creation of new jobs and higher economic growth – Austrians also expected security gains from joining the Union (Neuhold, 1995, pp.31ff). Even without acceding to NATO or the WEU, Austria may indeed count on additional protection provided by EU membership *per se*. It is almost inconceivable that members of the Union would sit idly by in the event of an attack on one of their number. The aggressor must rather reckon with at least becoming the target of political and economic sanctions by all of the EU states – a joint response which may hurt him considerably.

Another dimension of EU membership, its sociocultural effects, received scant attention in the Austrian debate preceding the referendum. Like the rest of Central Europe, the part of the Habsburg Empire that became Austria after the First World War did not fully participate in such crucial religious, philosophical, cultural and sociopolitical developments, as humanism, the Renaissance, the Reformation and, most importantly, the Enlightenment, as well as the French and the Industrial Revolutions (Hanák, 1988, pp.20ff). These developments have shaped a distinct (West) European identity which is based on a specific relationship between the citizen and his/her state, as well as between the individual and society. In turn, this is reflected in the West's individualistic concept of human rights, in the rule of law and in pluralistic democracy. Despite its undeniable deficiencies, the EU seems to be the best framework for promoting and strengthening these values. To Austria, membership in the Union offers a unique opportunity to overcome rather quickly its centuries-old backwardness in some areas.

For Austria, the task of establishing its place in the EU as a newcomer was complicated by the fact that, as the accession treaty entered into force, the Union started to become a moving target. In 1995 preparations began for the Intergovernmental Conference (IGC) which was to revise the Maastricht Treaty. This meant that Austria also had to define its position on numerous issues on the IGC's agenda.

Austria's Position after the 1997 Amsterdam and Madrid Summits: A Postscript[9]

Austria's EU Membership at the End of the IGC

Those who believe that the EU should become more political and that its membership should be enlarged could argue that the Union's heads of state or government addressed the 'wrong' priorities in Amsterdam (for a first analysis of the draft treaty see Wessels, 1997).[10]

On the one hand, the establishment of monetary union has run into difficulties that could hardly have been foreseen in February 1992, when the Maastricht Treaty was signed. For most EU members, including Germany, the driving force behind a 'hard' common currency which meets the so-called convergence criteria poses considerable problems. Many citizens of the Union have come to regard the Euro as a liability, rather than as an asset facilitating future economic progress. The unexpected change of government in France further complicated matters. On the eve of the Amsterdam summit, Chancellor Helmut Kohl and the new French socialist prime minister, Lionel Jospin, had still failed to agree on employment provisions to be included in the new treaty, and thus the 15 political leaders eventually settled for a compromise package on employment as well as on financial stability.

The Austrian government wants Austria to be among the first members of monetary union but is finding it difficult to comply with the admission requirements pertaining to the country's budget deficit and especially to its gross national debt.[11] As noted earlier, Austrians' initial enthusiasm for EU membership turned into disenchantment with the outcomes of membership. This has much to do with the fact that many of the expected benefits have failed to materialize – at least to the extent promised by some members of government.[12] Austria can thus be counted among the EU member countries where the Euro is the least popular.[13] In an obvious attempt to capitalize on this sceptical attitude, the *Freiheitliche Partei Österreichs* (FPÖ) has recently launched a *Volksbegehren* (popular initiative) calling for a referendum on the introduction of the single currency.[14] If more than 100 000 signatures are collected, parliament has to deal with the initiative, although it is not bound by its demands. From a legal point of view, it is a strange move, since Austria had already agreed to the provisions of the Maastricht Treaty on monetary union when it joined the EU. Nonetheless, the result of the *Volksbegehren* will be politically significant as a test of the present mood in the country concerning the performance of both the Union and the Austrian government.

On the other hand, with almost 20 million EU citizens looking for a job, unemployment had become a Europe-wide economic and sociopolitical problem of such magnitude that the Union's leaders, feeling that they could ill afford to ignore it, added a new Title on Employment to the draft treaty. However, the new articles are couched in rather general terms and do not provide for the funds necessary to launch major employment programmes at the Community/Union level. Consequently, there is a very real danger of creating exaggerated hopes among EU citizens; if these expectations are not met, they may well backfire against the Union, although the blame must lie with the member states which retain the chief responsibility in the employment sector. Although Austria has one of the lowest unemployment rates within the EU (4.4 per cent for 1997),[15] the Austrian government was among the most outspoken advocates of including provisions on employment in the Amsterdam Treaty.

One of the EU's recent priorities has therefore been the 'homework' to be completed under the terms of the Maastricht Treaty; while the other forced itself on to the EU's agenda as a result of previously unforeseen economic difficulties. By contrast, a 'proper' focus in terms of remedying weaknesses of the EU Treaty was placed on Justice and Home Affairs – matters of direct and growing concern for EU citizens. The EU's 'third pillar' will be partly 'communitarized', whilst cooperation in the remaining areas is to be improved. In addition, the *Schengen acquis* is integrated into the EU framework under a Protocol for 13 member states (excluding the UK and Ireland). Austria was one of those members that, from the outset, supported the strengthening of the 'third pillar' at the IGC.[16]

The IGC made modest progress at best in two other crucial issue areas. It failed to agree on a solution to the two central controversies in the field of institutional reforms – the size of the Commission and qualified majority voting in the Council. In the past the principles initially agreed upon for Communities consisting of three big and three smaller states were simply extrapolated whenever new members were admitted. Yet there are widespread concerns that, in the wake of the envisioned eastern and southern enlargement of the EU, the Commission may become too large to perform its tasks effectively. For instance, if each member were entitled to nominate at least one Commissioner, their number could increase up to 30. Furthermore, the current rules of weighted voting favour smaller members,[17] and the more populous member states are concerned that they may be outvoted by the smaller states in the future. In fact, with the exception of Poland, all the candidates for admission belong in this second category. Consequently, the larger EU member states have proposed various new systems that should allow them to safeguard and promote their interests.

In this discussion, Austria sided with the other smaller members which insisted on the right to appoint 'their' Commissioner. This is a somewhat puzzling attitude in view of the fact that all Commission members are required to be independent and must not accept instructions from the government of any member state. However, Commissioners are widely perceived as explaining and advocating 'their' country's positions at least informally in the Commission's decision-making process. In the same vein, Austria strongly opposed attempts to revise the voting rules within the Council to the detriment of smaller member states, arguing that the efficacy of this body could be enhanced without such changes. At the same time, Austria ought to have further allayed apprehensions about a 'German bloc' which were occasionally voiced when it was admitted to the EU. In the event, however, *Realpolitik* has resulted in small Austria and big Germany finding themselves in opposite camps in the institutional debate.

The European Council eventually postponed a genuine solution to these two thorny institutional issues until the completion of the EU's next phase of enlargement. This failure to reach agreement is bound to complicate the admission of new members, which was not on the Amsterdam agenda but loomed large in the background.

Further expansion to the east and also to the south is, in fact, one of the principal challenges and opportunities facing the EU. In particular, the accession of post-communist countries makes eminent economic and political sense, at least in a macroscopic perspective. From the economic point of view, the Union's enlargement to the east promises attractive markets and investment possibilities. In addition, it would strengthen Europe's role as a global actor in its cooperation and competition with the other two economic giants – namely, the US and the Pacific region or, more specifically, with the North American Free Trade Association (NAFTA) and the Asian-Pacific Economic Cooperation (APEC). On the political level, Western Europe also has a stake in the outcome of the transition processes in the eastern half of the continent (Neuhold, Havlik and Suppan, 1995). If they fail, the ensuing instability is likely to bring threats to, and dangers for, the security of other states as well; they could lead to the spread of terrorism, organized crime or mass migration. Armed conflicts may then spill over the borders of the countries in which they break out.

The most effective guarantee for the permanent success of the democratization and marketization of the post-communist states would undoubtedly be their admission to the EU. The Union's eastern enlargement, however, gives rise to certain problems. Unlike Austria and Sweden, the East-Central and Eastern European applicants would not become net contributors to the EU's budget; on the contrary, they would be entitled to payments from the Union's agricultural and structural funds. Although the concrete costs of the admission of new members cannot be assessed at this time, but will depend on which candidates are admitted, on when they are admitted and on the economic condition in which they find themselves on admission, the costs are likely to be substantial. Moreover, enlargement will result in the creation of winners and losers among not only new but also exisiting member states. The loss of both jobs and the competitiveness of labour-intensive enterprises as a result of lower wages in the Eastern bloc gives rise to particular concern in the existing EU member states.

Given the country's proximity to the former Soviet bloc, all these considerations are particularly relevant for Austria because of its vested interest in the political and economic stability of its post-communist neighbouring countries. Currently an EU border state, Austria would greatly benefit from an eastward shift of the Union's frontier and has therefore consistently advocated the EU's eastern enlargement.[18] However, Austrians do have acute apprehensions about the above-mentioned negative consequences. Hence Austrian politicians have argued that it is in the interests of both sides to have long transition periods in various areas in the accession treaties with the post-communist applicants.[19]

In addition to the stillborn crucial institutional reforms, progress with respect to the EU's second pillar must disappoint those who wish the Union to play a principal role in the areas of foreign and especially (military) security policy. The creation of a new *Troika*, a high representative[20] for the Common Foreign and Security Policy (CFSP) and the establishment of a policy planning and early warning unit are essentially cosmetic operations. The inclusion of the so-called Petersberg missions – humanitarian and rescue tasks, peacekeeping tasks and tasks of combat forces in crisis management including peacemaking – certainly represents a step in the right direction. The introduction of the possibility of 'constructive abstention' is a welcome deviation from the unanimity principle that governs the CFSP under the Maastricht Treaty. However, this less rigid rule does not apply to decisions which have military or defence implications. Most importantly, the integration of the WEU into the EU is merely mentioned as a possibility and requires a European Council decision to this effect. Consequently, the EU is still not an alliance in which members have to provide military assistance to each other in the event of an armed attack.

Austria supported the strengthening of the CFSP in principle but was among the member states which objected to endowing the Union with a 'defence identity'. As a result, EU membership remains compatible with permanent neutrality – the reason for Austria's somewhat inconsistent position on the development of the CFSP.

The Issue of NATO Membership

The principal challenge to Austrian neutrality thus arises not from the EU, but rather from the recent evolution of NATO. The Atlantic Alliance has adapted its strategic doctrine to the post-Cold War realities; in recent years, it has also moved 'out of area' by providing military support to the United Nations Protection Force, by helping to implement UN sanctions and by leading the Implementation Force and the Stabilization Force in former Yugoslavia. NATO has also moved into the area of cooperative security with non-member states, above all by launching the Partnership for Peace concept. Finally, the NATO heads of state or government invited the Czech Republic, Hungary and Poland to join the Alliance at their meeting in Madrid on 8 July 1997. By signing the Founding Act on Mutual Relations, Cooperation and Security with the Russian Federation in Paris on 27 May 1997, the Alliance had previously laid the foundations for a constructive relationship with Russia, although the latter has not abandoned its criticism of NATO's enlargement to the east.

With two of its post-communist neighbours on the road to membership – Slovenia, one of the favourites for the second round of enlargement, and

Slovakia, a hopeful candidate once the state of democracy improves in the country – Austria may sooner or later find itself almost completely surrounded by NATO members.[21] To join or not to join (the new NATO), is therefore the key question for the future of Austria's security policy – whether it is nobler (and wiser) to remain neutral or to be ready to take up arms together with others.[22]

On the one side of this debate are those who feel that Austria's security is adequately provided for by the country's permanent neutrality (defined restrictively and reduced to its military core obligations), and by its membership of the United Nations, its participation in the OSCE, its membership of the EU, its observer status within the WEU and its participation in NATO's Partnership for Peace as well as its membership in the new Euro-Atlantic Partnership Council. The proponents of this view point out that Austria is neither confronting – nor, in the foreseeable future, is likely to confront – any threats of armed attack by another state.

The more relevant non-military challenges to Austrian security can, they assert, be dealt with through joint efforts within the above-mentioned international institutional framework, into which Austria has been integrated without having to abandon its neutrality. This is also seen as the reason why the transformation of the EU into an alliance is neither necessary nor desirable. Austria is said to display sufficient international solidarity through its active neutrality policy, and especially through its contributions to peace-keeping and similar operations – for example, in Bosnia-Herzegovina and Albania. In other words, Austria still can perform a useful function as a neutral 'bridge-builder'. For its part, NATO continues to be viewed as a Cold-War military alliance that relies on nuclear weapons and is not immune from interventionist designs. If Austria eventually became surrounded by friendly NATO members or neutral neighbours, its neutrality would be more beneficial than ever, as Austrians would no longer have to worry about military security. By contrast, if Austria became a member of the Atlantic Alliance, it would contribute to a new division of Europe, could strain its relations with the Russian Federation, would run the risk of being drawn into conflicts of no direct concern to itself and would have to accept both unnecessary restrictions on its sovereignty and considerable expenses.

The advocates of joining NATO at the price of giving up neutrality have a counterargument against each of these points. In their opinion, an armed attack on Austria cannot be excluded and may occur as a bolt from the blue, especially from outside Europe. The logic of integration also calls for common defence. Austrian solidarity *à la carte* will not be appreciated by the other states that are ready to incur the high costs of repelling armed aggression. After the country's accession to the EU, there is little room for Austria's individual neutral 'bridge-building'.

This side of the NATO membership debate stresses the fundamental changes which the Atlantic Alliance has undergone. If Austria became a permanently neutral enclave within NATO territory, its neutrality would have no geopolitical function. Instead, it would constitute a nuisance for its neighbours, whose traffic and transport routes it would interrupt. NATO's progressive enlargement is perceived not as creating a new partition, but as overcoming the division imposed on Europe during the Cold War. If Austria took its independent defence as seriously as it should, the costs would be higher than if Austria relied on collective defence within the Atlantic Alliance.

In this debate, the *Österreichische Volkspartei* (ÖVP) and the FPÖ are in favour of NATO membership. The Liberal Forum would prefer to join the WEU, but does not reject accession to the Atlantic Alliance in principle. The Greens insist on maintaining permanent neutrality and reject entry into NATO. The factor which will be decisive for the future orientation of Austria's security policy is the attitude of the *Sozialdemokratische Partei Österreichs* (SPÖ). Many leading, as well as rank-and-file, SPÖ members still object to a change of course, but a discussion is currently underway within the party. In this connection, it ought to be borne in mind that the two governing parties, the SPÖ and the ÖVP, agreed in their coalition agreement of 11 March 1996 that the government would report on all security options open to Austria and submit the necessary recommendations to parliament by the end of the first quarter of 1998.[23]

The second crucial variable is public opinion, especially if it were decided to hold a referendum on an eventual accession to NATO. The average Austrian still seems to value neutrality highly. According to a recent opinion poll, 37 per cent oppose Austria's NATO membership, whilst only 18 per cent endorse it and as many as 45 per cent remain undecided or have no opinion on the issue.[24] The share of supporters increases to 28 per cent if the Atlantic Alliance were to include the reformed states of Eastern Europe.

Conclusion

To return to the initial topic of this chapter, it should have become clear that, notwithstanding its neutrality, during the Cold War Austria was never fully 'in between' the two blocs – that is, in a position of complete equidistance between them. Given the magnitude of the changes that have occurred in Europe since 1989, the conclusion is warranted that Austria's international status has undergone what amounts to its fourth qualitative transformation in the course of this century (Neuhold, 1996). Thus in 1918–19, the German-speaking core of a multi-ethnic great power became a small country of precarious economic viability; in 1938 the *Anschluß* meant that Austria disappeared from the map of sovereign states, re-emerging under Allied control in 1945. The history of Austria since it regained full independence under the terms of the 1955 State Treaty and the adoption of permanent neutrality in that year can be termed a political and economic success story and helps explain why many Austrians are reluctant to abandon neutrality. When it was admitted to the EU in a new Europe in 1995, Austria turned yet another page in its eventful history. It may be argued that, once again, a new chapter will be opened if and when Austria joins a military alliance and relinquishes its neutral status.

Notes

1 This neglect was reflected in the share of its GNP Austria spent on defence, which was considerably lower than that of comparable countries. Concrete figures can be found in the annual Military Balance published by the International Institute for Strategic Studies and the SIPRI Yearbooks on World Armaments and Disarmament published by the Stockholm International Peace Research Institute.

2 However, the neutrals are not completely 'out' as 'bridge-builders'. Thus the World Trade Organization established its seat in Geneva; the agency that will ratify compliance with the 1996 Comprehensive Test Ban Treaty will be located in Vienna; and Presidents Clinton and Yeltsin picked Helsinki for their meeting in March 1997.

3 For the text see Neuhold, Hummer and Schreuer (1991, p.500). On the political and economic background of Austria's decision to 'go it alone' in 1989, see Schneider (1990).

4 In Austria, 66.58 per cent voted in favour; the corresponding figures for Finland, Sweden and Norway were 56.9, 52.3 and 47.8 per cent, respectively (Kaiser *et al.*, 1995, pp.76ff). On the EU's 'EFTA enlargement' in general, see Pedersen (1994). Although Switzerland had also applied for admission to the EC in 1992, it did not enter into accession negotiations with the EC/EU after Swiss voters had rejected membership in the European Economic Area in December 1992. On the Austrian referendum, see Pelinka (1994) and Ogris (1995).

Enthusiasm for EU membership in Austria cooled quickly after the country's accession to the Union on 1 January 1995. According to a poll four months later, only 37 per cent regarded membership as advantageous, 28 per cent rejected it and 35 per cent were indifferent or had no opinion (*Kurier*, 21 April 1995). In mid-May 1995 another opinion survey revealed that only 39 per cent would have voted for and 47 per cent would have voted against EU membership. Austria's accession to the EU had fulfilled the expectations of just 24 per cent of the respondents, while disappointing 57 per cent (*NEWS*, (20) 18 May 1955).

5 Like the then Belgian Foreign Minister Willy Claes (*Der Standard*, 8 October 1993).

6 The same applies to the CFSP *acquis communautaire*, the joint actions decided so far and the agenda in the field of security policy, with the possible exception of the control of military exports (Zemanek, 1995, pp.16ff).

7 '... including the *eventual* framing of a common defence policy, which *might in time* lead to a common defence' (Art. J.4, paragraph 1, emphasis added).

8 On the legal aspects, see Hummer (1994).

9 The concluding part of the paper ('Austria Still Between East and West?') read by this author at the 1995 conference, at which most of the contributions to this volume were originally presented, dealt with Austria's position on some of the key issues on the agenda of the EU's IGC, which had, at the time, not yet started. Those comments have since become obsolete and have therefore been replaced by a brief and tentative summary of the impact of two recent high-level political events on the future of Austria's international status – the Amsterdam meeting of the European Council in June and NATO's Madrid summit in July 1997.

10 The above critical assessment is not to deny that useful, but limited, progress was achieved in numerous sectors in the draft treaty.

11 At the time of writing, the Austrian Institute of Economic Research (*Österreichisches Institut für Wirtschaftsforschung*) expects Austria's 1997 budget deficit to comprise 2.8 per cent of GDP, which is below the 3 per cent convergence limit. By contrast, the Finance Ministry estimates Austria's public debt at 70.8 per cent of the country's GDP for the current year, so that Austria will clearly exceed the 60 per cent threshold. I am indebted to the Institute for these up-to-date figures.

12 See note 4.

13 According to an EU-wide opinion poll of November 1996, 41 per cent of the Austrians interviewed oppose and some 35 per cent support the Euro. Only the Danes, Swedes, British and Finns are more critical of monetary union. The EU average is 33 per cent against and 51 per cent in favour of the Euro (*Profil*, [35], 25 August 1997). A more recent survey of May 1997 showed 41 per cent supporting and 42 per cent rejecting the Euro (*Kurier*, 13 June 1997).

14 The *Volksbegehren* was held from 24 November to 1 December 1997.

15 According to the forecast by Austrian Institute for Economic Research to which I am indebted for this information as well.

16 See the guidelines for the IGC adopted by the Austrian government: *Österreichische außenpolitische Dokumentation. Texte und Dokumente*, (4), August 1995, pp.7–50, esp. pp.39–48.

17 For instance, Luxemburg, with a population of approximately 400 000, has two votes, while Germany, with about 81 million inhabitants, has ten votes.

18 For example, in Federal Chancellor Franz Vranitzky's governmental declaration of 11 March 1996: *Österreichische außenpolitische Dokumentation. Texte und Dokumente*, (2–3), July 1996, pp.15–18 at p.16.

19 For instance, by Vice-Chancellor and Foreign Minister Wolfgang Schüssel (*Die Presse*, 9 September 1997).

20 Since he or she will not be a ranking political personality but a high EU official, the Secretary-General of the Council, in practice he or she will not be quite so 'high', however.

21 The exceptions are Switzerland and Liechtenstein.

22 The present chapter aspires to do no more than summarize some of the principal arguments in this debate. For a more detailed discussion of (future) Austrian security policy see Neuhold (1997) and the literature quoted therein.

23 *Österreichische außenpolitische Dokumentation. Texte und Dokumente*, (2–3), July 1996, pp.5–14 at p.8.

24 *Die Presse*, 12 September 1997.

Bibliography

Bielka, Erich (1983), 'Österreich und seine volksdemokratischen Nachbarn', in Erich Bielka, Peter Jankowitsch and Hans Thalberg (eds), *Die Ära Kreisky. Schwerpunkte der österreichischen Außenpolitik*, Vienna: Europaverlag.

Cede, Franz (1995), 'Österreichs Neutralität und Sicherheitspolitik nach dem Beitritt zur Europäischen Union' , *Zeitschrift für Rechtsvergleichung*, **36**.

Cornett, Linda and Caparaso, James A. (1992), '"And still it moves!" State interests and social forces in the European Community', in James N. Rosenau and Ernst-Otto Czempiel (eds), *Governance without Government: Order and Change in World Politics*, Cambridge: Cambridge University Press.

Danzmayr, H. (1991), *Kleinstaat auf der Suche nach Sicherheit. Eine Analyse sicherheitspolitischer Konzepte Österreichs und der Schweiz*, Vienna: Wilhelm Braumüller.

Eekelen, Willem van (1993), 'Die Westeuropäische Union und die europäische Sicherheit', in Kurt R. Spillmann and Mauro Mantovani (eds), *Die sicherheitspolitische Integration in Europa als Herausforderung für die Schweiz*, Zurich: Eidgenössische Technische Hochschule.

Fasslabend, Werner (1993), 'Die Heeresreform 1992 – Antwort auf neue Bedrohungsbilder und sicherheitspolitische Herausforderungen', *Österreichisches Jahrbuch für Politik 1992*, Vienna: Verlag für Geschichte und Politik.

Ghebali, V-Y. and Sauerwein, B. (1995), *European Security in the 1990s: Challenges and Perspectives*, New York and Geneva: United Nations.

Hanák, Péter (1988), 'Schöpferische Kraft und Pluralität in der mitteleuropäischen Kultur', in Hans-Peter Burmeister, Frank Boldt and György Mészáros (eds), *Mitteleuropa – a Traum oder Trauma?*, Bremen: Edition Temmen.

Hummer, W. (ed.) (1994), *Die Europäische Union und Österreich*, Vienna: Verlag Österreich, Österreichische Staatsdruckerei.

Jürgens, T. (1994), *Die gemeinsame Europäische Außen- und Sicherheitspolitik*, Cologne: Carl Heymanns Verlag.

Kaiser, Wolfram, Visuri, Pekka Malmström, Cecilia and Hjelseth, Arve (1995), 'Die Volksabstimmungen in Österreich, Finnland, Schweden und Norwegen: Folgen für die Europäische Union', *Integration*, **18**.

Kluth, W. (1995), *Die demokratische Legitimation der Europäischen Union. Eine Analyse der These vom Demokratiedefizit der Europäischen Union aus gemeineuropäischer Verfassungsperspektive*, Berlin: Duncker & Humblot.

Krejci, H., Reiter, E. and Schneider, H. (eds) (1992), *Neutralität. Mythos und Wirklichkeit*, Vienna: Signum Verlag.

Menasse, R. (1993), *Das Land ohne Eigenschaften. Essay zur österreichischen Identität*, 3rd edn, Vienna: Sonderzahl Verlagsgesellschaft.

Mlynar, Z., Heinrich, H.-G., Kofler, T. and Stankovsky, J. (1985), *Die Beziehungen zwischen Österreich und Ungarn: Sonderfall oder Modell?*, Vienna: Wilhelm Braumüller.

Neuhold, Hanspeter (ed.) (1987), *CSCE: N+N Perspectives: The Process of the*

Conference on Security and Co-operation in Europe from the Viewpoint of the Neutral and Non-Aligned Participating States, Vienna: Wilhelm Braumüller.

Neuhold, Hanspeter (ed.) (1991), *The Pentagonal/Hexagonal Experiment: New Forms of Cooperation in a Changing Europe*, Vienna: Wilhelm Braumüller.

Neuhold, Hanspeter (1994a), 'Österreich in einem neuen Europa – Versuch einer Standortbestimmung', in Konrad Ginther, Gerhard Hafner, Winfried Lang, Hanspeter Neuhold and Lilly Sucharipa-Behrmann (eds), *Völkerrecht zwischen normativem Anspruch und politischer Realität. Festschrift für Karl Zemanek zum 65. Geburtstag*, Berlin: Duncker & Humblot.

Neuhold, Hanspeter (1994b), 'Security Challenges and Institutional Responses: An Austrian Perspective', *The International Spectator*, **XXIX**, (3), July–September.

Neuhold, Hanspeter (1994c), 'Conflicts and Conflict Management in a "New" Europe', *Austrian Journal of Public and International Law*, **46**.

Neuhold, Hanspeter (1995), 'Perspectives of Austria's Membership in the European Union', *German Yearbook of International Law*, **37**.

Neuhold, Hanspeter (1996), *Austria on the Threshold of the Twenty-First Century: Another Change in International Status?*, Oslo: Europa-prorammet.

Neuhold, Hanspeter (1997), 'Optionen Österreichischer Sicherheitspolitik', *Österreichische Militärische Zeitschrift*, **35**.

Neuhold, H., Hummer, W. and Schreuer, C. (eds) (1991), *Österreichisches Handbuch des Völkerrechts*, vol. 2. *Materialienteil*, 2nd edn, Vienna: Manzsche Verlags- und Universitätsbuchhandlung.

Neuhold, H., Havlik, P. and Suppan, A. (eds) (1995), *Political and Economic Transformation in East Central Europe*, Boulder Col., San Francisco and Oxford: Westview Press.

Ogris, Günther (1995), 'Die EU-Volksabstimmung' in Josef Rauchenberger (ed.), *Entscheidung für Europa. Österreichs parlamentarischer Weg in die EU*, Vienna: PR-Verlag.

Pedersen, T. (1994), *European Union and the EFTA Countries*, London and New York: Pinter Publishers.

Pelinka, A. (ed.) (1994), *EU-Referendum. Zur Praxis direkter Demokratie in Österreich*, Vienna: Signum Verlag.

Regelsberger, E. (ed.) (1993), *Die Gemeinsame Außen- und Sicherheitspolitik der Europäischen Union. Profilsuche mit Hindernissen*, Bonn: Europa Union Verlag.

Schneider, H. (1990), *Alleingang nach Brüssel. Österreichs EG-Politik*, Bonn: Europa Union Verlag.

Stourzh, G. (1985), *Geschichte des Staatsvertrages 1945–1955. Österreichs Weg zur Neutralität*, 3rd edn, Graz, Vienna and Cologne: Verlag Styria.

Straßer, H. (1972), *Der Weg Österreichs zu den Verträgen mit Brüssel*, Vienna: Österreichische Gesellschaft für Außenpolitik und Internationale Beziehungen.

Verdross, A. (1978), *The Permanent Neutrality of Austria*, Vienna: Verlag für Geschichte und Politik.

Weidenfeld, W. (ed.) (1993), *Demokratie und Marktwirtschaft in Osteuropa. Strategien und Optionen für Europa*. Gütersloh: Verlag Bertelsmann Stiftung.

Wessels, Wolfgang (1997), 'Der Amsterdamer Vertrag – Durch Stuckwerksreform zu einer effizienteren, erweiterten und föderalen Union?', *Integration*, **20**.

Zemanek, Karl (1991), 'The Changing International System: A New Look at Collective Security and Permanent Neutrality', *Austrian Journal of Public and International Law*, **42**.

Zemanek, K. (1995), *Österreichs Neutralität und die GASP*, Saarbrücken: Europainstitut der Universität des Saarlandes.

PART IV
WHITHER AUSTRIA?

12 Between Collectivism and Liberalism: The Political Evolution of Austria Since 1945

Peter Pulzer

The reconstitution of an Austrian state in 1945 took place under a number of shadows – not only that of Allied military occupation, although that was the most threatening, but the many shadows of Austria's many pasts. The history of Austrian state formation had been one of failure over the centuries. Whether there was a recognizable Austrian state at all within the Holy Roman Empire is disputed by historians. Beyond a rudimentary military command and an administration largely restricted to collecting taxes, little bound the various territories inherited by the Habsburgs. Only in the second half of the eighteenth century under Maria Theresia and Joseph II was there an attempt to build a rational, comprehensive bureaucratic structure. The first genuinely Austrian state, the Austrian Empire of 1806, was the product of military defeat, setting the precedent for its successors. This Empire was a sovereign state, unlike the component parts of the Holy Roman Empire, but as the dominant member of the German Confederation, created in 1815 after the defeat of Napoleon, it still lacked a complete and unambiguous identity. It was both Austrian and German; indeed, under its chancellor, Prince Metternich, any loyalty other than to the state and the dynasty was frowned upon. Any German nationalism, directed at creating a nation-state on the principle of self-determination, was incompatible with the principle of dynastic legitimacy; any non-German nationalism among the subject peoples of the Austrian Empire posed a similar threat. For Metternich the primacy of the state over the nation was an unalterable principle.

That this principle was becoming increasingly untenable in the course of the nineteenth century was shown first by the revolution of 1848–49 and then by the Prussian victory at Königgratz in 1866, which separated Austria from the rest of Germany and from the rudimentary nation-state proclaimed in the form of the German Empire of 1871. Yet, although this Empire – a dual monarchy after the *Ausgleich* of 1867 – had representative institutions and, after 1906, universal male suffrage in its Austrian half, it could survive only if, as under Metternich, nation was subordinate to the state – a state that depended on the dynasty. The charisma of the Emperor Francis Joseph notwithstanding, the Habsburg monarchy lacked a constitutional consensus. The proof of this came with the military defeat of 1918 which completed what the military defeat of 1866 had begun.

The great paradox of this epoch is that Austria did not lack an urban civil society or modern schools of thought of great intellectual vibrancy. While the grandfathers of European liberal thought came predominantly from England, Scotland and France, many of the dominant liberal ideas of the twentieth century, especially in economics, have their origins in Vienna. The entire Austrian school of economics, admittedly not a uniform body of thought, has had a worldwide impact in its emphasis on the sovereignty of the rational individual and its distrust of the state. The roll-call of Carl Menger, Eugen von Böhm-Bawerk, Ludwig von Mises, Friedrich von Hayek and Karl Popper – an arbitrarily incomplete roll-call – suggests some dissonance between the structure of state and society on the one hand and the intellectual ferment within it on the other. It is more plausible to speak of a liberalism from Austria than of one in Austria. Its influence spread throughout the English-speaking world and trickled back to Central Europe slowly and partially.

Although many of the great minds of Austrian liberalism developed their theories in the inter-war years, neither the politics nor the economics of Austria in those years could be said to be liberal. The Constitution of the First Austrian Republic was certainly a model of liberal orthodoxy, but the political conventions were those inherited from the practice of the Empire. Austria was a republic not of *citoyens libres*, but of members of collectivities, dependent on group membership for their identities, their access to benefits and for their guides to behaviour. In the Empire the dominant collectivities had been ethnic. Now they were based on class, religion and ideology. Austria was no closer to a constitutional consensus than under the Empire – indeed, in some respects, further removed from one, for the question whether post-Imperial Austria was a viable state dominated public debate. After 15 years the democratic republic collapsed in civil war; after four more years of the dictatorship that followed, Austria succumbed – not unwillingly – to the pressures of the Third Reich.

In 1945 it was once more the fortunes of war that determined the shape of an Austrian state. Pan-Germanism was no longer an option; apart from anything else, it was unacceptable to the victorious Allies. For the first time in history, therefore, the potential for a consensus on national identity existed. State and nation could, if matters were handled sensitively, coincide. They were, as the record shows, handled in such a way that an Austrian nationality, identity and constitutional consensus did indeed emerge and, by the 1970s, their existence could no longer be doubted. The conflict between state and nation was a thing of the past. There was, however, a price to be paid for this achievement – one that delayed, although it did not prevent, the emergence of a more liberal domestic order.

The pressures making for consensus in the early post-war years were threefold: the burden of the four-power occupation, the need for economic reconstruction and the imperatives of ideological reconciliation. The occupation was ended by the State Treaty in 1955, but the obligation to maintain neutrality meant that foreign policy options remained restricted. Economic reconstruction, though it proceeded more slowly than in the Federal Republic of Germany, also brought peacetime normality to most Austrian citizens by the end of the 1950s, helped by the wage–price agreements of 1947–51 which were finally institutionalized in the Joint Commission established in 1957. The mechanisms for ensuring consensus on foreign and economic policy also contributed to ideological reconciliation. From 1945 to 1966 Austria was governed by a grand coalition of the two major parties (the ÖVP and SPÖ), which put a further premium on unanimity in policy-making. Macro-politics therefore reflected the practice of the Joint Commission, in which the three main chambers and the trade union federation (ÖGB) strove to achieve unanimity on wages and prices. This did not mean that the ideological camps that had dominated the First Republic disappeared, but their teeth were drawn. Party membership was extraordinarily high by Western standards and there were very few interest groups or leisure associations that were not affiliated – or at least identified with – one or other of the two parties. In some cases, they were also close to the third (pan-German) political force, which went under the name of the Freedom Party (FPÖ) from 1956 onwards. Each of the government departments and each corporation in the large public sector became the domain of one of the coalition parties. The *Lager* survived not as militias, but as mutual benefit societies. Party membership was now a pass to a job or a flat.

Above all, reconciliation meant a conspiracy of silence about the past. The civil war of 1934 was consigned to an *oubliette*. The commemorations on its 50th anniversary caused some surprise and embarrassment; they also revealed a good deal of ignorance on the part of the younger generation. Austria's part in the Third Reich was even more energetically repressed, not least in the desire to attract the votes of former Nazi Party members. Here, too, the 1980s provided a rude shock in the form of the international debate about President Waldheim's wartime career. All these developments might indicate a suffocating avoidance of controversy and an attempt to stifle the types of conflicts that are inherent in a modern, mature society. Austria seemed to be permanently ruled by a cartel of no doubt enlightened, conscientious functionaries, *de facto* accountable to no one as long as the majority of Austrians preferred the role of subjects to that of citizens.

And yet this is only half the story, for throughout this period there were as many currents leading in the direction of greater liberalization. The first of these was an indirect consequence of the Cold War. Europe was now divided into East and West, with no room for states that might have an ideological preference for *Mitteleuropa*. Although inhibited, first by military occupation and then by neutrality, from formal adherence to the Western military alliance, Austrian governments made it clear that their countries belonged to the West in every other respect. In practical terms, that meant being part of the capitalist world order. Unlike the Soviet satellites, Austria took part in the European Recovery Programme which tied its trade flows to the West, required steps towards currency convertibility and a general adaptation towards the principle of a market economy. Although, as we have seen, the Austrian economy remained more highly regulated, with a larger public sector than was usual in Western Europe and with rather more of its foreign trade being conducted with the Soviet bloc, Austria became a trading state like any other in Western Europe, linked into an increasingly liberalized flow of people, money, goods and services. Under Richard Kamitz's tenure of the Ministry of Finance (1952–60), the foundations were laid for an economy characterized by low inflation, steady growth and full employment, and Austria began to participate in the consumer affluence of Western Europe. All formal commitments took Austria further in that direction: foundation membership of the European Free Trade Area (EFTA) in 1957 and the Free Trade agreement with the EEC in 1972. Each of these steps bound Austria more closely with economies that were less closely regulated than its own. The final step was the decision in 1994 to join the EU, which is considered below.

In terms of social structure and political culture, Austria also followed the Western European pattern even if at some remove. Industrialization, which had begun to accelerate under the Third Reich, made for an urbanized society, especially in the Western *Bundesländer*. Austria shared in the boom in secondary and tertiary education that, like urbanization, helped to open hitherto closed minds. The decline of agricultural employment and the growth of a mainly private-sector service economy further reduced the numbers of those who fitted into the traditional political *Lager* by heredity or environment. Affluence encouraged foreign travel: Austria now exported tourists, as well as importing them – another factor undermining the mental isolationism of a small nation, whose complacency sometimes hid suspicion of the outside world.

Very slowly these processes resulted in a loosening of the electoral blocs, although it was only in the 1980s that a serious degree of electoral volatility became evident. It was a development characterized by small steps. The first sign came with the ending of the grand coalition in 1966, when the ÖVP gained an absolute majority of seats, but not of votes. The second sign came with a peaceful alternation of power – the first since 1920 – when the SPÖ gained a plurality of votes and seats and formed a single-party government in 1970. This was confirmed in office with absolute majorities on three occasions, in 1971, 1975 and 1979. This decade-long SPÖ hegemony was a form of liberalization in two respects. It showed that voters no longer needed each of the major parties to control the other. Political trust was an established feature of the polity. It also showed that they were less afraid of the kind of open, urban, cosmopolitan society that Bruno Kreisky, a scion of the Jewish upper middle class of Habsburg Moravia, symbolized. There had been a small but decisive swing from the cautious conservatism of the reconstruction years, but no breaking of the mould of party politics. Between 1966 and 1983 the two main parties invariably won over 90 per cent of the vote between them. There was only one instance of electoral self-emancipation during this period, although in retrospect this turned out to be highly significant – namely the 1978 referendum on nuclear power, in which a narrow majority voted against the pro-nuclear policy supported by both major parties and almost all established interest groups.

In the 1980s two further stages of liberalization began, simultaneous rather than inter-connected, but nevertheless combining to reduce the distance between Austria and the Western European norm. The first arose out of the crisis in the nationalized industries, which led to a slow process of deregulation, privatization and, above all, managerial appointments made on the basis of merit rather than on party patronage. The Austrian economy of 1995 is considerably more marketized than that of, say, 1980. The second aspect of recent liberalization is that of party fragmentation. It liberalizes in the sense that it marks a further stage in the disintegration of the *Lager* and emergence of voters who make a choice. It also liberalizes in the sense that two of the three beneficiaries of the disintegration proclaim programmes are, in different ways, liberal. This applies to the Greens, who entered parliament in 1986 and to the Liberal Forum, which entered parliament in 1994, but had made an impact at *Landtag* elections in the preceding legislative period.

The third and most significant beneficiary of *Lager* disintegration is the FPÖ which, under the leadership of Jörg Haider, advanced from 5 per cent to 22 per cent between 1986 and 1995, and won 27 per cent in the election of 1996 to the European Parliament. To what extent has it contributed to the liberalization of Austria? Much of its ideology is manifestly illiberal. In its nationalism, its xenophobia, its cultural philistinism, its anti-pluralism and, above all, in its defensive and apologetic attitude towards Austrian participation in the Third Reich it is a throw-back. Its effect in these respects is to resist, and even reverse, the liberalizing trend of the previous quarter-century. But there are other respects in which its effect is, as Marxists would once have said, 'objectively' liberalizing. Its economic programme is not that of the traditional radical Right, with its emphasis on corporatism and protectionism, but rather one that advocates enterprise, deregulation and meritocracy. It appeals at least as much to the ambitious and the successful among the middle and skilled working classes as to the so-called modernization losers. It also assaults those remaining citadels of Austrian corporatism – the economic chambers with their compulsory membership and their *nomenklatura* of party hacks. It articulates a range of discontents, many of them irrational and some of them contradictory, but one of them is resentment of the closed political class in the cartel that, at times, has been not only corrupt, but corrupt with impunity.

The logical conclusion of Austria's cautious liberalization came in 1994, with the referendum that gave a two-to-one majority in favour of EU membership. While the collapse of communism and the ending of the Soviet veto on EU adherence were necessary conditions for this step, they were not sufficient. EU membership, and public support for it, was the logical outcome of the transformation of Austrian society, its integration into the world economy as an active trading nation and its ideological absorption by the West. Phases of disillusionment with the consequence of EU membership do not negate this conclusion.

Fifty years after the restoration of Austrian independence, 50 years during which Austrian statehood has been legitimated by a constitutional consensus and a sense of nationhood, Austria stands Janus-like: more liberal than it has ever been in its history, less liberal than many of its European neighbours. The Joint Commission still exists, although its remit is much reduced. The Chambers remain in place, buttressed by compulsory membership, although their authority and role are diminished. Since 1987 Austria has again been governed by a grand coalition, after an interlude of alternation, although the range of issues exempt from the unanimity rule has widened. Austrian privatization can take on a surreal form, as when the *Creditanstalt* was 'privatized' in January 1997 through a takeover of a 'black' state-owned bank by a 'red' one. Austrian cultural life is again creative, writers and producers are again provocative, the cupboard containing the skeletons of the past is no longer locked. Public life is no longer dominated by utopian or nihilistic ideologies with an exclusive claim to truth, but there is also a strong demagogic and populist presence. Liberalism has made a breakthrough that is probably irreversible, even though it is incomplete. Unlike the liberal breakthrough of 1867–79, it is backed by wide popular support.

Index